FLOURISH

FLOURISH

The Extraordinary Journey Into Finding Your Best Self

ANTONIA CASE

BLOOMSBURY CONTINUUM
LONDON · OXFORD · NEW YORK · NEW DELHI · SYDNEY

BLOOMSBURY CONTINUUM
Bloomsbury Publishing Plc
50 Bedford Square, London, WC1B 3DP, UK
29 Earlsfort Terrace, Dublin 2, Ireland

BLOOMSBURY, BLOOMSBURY CONTINUUM and the Diana logo are trademarks
of Bloomsbury Publishing Plc

First published in Great Britain 2023

A catalogue record for this book is available from the British Library

Library of Congress Cataloguing-in-Publication data has been applied for

ISBN: HB: 978-1-4729-7971-1; TPB: 978-1-4729-7970-4; eBook: 978-1-4729-7974-2;
ePDF: 978-1-3994-0811-0

2 4 6 8 10 9 7 5 3 1

Typeset by Deanta Global Publishing Services, Chennai, India
Printed and bound in Great Britain by CPI Group (UK) Ltd, Croydon CR0 4YY

MIX
Paper | Supporting
responsible forestry
FSC
www.fsc.org FSC® C171272

To find out more about our authors and books visit www.bloomsbury.com
and sign up for our newsletters

CONTENTS

PREFACE

'We must let go of the life we have planned, so as to accept the one that is waiting for us.'

—Joseph Campbell

D O   Y O U   H A V E   A   feeling that there's something missing in your life, but you just can't put your finger on exactly what it is? That there's something waiting for you, but you don't know what to expect or find? That there's a gap, a space, but you can't fathom how this gap could be filled? You may feel that with some quiet time, or some words of wisdom, you might finally locate it, and then you'd be on your way – you'd know what to pursue and why.

In my hometown, there was a woman who waited. From the car window I'd watch her every morning before school. She'd stand on the footpath outside her home and look every which way up and down the street. 'What is she doing?' I asked my mother as we were driving past one day. 'Oh,' my mother replied in a quiet voice, 'she is waiting.'

It soon became obvious that this woman's wait might go on for some time. It was also clear that she didn't know what she was waiting for. I don't believe that her wait had a sense of looking for something that had gone missing, like the way one searches high and low for a lost key. It was more of an existential wait – a sense of displacement, almost as though she had lost a part of herself and was waiting for it to return.

The Danish existentialist philosopher Søren Kierkegaard thought it possible to lose the self: if you take no responsibility or ownership for yourself, selfhood withers. 'The greatest hazard of all, losing the self, can occur very quietly in the world, as if it were nothing at all,' he wrote. Simply define yourself by the clothes you wear, the car you drive and the properties you own, and before you know it, you'll turn around and discover that you've waltzed into old age. You may well be a human being, but you are not a self, he claimed, unless you have self-awareness, taking ownership and responsibility for who you are and projecting yourself into the person you wish to become.

So, what should you do with your life? It might sound like an overwhelming question, but one of the most influential thinkers of modern times, Friedrich Nietzsche, saw such ruminations as of vital importance. What is important to you? What matters? What makes for a good and meaningful life? What do you prioritize, and why? These values are acted out in the choices you make – they underpin your aspirations, goals and actions.

It's during the moment when you feel restless and discontent that Nietzsche implores you to get up close to this feeling and to study it. He regards any form of questioning as a sign of good mental health. When you stop one day and say, 'What am I doing with my life? Is this a good way to live? How could I be doing things better?' then you are beginning to ask the right questions.

Restlessness and questioning indicate an unease, a sense that things could be better. It could be little more than a vague feeling that there's something out there that'd make your life richer, even if you're currently at a loss to what that might involve. You sense that by doing something, or learning something, or changing something, your life could be markedly improved. But for some reason, the 'what' keeps eluding you.

This brings me to a family I once met in Paris who lived in darkness. Come night-time, the four family members would patter between the darkened walls of their apartment, sorting out clothing and packing things away, as effortlessly as we move under electric lights. They'd learned to live in the shadows and to see their familiar world anew. I should note that the family could well afford electric lighting. They simply preferred to time their waking hours with the rhythm of the sun – rising early, retiring early. When I enquired as to why they lived like this, they mentioned the need to create the right conditions for a good life. One does not just stumble into the good life, they proclaimed, it had to be actively managed.

The idea of a life being one that is actively managed wasn't something I was accustomed to. Like most, I came from a family where things were done a particular way because that was the way things were done. During summer storms, when the lights blew and the house was flooded in darkness, we'd stumble about, looking for torches and lighting candles, all the while cursing the loss of our familiar bearings. To deliberately plunge oneself into darkness each night seemed utter madness, until I started to mull it over some more. I started to reflect on the assumptions and conditions of life that I had hitherto taken for granted, such as ever-present overhead lighting. It made me think about how much of life 'just is' and why perhaps sometimes it might well be improved by not being 'this way' at all. By that, I mean perhaps everything in our life could be looked at from another angle, particularly if we think things could be, well, better.

Although this will hardly be news to you, it's still worth mentioning that you only have one life. You want to make sure you do your best with it. You don't want to get to the end and realize with a jolt that you'd kind of blown it; that you hadn't taken advantage of this precious gift; that you'd unthinkingly wasted your time. Because if you are someone who tries hard, means well and is willing to put in the hours – and I'd like to think that most of us fall into this category – then you want to know how best to make use of your time.

But we can fall into the trap of thinking that a good life means following some sort of scripted module for personal improvement. Self-help literature abounds with ideas on ways to live a better life: 'The most powerful goal achievement system in the world'; 'Five steps to realizing your goals and resolutions'; '12 months to $1 million'; 'The Personal MBA'. Most of it punches out advice on goal setting, productivity, time management and procrastination busters. But the problem with this is that it leaps over the 'What am I doing with my life' problem and sprints towards the next hurdle, which is 'How do I achieve it?' Armed with the kind of advice this approach offers, you can certainly take flight, and you can definitely achieve goals, but you'll probably land back in the bare patch, burdened with the same restlessness and unease, and asking yourself, 'Is this really what I want to do with my life?'

For some, the art of flourishing involves committing time and energy to productive endeavours that lead to a healthy bank balance and ensure a steady stream of material possessions. The good life is about buying stuff and finding the means to pay for it. This may involve the titillation of owning a shiny black car or a smart-looking house, sending the kids to private school, or taking many trips away to be pampered at a resort. Such types set their sights on ownership, and every decision thereafter is funnelled in this direction – investing in property, putting money into high-yielding savings accounts, dutifully paying off the credit card each month.

But you need to ask yourself: do I want to live my life pining for something else? Constantly thinking, 'Once *this* happens, then I will be happy.' Once I buy a house, or get a pay rise, or finish the renovations, then I will be happy. Or for some, it may extend to finding a partner, losing weight, having a child, stopping work, finding work, or finding meaningful work; once I find my passion, then, only then, will I be happy. Happiness, in this context, is a place sometime, somewhere in the future.

Ancient Greek philosopher Epicurus would likely have taken exception to this way of living. 'Do not spoil what you have by desiring what you have not; remember that what you have was once among the things you only hoped for,' he wrote. Always pining for the 'next thing', thought Epicurus, will set you on a course of eternal dissatisfaction. Desiring what you do not have dilutes appreciation for what you do have. And even if you were able to secure all your desires, then it just puts you back at square one – desiring the very next thing. It's called the 'hedonic treadmill' and it lurks in our subconscious, etched into the seeking part of our brains. So what did Epicurus suggest we do instead?

Epicurus lived on bread and water, declaring, 'Plain fare gives as much pleasure as a costly diet, when once the pain of want has been removed, while bread and water confer the highest possible pleasure when they are brought to hungry lips.' He saw happiness as the absence of pain, both mental and physical, and sought to pursue it by quelling desires that made him feel jealous, envious, or dissatisfied. For him, a life without desires was the ultimate pleasure. But few in modern society would agree with Epicurus that the path to happiness is a spartan life of few pleasures. Eating crud and living on next to nothing doesn't sound like much fun. So what *is* the answer?

My quest to find answers led me to launch a philosophy magazine, *New Philosopher*, and then an ad-free women's magazine, *Womankind*. In the days when news agencies stood at most high street corners and magazines were sold in supermarket chains and bookstores, there was a raft of such publications presenting readers with a life full of, well, consumption. Funded by advertising dollars, these magazines showcased the good life as lived by celebrities, and focused on fashion, finance, cosmetics and entertainment. For me, though, this was a paltry version of the good life. It was for this reason that I started my own magazines a decade ago.

The question of how best to live a good and meaningful life has in many ways taken shape in their pages. At the time of their creation, their underlying motive – to look at this forever questioning – felt somewhat revolutionary, especially in the face of media that seemed to me to be on perpetual repeat – the same faces in the spotlight, the same insistence that what is good for the economy, the roads and our bank accounts is also good for the human spirit. Our magazines aimed to pull the rug out and shake it up a little. And to see what resettled.

My research has since led me down many paths and across continents. I have been on a personal quest to test determinism at its core, by forcing change in an effort to wrest myself from my life's momentum that, like an underwater current, seems to be constantly pulling me in a particular direction. I have tried to decondition myself, to expel the influences that moulded and shaped me. I have interviewed hundreds of experts from around the world in a bid to investigate happiness and meaning across cultures. And I have debated personal identity with philosophers who scoff at the suggestion that one can find one's 'true self', or that there lies an 'inner self' waiting to be discovered.

But if flourishing is not prescriptive, if it can't be put in a box, or jotted down in list form, then it is indeed an individual journey. Nietzsche was one to stress this point. 'At bottom every man knows that he is a unique being, the like of which can appear only once on this earth. By no extraordinary chance will such a marvellous piece of diversity in unity, as he is, ever be put together a second time. He knows this, but hides it like a guilty secret. Why?' Nietzsche thinks the reason we shy from the glory of our unique selves is out of fear of others' opinions, so we think and act with the herd and do not seek our own joy. And while some may act this out due to shyness, mostly we do it out of laziness. We are too lazy to explore our exceptional uniqueness, to discover what it is that we, each of us a 'unique being', wish to do in this one extraordinary life that has been gifted to us at this moment in human history. Nietzsche goes on to say: 'The man who does not want to remain in the general mass, has only to stop "taking things easily". One needs to follow one's conscience, which cries out: "Be yourself! The way you behave and think and desire at the moment – this is not you!"'

To flourish, suggests the philosopher, we need to unchain ourselves from the opinion of others and the fear of standing out. We must conquer laziness and set forth on a journey to find our true genius. In the infinity of time, we exist in a brief span – 'today' – and 'we must reveal why we exist', demands Nietzsche. 'We have to answer for our existence to ourselves and will therefore be our own true pilots, and not admit that our existence is random or pointless.' But this quest to find your unique self may take you on a journey, and it may involve giving up the security of knowing. 'Why cling to your bit of earth, or your little business, or listen to what your neighbour says?' he coaxes.

It can be unnerving to think that you, and you alone, will determine the course of your life. It's more comforting to think that other people can make that decision for you, or that your fate is in some way predetermined by your upbringing, your education, your peers, society, the time into which you were born, your family wealth, your personal network, your health, your habits, your fears and your sorrows. But Nietzsche would shun this as nonsense and would probably call you lazy. 'No one can build the bridge over which you must cross the river of life, except you alone.' While we can wait for others to guide us, we risk losing ourselves. 'There are paths and bridges and demi-gods without number, that will gladly carry you over, but only at the price of losing your own self: your self would have to be mortgaged, and then lost.'

When restlessness mounts and you find yourself seeking, but don't know where to look, or what it is exactly that you wish to find, US mythologist Joseph Campbell likens it to being in a forest and hearing the enchanting notes of music from afar. Do you stop to listen? Or do you, consumed by your own thoughts and worries, continue on? 'Stop,' he implores. 'Listen.' Even if just for a moment.

The enchanting music is your bliss, and bliss is your signpost pointing the way. In Sanskrit, writes Campbell, the three terms that represent the brink, the jumping-off place to the ocean of transcendence, are: Sat-Chit-Ananda. 'The word "Sat" means being. "Chit" means consciousness. "Ananda" means bliss or rapture,' he writes. 'I thought, "I don't know whether my consciousness is proper consciousness or not; I don't know whether what I know of my being is my proper being or not; but I do know where my rapture is. So let me hang on to rapture, and that will bring me both my consciousness and my being." I think it worked.'

In other words, while philosophers continue to struggle to define consciousness, and while debate still rages in philosophy departments as to what is a self, what we can grasp within this life is our bliss. What uplifts you? What makes you breathless when you talk about it? What did you gravitate to as a child? Such questions, of course, may be difficult to answer – and it's easy to slouch your shoulders and declare, 'Nothing... See, that is the problem.' But these questions are merely the jumping-off point.

'Our life has become so economic and practical in its orientation that, as you get older, the claims of the moment upon you are so great, you hardly know where the hell you are, or what it is you intended. You are always doing something that is required of you,' writes Campbell. When Campbell pored over his lecture material and writings spanning a period of 24 years, he noticed something odd. Over that quarter of a century, Campbell had grown as a person, he'd changed, progressed, and much had happened in his life. He'd worked as a professor of literature at a women's college and had married a former student, who was a dancer. But when he reviewed his writings over that time frame, he noted: 'There I was babbling on about the same thing.' Campbell was struck by the continuities that ran through his notes. He was 'on topic' so to speak, and this continuity, or thread, is what he calls his Personal Myth. It was his bliss station.

Indeed, what we can grapple with – and test, and chart – what we can compose songs and sing about, and tell our grandkids about, is our joy, or bliss. 'Where is your bliss station? You have to try to find it,' urges Campbell. 'Follow your bliss,' he insists. Because this is your destiny in waiting.

The nineteenth-century German philosopher Arthur Schopenhauer may have seen it as more akin to a personal narrative, the plot of the novel about one's life. Whichever term you might prefer, the questions are much the same: what recurrent ideas or dreams have you had in your life? When you leaf through past diary entries, what themes recur? What is on your to-do list year after year after year? What inspires you most in books and films? In other words, what are you babbling on about? Find out, and follow it, is Campbell's message. Follow your bliss.

At university, Campbell was a successful track and field athlete. He could sprint a half mile faster than almost anyone else in the world at the time. He found his bliss in sport, in both training and competing. But after university, he couldn't find a job. So instead, he rented a shack in the woods and retreated from life. He read books for five years, dividing his day into four three-hour periods, and reading up to nine hours each day. 'I followed the path from one book to another, from one thinker to another. I followed my bliss,' he explains, 'though I didn't know that that was what I was doing.'

But it takes courage to do what you want, he stresses. 'Other people have a lot of plans for you. Nobody wants you to do what you want to do. They want you to go on their trip, but you can do what you want. I did. I went into the woods and read for five years.'

There were days when Campbell wished someone could give him the answer – knock on the door of his cabin and tell him what he should do with his life. He was searching in his books for a message, and it would have been easier to find if someone had given him a clue – start here and follow the path in this direction. But Campbell knew that the call to your own adventure begins and ends with you. 'Freedom involves making decisions,' he writes, 'and each decision is a destiny decision. It's very difficult to find in the outside world something that matches what the system inside you is yearning for.'

From 1929 to 1934, he read, among others, Mann, Nietzsche, Spengler, Schopenhauer, Kant, Goethe and Jung. Finally a message arrived, asking him if he'd like to take a job teaching literature. Campbell instinctively knew it was time to go back into the world and share what he had learned.

Most of our decisions in life centre on the core requirements of survival. We need food, water, shelter, clothes; we need security, a good job, adequate health and a place to live. We need love and friendship, a sense of family and connection, and also, for many, a level of respect in society, which may fall into the need for recognition, status or prestige. These 'needs' are set out graphically in Abraham Maslow's 'hierarchy of needs' pyramid, with its pinnacle being 'self-actualization', or the desire to become the most that one can be. This is the top of the pyramid, and it is often only sought once the other needs have been met.

But Campbell was puzzled by Maslow's value system. 'I looked at that list and I wondered why it should seem so strange to me,' he writes. 'A person who is truly gripped by a calling, by a dedication, by a belief, by a zeal, will sacrifice his security, will sacrifice even his life, will sacrifice personal relationships, will sacrifice prestige, and will think nothing of personal development; he will give himself entirely to his myth.'

This happens when one experiences the call to one's own adventure. It happened for Campbell, and he entered the woods. He shunned Maslow's value system and turned his back on what was expected of him by his parents, teachers and friends. He relinquished his place in society, his security, to say nothing of prestige. 'If the call is heeded,' writes Campbell, 'the individual is invoked to engage in a dangerous adventure. It's always a dangerous adventure because you're moving out of the familiar sphere of your community.'

Campbell sees countless parallels in folklore, myths and legends, where a central character moves out of the known sphere into the great beyond. In his book *Pathways to Bliss* he describes a Native American Navajo tale of two brothers searching for their father, the sun, called 'Where the Two Came to Their Father'. Their mother warns them, 'Do not travel too far from home.' But more importantly, she implores them never to travel northwards due to the monsters, saying, 'You may go eastwards, southwards and westwards, but don't go north.'

The brothers, of course, head north, forging, for the first time in their life, their own path. The boys aim to travel to their father to source weapons to help their mother fight the monsters. They travel to the edge of the known world, and step beyond the threshold into the desert, where the landscape is shapeless and devoid of features. 'I call this crossing the threshold,' writes Campbell. 'This is the crossing from the conscious into the unconscious world.'

The boys meet an old lady called Old Age, and she says, 'What are you doing here, little boys?' They tell her they are going to visit their father, the sun, and she says, 'That's a long, long way.

You'll be old and dead before you get there. Let me give you some advice. Don't walk on my path. Walk off to the right.' The boys start walking as she told them, but shortly forget about Old Age's advice, and end up walking on her path instead.

To leave the known path is often depicted in mythology as akin to entering the dark woods, plunging into the ocean, or traversing the desert. Crossing the threshold into the unknown may involve relinquishing the security of a successful career, for example. 'It may be depicted as an ascent or a descent or as a going beyond the horizon', writes Campbell, 'but this is the adventure – it's always the path into the unknown, through the gateway or the cave or the clashing rocks.'

Nietzsche concurs that the path to finding your unique self, to unveiling your true being, will not come easily. This 'digging into one's self,' as he puts it, 'this straight, violent descent into the pit of one's being,' will be troublesome and dangerous. He warns us that to begin this journey of self-exploration will be perilous and marked with potholes.

The boys continue to walk on Old Age's path, forgetting what she said, and they grow old and tired, barely able to put one foot in front of the other. Sometime later they meet Old Age again, and she reprimands them for ignoring her advice. 'Forge your own path and stay off mine,' she bellows. And this time they obey, and in doing so they eventually find what they were searching for: their father.

'If you follow your bliss,' continues Campbell, 'you put yourself on a kind of track that has been there all the while, waiting for you, and the life that you ought to be living is the one you are living. Wherever you are – if you are following your bliss, you are enjoying that refreshment, that life within you, all the time.'

Many times, however, you will hear the call of enchanting music, but you will refuse it. You may think about Maslow's value system and feel overwhelmed by the enormity of what you are giving up – security, connection, prestige and recognition. How will I make money? Where will I live? When one experiences fear of the unknown, one may refuse the call to one's adventure, and, as Campbell argues, 'the results are then radically different from those of the one following the call.' Sometimes, 'when the call isn't answered, you experience a kind of drying up and a sense of life lost.' Sometimes when the call isn't answered, banality sets in.

It's not all lost, however. In life we are called to our own adventure repeatedly. It doesn't just happen once in a lifetime. It's a cycle, and sometimes we may be up to the task, other times not. 'What I think is that a good life is one hero journey after another,' concludes Campbell. 'Over and over again, you are called to the realm of adventure, you are called to new horizons. Each time, there is the same problem: do I dare? And then if you do dare, the dangers are there, and the help also, and the fulfilment or the fiasco. There's always the possibility of fiasco. But there's also the possibility of bliss.'

That brings me to a man I interviewed in my younger years as a junior journalist for a finance magazine. Three men, armed with different trading strategies, had been given $5,000 each to trade on the stock market for three months. One of them was a technical trader, another was a contrarian, and the third was a buy-and-hold investor. Which trading strategy was superior? I interviewed them, recorded their results, and plotted their successes and failures. While two of the men could have been pulled straight out of a trading game box, the third man was more memorable. My phone interviews with him sometimes lasted for hours. He talked in tangents, often about neither trading nor the stock market. He seemed to be confused about the meaning of his life, what he should do, how he could make a success of it. He seemed to want to do something, and urgently, but couldn't for the life of him work out exactly what that was. To me as a twenty-something, this forty-something man seemed almost insane by yearning after something that he couldn't quite define. And why did he think I had the answers? I don't really think he did, but he was happy to ponder any scraps of ideas I had to offer before I desperately tried to get him off the phone, my editor raising his eyebrows at me over the partition as I hung up after another marathon call.

The reason he stuck in my memory is that some years later I came across his name again, quite by chance. He'd helped launch a financial company – whatever it did, I am at a loss to remember, but it was building wealth rapidly, and it was constantly mentioned in the financial news. I imagined at the time that he'd be very successful by now and leading a large team of people. I think back to those phone conversations, to his evident agitation, his questioning, and I can't help but think that Nietzsche would have applauded him as someone who was digging deep. And in the end, he found gold.

But there is no set point in a life – no point where we can say, 'This is it, I am flourishing!' Instead, we are on a conveyor belt moving forward towards our ultimate end, passing scenes of bliss and rapture followed by frustration and deep despair. But both Nietzsche and Campbell would concur on this one: life is about seeking what matters, finding your individual footprint – for this is your way forward. While hedonists may interpret this as toasting the good life with a champagne flute in hand, Campbell has a different take on it. He deliberately rephrased 'follow your bliss' to 'follow your blisters'. In other words, follow your purpose, that which matters, and it will, oh yes it will, come with blisters.

I remember one cold evening meeting a snowy-haired Nordic couple at the base of the Atlas Mountains of North Africa. Shoeless and penniless, the couple worked on fruit plantations to fund their travels, sleeping at night in a tent too small for two people. While our group were safely tucked inside our tourist cabin in the evenings, a small flickering torchlight in the surrounding plains signalled the whereabouts of this couple, somehow battling it out on the plains, the tent's skin stretching against the relentless force of the chergui wind. At dawn, our group rose early and set forth with the goal of scaling the second highest mountain in Morocco. Wearing sensible hiking boots, and with some of our company carrying professional hiking sticks, our group wound up and up the trail, and, come lunchtime, we arrived at a bend where once again we were accosted by this strange couple, now at least wearing sandals in the chilly air, and beaming at us as though we had just happened to pass them out on a Sunday stroll. And then again, further along the trail, now just kilometres from the top, as our group stood together all peering vertically towards the peak, I spotted them again, within the clouds, surveying the landscape from the pinnacle. They had blazed their own trail – and just as there isn't one way to scale a mountain, there isn't one way to live a life.

Many years ago, I quit my corporate job in the city. It had been secure and well paid, with good prospects and endless avenues for career advancement. But I was restless – I had heard the call. I switched off the soundtrack to my old life; I switched off the media, the internet; and I turned my back on my obligations and duties. I embarked on a journey that took me winding through unknown city streets, across mountains and into the desert. I was on a quest to both lose and find myself. And in the end, whatever came of it, I would have forged my own path.

I hope that, by sharing this story, it will inspire you too to heed the call. As Nietzsche says, the true path is the one which is currently darkened, where you don't know what's around the bend. 'There is one road along which no one can go except you,' he urges. 'Do not ask where it leads – go forward.'

CHAPTER 1

Brisbane, Australia

'But to be quite oneself one must first waste a little
time.'

—Elizabeth Bowen

I DON'T PLAY GOLF, but it's 7.23 a.m. and tee off is in seven
minutes. From the driver's seat, I see a huddle of figures in the
morning mist. My boss has issued clear instructions to whip the
credit card hard: 'These guys are a big deal. They sell a tank load
of our funds. Be sure to give them a good time.' By mid-afternoon,
this band of golfers will be merry drunk. By early evening, they'll
barely hold themselves up against the bar. A good day on the golf
course will mean a surge in sales of lifetime annuities. A gold star
for me.

But the car seat holds me in its embrace. Rising mist billows
over sea-green grass, dwarfing the skyscrapers in the distance.
Bloated faces appear and disappear. A man decked head to toe in
white glances at his oversized watch. The clock on the dashboard
ticks to 7.25.

A rare and somewhat baffling aspect of being human is our
ability to gaze back upon ourselves – as the English philosopher
John Locke called it, to be a 'self to itself'. We can be a self and
analyse ourselves at the same moment. And in so doing, we turn
ourselves into an object, much like we may view an apple or a
pear. And we may wish to be a little more like this and a little less
like that – and sometimes who we see is not who we wish to see
at all. And it is this gap – between who we are and who we ideally
wish to be – that haunts us. It's the reason we write out New

Year's lists with gusto, and why we fall victim to jealousy when other people attain their dreams but we don't. In *The Gay Science*, Nietzsche declares: 'What does your conscience say? "You shall become the person you are."'

I hazard a glance at myself in the rear-view mirror. My face is dusty with makeup, and a lime-coloured cap is perched reluctantly on my forehead. Behind the car, three latecomers walk briskly towards the group, with handshakes all round when they get there. The mist clears for a moment, and I count them – well over 20 now, mostly men.

My mind goes over the possibilities. 'Yes, yes, I did get here on time. I made it. I just couldn't get out of the car,' I could say.

'You what? You couldn't get out of the car?'

'Yes, that's right. My hand was just lying there, I couldn't get it to move. And so I just sat there, watching everyone through the windscreen. Even Jerry.'

Jerry was the founder of the dealership. Even my boss got tense in Jerry's office. He'd mask his nervousness by being too familiar, doing things like delving into Jerry's golf bag hidden in the corner under the plastic blinds. And with a salesman's intuition, he'd pull out Jerry's favourite golf club, raise it in the air, and declare, 'Now this, this is a beauty!' Squinting with one eye, my boss would wiggle his bum and send a golf ball hurtling down the carpeted hallway, shooting past the girls at reception, and smacking into a white plastic cup.

Jerry was the quintessential 'rags to riches' type. Uneducated and humourless, he'd built a multi-million-dollar business that employed hundreds of financial advisers. Millions of dollars flooded through that dealership, with its yellowing walls, and my boss always got a yearly slice of that golden pie. Because golf, he'd figured out, was the way to Jerry's heart and, through that, to his cheque book. 'Find out what makes a person tick,' he said to me one day while we were stopped at traffic lights, on the way to some sales appointment in the suburbs. 'Find out what makes them feel important. Sniff it out.' He tapped his nose with a superbly manicured nail. 'Once you know what makes someone feel important, then you will know how to sell to them.'

I see Jerry's broad head within the mist-shrouded pack. He grapples for a phone in the pocket of his white golf shorts. The man at his side, like a hound, picks up the whiff of impatience. He glances at his watch. He mutters something, and Jerry scowls. Tee off is in two minutes and 31 seconds.

I look at the latch on the door, but my hand is a dead weight in my lap. I spot my reflection in the rear-view mirror and shake off the cap.

The American psychologist Abraham Maslow warned that you can enter a state of incongruence, where there is a gap between your actual self and your ideal self, between who you are and who you ideally wish to become. This gap sometimes explains the mid-life crisis, the sudden life lurch where a person you once knew has taken an unexpected detour. It can explain the person who is depressed, anxious, pent-up, who can't seem to get out of bed in the morning, who has lost a certain spring in their step. When the actual self and the ideal self are incongruent, Maslow predicted maladjusted behaviours. You may have seen it first-hand. A couple you once knew who 'had everything' – kids, a renovated house, a swimming pool – suddenly, they split up. They're bickering, and then he takes off with a divorcee in town. Marriage counsellors, even close friends, might just put it down to 'irreconcilable' differences, but when a couple has been together for some 20 years, incompatibility is not at the heart of it. Incompatibility hits lovers within weeks, or at most months, of meeting each other. But if a couple can get through children and home renovations, then it's something else, and Maslow would point the finger at 'incongruence' – that gap between the actual self and the ideal self. It's an individual thing; one person in the partnership is yearning to close that gap, and the easiest way, they think, is to ditch the marriage. But it's not as simple as this. Often, by ditching the marriage, financial constraints force the couple to go further into entrenched routines, staying in jobs they detest, plugging away. There's no time to 'try something new'; you don't go through an expensive divorce and then decide to take up photography full-time. Try convincing the new partner about that.

On the flipside, a good friend unexpectedly decides at a later age to study to become a doctor, and at 45 is sitting in their surgery seeing a string of patients. But this friend, you notice, hasn't just changed their job: they seem suddenly transformed, more caring, more compassionate, more in tune with others' needs, less envious. What you are witnessing here is a state of congruence, or what Maslow described as 'self-actualization'. Your friend has self-actualized, and all those externalities could be envisaged as sun rings around a more cohesive self.

But self-actualization is not gained in 90 days. Rather, it's a lifelong project. It is a growing into your own skin, or, as the German psychiatrist Kurt Goldstein first noted back in 1939, it is the 'tendency to actualize, as much as possible, the organism's individual capabilities in the world'. It is our primary drive, our mission, that we undertake minute by minute – 'every individual, every plant, every animal has only one inborn goal – to actualize itself as it is'.

To be honest, I had only myself to blame for the job. When the position was advertised, I cold-called the manager, who became my boss. He picked up the call from a packed underground lunchroom, barely making out my chirping voice at the end of the line. But I'd boldly called him, and it was a sales job after all. Pushy types with no regard for protocol or standing in line are typically star performers, the ones who get the deals over the line. And so, within no time, I was flown interstate to meet his boss, deep-breathing in the lift to the 50th floor as my heart thumped wildly in my chest – to be awarded a salary 100 per cent higher than my previous one, along with a company car and a fuel and clothing allowance. Within a year, I'd doubled my salary and was granted my own glass office hovering a hundred metres above ground level. In my matching pant suit, I listened to my boss debating my new sales name with his overly pretty assistants, and suddenly booming, as if summoned by the gods, 'Touchdown Toni!'

I'd become Touchdown Toni, searching for a convertible Mercedes-Benz on the internet. Personally, I was partial to the sky-blue one. I test-drove a few and compared features, and I remember asking the sales guy what kind of people buy these sorts of cars. 'Are they people like me?' I enquired, curious to know what sort of person I'd become. A hundred metres below me, at ground level, there appeared a footpath, snaking back and forth to my apartment on the riverfront. There were no other points of interest on the horizon; it was short, clearly marked.

But here I was driving the executive car, parking in the underground car park, running my security pass through the turnstiles, clocking on for the day, rocketing up the lift, collecting my daily schedule from my assistant, comparing my gnawed-down fingernails with her highly manicured ones, realizing that my single pair of black boots probably shouldn't be worn every day. And I was soon to learn why the job came with so many car-related perks. My schedule was a not-a-minute-to-spare run of appointments, from the west of the city to the east, and from the north to the south, a red circle outlined on the city map around tiny offices and reception areas, cafés and boardrooms, my assistant Kelly commandeering my every step from her air-conditioned sanctuary in the sky: Building 1 in King Street at 11.45 a.m., to Building 1200 in Campbell Parade by 1.20 p.m. I was the miniature blue car on the toy racetrack, pushed hither and thither by a fingernail dug deep into my spine. Suddenly I was speeding through streets, in and out of corporate foyers, the clock ticking. 'Touchdown Toni, it's Kelly. I've booked you on a plane to Rockhampton tomorrow. You've got a presentation to 30 people?' In sticky 40-degree heat, my single pair of ill-fitting boots got worn down fast.

Human beings need to find food and shelter, to care for their family, to meet basic needs, but there must be more to a life than this. We need only think of Michelangelo's *David* or Tolstoy's tome of literary works. Maslow claimed that a primary aim in life is to attain your highest potential as a human being based on your unique talents, your disposition and your life situation. Much like when you're eight years old and you dream of becoming *this* sort of person. One day, you dream, you will become what you deem to be a success, and your life will matter, and it's this yearning to 'become' that we must keep fresh and spirited as we move through the decades.

Maslow cited Henry David Thoreau, the nineteenth-century American writer who left his community to live a spartan life in a log cabin – to 'live deliberately, to front only the essential facts of life'. Away from city life and ordinary pursuits, Thoreau was commended by Maslow for finding his true goals in life and following them, even while he had to reject the norms and customs of his day. Thoreau lived in a log cabin with few possessions. He wrote, read and meditated. To eat, he fished and collected fruit and vegetables. Thoreau discovered his purpose in living simply, abandoning illusions of fame, success and wealth. 'As you simplify your life,' writes Thoreau, 'the laws of the universe will be simpler.'

Unlike other prisoners within the corporate compound, I didn't get to run around the perimeter in my lunch break. While they got fresh air, jogging in their runners and tights, I'd be ordering my fourth latte of the day with an adviser Kelly had arranged for me to meet. We'd sit in some fishbowl café and watch other corporate prisoners rotate, huffing and puffing, knowing their own clock was ticking. On the table, I'd have my list of funds for sale – the 'Liquid Lifestyle' lifetime and the 'fixed-term' annuity – and the adviser would be looking at his watch, thinking about his kids, and his wife, and the fact that these damn salespeople were always taking up his time. But as the French philosopher Jean-Paul Sartre once warned, we tend, in existentialist terminology, to 'live in bad faith', knowing that this life is someone else's creation, a construct that we've taken on unthinkingly like some bad tattoo drilled into our skin. We try to rub it off, but it's there, the ink pierced into our skin permanently – or so we think.

While we were on the way up to our 30th-floor executive office one Tuesday, my boss asked me for my elevator pitch. 'You don't have one?' he gasped in feigned surprise as I shook my head. 'You need one, and you need to perfect it.' That day I was to learn an elevator pitch, a 30-second spiel I would rehearse and then broadcast to strangers about myself. A good elevator pitch, he insisted, could impress a stranger in the time it takes an elevator to rocket from ground floor to level 30. 'Practise it now,' he said, seizing the moment. 'Give it to me.'

Rapid-fire introductions, like the elevator pitch, often come with a lot of nouns, as though the more nouns one has in life, the more impressive one is. Sum yourself up in a couple of words. Users of social media do it to introduce themselves online. 'Surfer, father, film director.' 'Banker, golfer, traveller.' You're unlikely to see someone list their personal ideals, the goals for which they strive, or the principles that govern their behaviour – 'Integrity, lover of virtue, equality, freedom.' The way we define ourselves has altered over time, and probably not for the better. Today we classify ourselves into groups – norms and averages – like sociologists. We don't think of ourselves as pursuing an ideal, or a standard of perfection or excellence.

There was a time when ideals formed the basis of the study of society. Indeed, the author Daniel J. Boorstin argues that American historians were once preoccupied with ideals. The struggle for US independence and for the Constitution was written about as a struggle for the ideals of liberty and democracy. But over the past century, social scientists have thrown away the individualized portrait in favour of collecting statistics or facts about people, from which to derive medians and averages. With this data, social scientists built up group caricatures of people in society: the junior executive, the suburban housewife, the sales manager. These oversimplified sociological concepts were very helpful for advertisers, marketers, social reformers, and whoever else could make use of them in building images. 'Such caricatures became the image into which an individual was expected (and often tried) to fit,' writes Boorstin. 'These soon dominated the ways in which literate Americans thought about themselves. Americans tried to fit themselves into the social science images.'

This subtle change in the way individuals began to define themselves was a godsend for the advertising industry: conversion rates soared and profits ballooned. Imagine the difficulty of selling a pair of expensive shoes to a man pursuing the ideal of virtue; or selling an overpriced car to a woman inspired and driven by the ideal of charity or peace. Instead, advertisers were able to split the populace up into nice little groupings and hit them hard with images that appealed to their sense of identity: the 'banker/golfer' sports a luxury watch and drives a prestige car.

Boorstin notes: 'Naive emphasis on ideals had at worst tempted men to unrealistic pursuit of an abstract standard of perfection: emphasis on modes and images now tempts us to pursue the phantoms of ourselves.' Indeed, like a dog chasing its tail, we are intent on collecting images and forming an identity that represents what we already are.

But here in the lift with my boss, the thought of describing myself in 30 seconds came with a feeling of horror. It had all the hallmarks of a 30-second radio advertisement, except, rather than selling lifetime annuities, this time the advertisement is about me. When did I become a product to sell?

The clock hits 7.29 a.m. on the golf course, and I don't have my sales face on, my marketing personality. If I manage to open the car door, I worry I will exit as me, as visibly ill-suited to the role as if I had been wearing pyjamas. Normally, I'd rehearse my lines in the car ride, the 'elevator pitch', always aware of adding the sales comment, 'You know, we were thinking seriously about ditching that annuity, thinking no adviser is going to understand it – it's complex, you know, with the derivatives inbuilt, it's not a standard fund – but you know it's our star performer these days; the advisers really "get it". Marty, surely you've been taking secret golf lessons? Because that was one heck of a swing!'

But if I take a moment to reflect on what actually happened, I can see that the fissures began inside a room tucked deep within corporate walls. Glass sliding doors surrounded a long rectangular table, its polished wood gleaming. Our two assistants were already neatly tucked into matching chairs, arriving bright and early as was customary. It was one of the first team meetings we'd had, and it had been months since I'd started. My assistants giggled as they revealed how they psychoanalysed interview candidates from the shoes they wore. 'We saw your black boots at the interview,' they sniggered. 'And what did this say about me?' I shot back, having not had a moment to buy a replacement pair since I'd started. 'We saw you as hard-working,' they replied, stifling a giggle as my boss paraded in at 8.30 a.m. sharp, clearly exhilarated at the prospect of spending time in a small room with the three of us. He seated himself at the vacant head-of-table space, immune to the cupboard-feel of the inner sanctuary, its impenetrable white walls, its air devoid of oxygen from weeks-old coffee breath circulating through 30 floors of office workers.

To outsiders, I suppose I was a 'success'. I had a well-paid job and an assistant, and I got to drive an executive car and put lunches on the firm's credit card. But what is a 'success' exactly? In the Middle Ages, the word 'success' did not even exist. Success in the sixteenth century meant to 'follow or succeed something'; in other words, something happens if I do this. To distinguish oneself as 'successful' was not possible. Back then, to describe someone as successful was as nonsensical as calling them 'purple'.

I first noticed the sensation in my face. And then in my hands, my heart, thumping; it was fear, cold-blooded fear, and it was rippling through my bloodstream. Before my boss could utter a word, I stood up and muttered something incomprehensible about feeling ill. I exited the glass cupboard and rushed headlong out of the boardroom and into a wider glass bowl. I got into the lift. I grabbed my phone and called my boyfriend Zan, the signal radiating across to his office tower. I stood, my face pressed against the glass, hovering hundreds of feet above ground level. And as I shot down the elevator shaft, I screamed, 'I'm not Touchdown Toni. I don't know who she is, but this is not her!'

I now watch Jerry from behind the windscreen in a state of congruence. Jerry, the suburban kid who got teased at public school. I see him as a boy perched on the toilet reading the

Financial Times, titillated by the world of corporate money and broking deals. 'He was born in a suit,' declares his proud mother to friends over the back garden fence. And as soon as Jerry exited out of school, he was in the office, eating ham sandwiches at his desk and saving up to buy his first-ever polished golf clubs, the same ones that the professionals use.

The clock hits 7.30 a.m., and the group now seems far beyond the 20 golfers I counted earlier. They are huddled together so tightly in the morning glare that all I see is an expanse of white light, like an aura. I stare into it, tapping my phone with a nervous hand. 'I couldn't get out of the car. Yes, I know it doesn't make sense. But it just happened.'

How do you strip yourself of an identity once it's got you by the collar? Studies show that the people who experience the most purpose at work have jobs that align with the way they view themselves. Swiss psychiatrist Carl Jung once wrote: 'I have frequently seen people become neurotic when they content themselves with inadequate or wrong answers to the questions of life. They seek position, marriage, reputation, outward success of money, and remain unhappy and neurotic even when they have attained what they were seeking. Such people are usually confined within too narrow a spiritual horizon. Their life has not sufficient content, sufficient meaning. If they are enabled to develop into more spacious personalities, their neurosis generally disappears.'

To self-actualize is to be content with yourself, driven by your own goals, and not waylaid by the demands of others, including broader society as a whole. By analysing people who he believed were self-actualized, Maslow came up with a number of key personal traits. Self-actualizers accept their own flaws, are comfortable being alone, do not aim to be liked but rather are true to themselves. They also, he believed, see the world afresh, like children, and can have 'peak experiences' that may be as simple as delighting in a sudden shaft of sunlight from behind a cloud. Of course, the path to self-actualization will not come without its pain and setbacks, warns Maslow. Often, we must uncover difficult parts of ourselves in order to grow – there are often many fears, phobias, or habitual triggers that need to be pulled apart if one is to become the best version of oneself; or, as Maslow wrote, 'This tendency might be phrased as the desire to become more and more what one is, to become everything that one is capable of becoming.' Maslow listed philosophers, poets, politicians, writers – people like William James, Abraham Lincoln, Thomas Jefferson, Aldous Huxley and Baruch Spinoza. He could well have added Jerry.

After work one day, I met Zan at a city train station. We were heading out, wanting to get out of the loop of work. I arrived first, and the station was already teeming with workers trying to beat rush hour on a Friday afternoon. In the distance, I hazarded a glance at his tall outline arriving on the concrete platform, his shoulders squared off in his navy suit, the necktie choking his throat. Unabashedly, he first ripped off his tie, then undid a couple of buttons and pulled his shirt over his head. He unbuttoned his trousers and wrestled with a replacement pair of khaki army shorts. Then, spotting me at the last moment, he strolled, shirtless and shoeless, across the platform with his suit rolled under one arm. 'Are you hot?' I enquired, trying not to sound alarmed. 'No,' he replied, 'just ill-suited to this life.'

The train pulled up to the platform at 4.43 p.m., two minutes late, and we boarded, finding a seat facing backwards, watching our past pulling away from us. With my face slumped against the windowpane, I couldn't fathom what was plaguing me so much; I felt like my time had been somehow stolen, like a thief stealing a wallet from a backpack. I realized that from the moment I opened my eyes in the morning until the second I closed them at night, I was 'on schedule' – preparing for work, checking my diary, driving from one meeting to the next, working on my laptop, answering emails, my day subdivided into smaller and smaller units of efficient time. High-speed communication technologies seemed to only heighten this phenomenon, putting more and more items on my 'to-do' list. But what would idle time involve exactly? I pondered, as I observed blank-faced commuters out of the window, caught up in their own troubles, waiting for a go sign at traffic lights. What would my mind think about if it wasn't 'on schedule', when it was free to ponder and explore? Had part of my inner self been dulled, tuned out? Had my imagination and spontaneity withered? Had I lost something of my inner self?

The clock hits 7.32 a.m., the golfers have started to tee off, and I feel like I've slipped over the edge of something grand, like a cliff face. Something, indeed, is shifting within me.

Interestingly, Kierkegaard uses the cliff face as a metaphor. He thinks that when we literally stand at the edge of a cliff and peer over its edge, we are not only terrified of falling – at the same time, we also fear succumbing to the impulse to throw ourselves off. At the cliff face we experience our own freedom first-hand. Here, you can do whatever you please – move forward into the yawning abyss, or remain where you are. It's up to you. The realization that you have the absolute freedom to decide the course of your life – to jump or not jump – is as dizzying as vertigo, thought Kierkegaard, who proposed that we face the same anxiety in all of life's choices. Every action we take is a choice, decided by us and no one else. Kierkegaard's argument that life is a series of choices – and that these choices bring meaning (or not) to our life – is the cornerstone of existentialism. Rather than offloading the responsibility onto society or religion, each individual is solely responsible for making their life meaningful and living it authentically.

My hand is on the gearstick, and I shove the car into reverse. The wheels crunch against the gravel as the axle pivots. I pause as a merry-faced golfer makes his way through the gates into the compound, before levelling my foot hard upon the accelerator. I don't look back. I don't ponder the consequences. I am just moving, my fingernails dug into the gearstick. I steer away from the mirage of a conventional life of stable income and yearly bonuses.

And upon the freeway proper, I step resolutely upon the accelerator. My shoulders are hunched and my corporate cap is crumpled under my black boots. I have just jumped into the abyss.

CHAPTER 2

Leaving Home

'One of the most powerful wellsprings of creative energy, outstanding accomplishment, and self-fulfilment seems to be falling in love with something – your dream, your image of the future.'

—E. Paul Torrance

I AWAKE TO THE sound of wheels skidding, followed by the clang of steel meshing into steel, a collision so violent that the apartment floor shakes. It is 5 a.m. on a Sunday morning. I fling open the balcony doors. Early sunlight casts a crimson pallor over the Brisbane River. It is hot and sticky, and the empty streets are already consumed by thickening air. Below me, a deformed metal sculpture is circled by two figures hopping from leg to leg. My executive car, the first time I'd parked it on the kerb outside, is now a heap of misshapen metal.

I grab my coat and, shoeless, take the lift down to ground level. There is an intense smell of rubber in the air, and the foreign chatter of an unfamiliar language. Two Nigerians, brother and sister, had arrived in the country the day before. They stand wide-eyed and apologetic. I look into the clear black of their eyes and smile, knowing that I only have them to thank.

Imagine you walk into a room and meet someone, who beckons you to sit down on a couch. This person smiles, makes polite small talk, and asks you how you are feeling. And then this person introduces themselves to you as you. 'You can't be me,' you say to them. 'I'm me.' But they refuse to accept this and continue to insist that they are, indeed, you. There is a peculiar similarity between the two of you, this you must admit, but there are major differences too. This person dresses in a way you admire, and, oh yes, they suddenly start discussing a topic that's secretly meaningful to you. It is impossible that this person is you as there are too many differences. However, when they enquire about your past, they seem to know it intimately, but odder still, they seem to have memorized your dreams – better, shall you say, than you yourself, if that is at all possible. 'Oh yes,' they say, and nod knowingly.

The person who insists that they are you takes you to a mirror on a wall, and you stand side by side, and then they move behind you and place their face above yours in a tower-like formation. There's a confidence in their eyes, a sense of direction, a calmness that is missing in your pale and jittery profile. There is no doubt that they carry themselves better than you. You stand in their shadow.

You feel time escaping, and with a pressing agenda of tasks to do, you know you should excuse yourself and leave, but for some reason you're not compelled to do anything but stand alongside this person who says that they are you. For once, it's nice, you admit, to have a sense of it being all about you. As well, you find that you are not pulled by time, or – perhaps for the first time in your life – by anything at all. You relax and simply 'be' with this person; it's comforting to exist quietly, to not go anywhere, to just be.

As soon as you leave the mirror and return to the sofa, according to the humanistic psychologist Carl Rogers, you'll have entered a state of incongruence, or separation, between who you are and your 'ideal' self, or the person you wish to become. You'll have returned to a state of separation, and you may feel the tension rise. Perhaps it's from a longing to return to the mirror, or at least to return to a state of being a shadow of your ideal self – but alas, you sink despondently into the sofa's cushion. How do you cross the floor to become this person? How can you go from where you are today to the person you most want to become? Sigmund Freud, the founder of psychoanalysis, always said that a problem can't be solved by the same consciousness that created it. So, here, the issue is this: if it's you that's doing the thinking, then surely you can't know the answer to this paradox of identity? If you are in search of your ideal self, then you have to take yourself out of the picture.

———

The plane battles the turbulence, and I can't help but stare at the fidgeting hands of the woman beside me tap, tap, double-tap, tap, tapping on her phone. A person from the eighteenth century might hazard a guess that this woman, clad in a blue jumpsuit, had some form of 'irritable hand' syndrome, a forever twitch – seemingly at the mercy of some higher power. I open my notebook and attempt to compose my thoughts for the journey ahead. Is it possible to change who you are?

As the plane steadies, and the nervous coughing of a man behind me momentarily ceases, I'm still transfixed by the movements of this woman who stares ahead, expressionless, her fingers constantly tapping. The air stewards wheel out a trolley full of food and drink – muffins, toasties, tea and coffee – and click it into place before the plane takes a lunge to the right. One of them leans down to ask us if we want something to eat or drink. I take a muffin and a coffee for Zan, while the woman next to me shakes her head without even a glance.

Psychologists have forever worried about why we do the things we do. What drives our behaviour? How is it that some people are motivated to pursue their dreams, while others stumble about in a maze of indecision? One man watches six hours of television a day, while another gets up at 5 a.m. to go for a run. One woman fulfils her childhood dream of becoming a well-known painter after years of studying, applying herself, networking, exhibiting, selling, while another woman with the same dream, and perhaps more innate talent, works downtown in a government agency, rarely finding the time to pick up a brush. There's more than genetics, or opportunity, or timing, or luck, or money at play here. You only have to consider those who defy all the odds to get what it is that they want in life, from self-made billionaires at one extreme to drug addicts at the other. We all have dreams. We all want something out of this life of ours. But why is it that some people can muster the motivation and willpower, while others keep writing out the same New Year's resolutions year after year after year?

There are plenty of books on the topic, but there's something lacking in the literature for people who, like me, want to break free of the prison of the self, adopt new behaviours, achieve childhood dreams, or simply gain a subtle shift in perspective. Putting it more simply: how do you go from who you are today to who you want to be in the future? How do you close the gap between your real self and your ideal self – a quest that shouldn't be relegated to the bottom shelf, sidelined as the trivial and self-centred pursuit of the privileged few? Carl Rogers, regarded in the field as one of the most eminent psychologists of the twentieth century, thought the desire to 'become' your ideal self should be none other than the prime mission of your life. For Rogers, humans have one principal motive, and that is to self-actualize, to reach their full potential – a mission that he optimistically believed we all could achieve. According to him, we are in congruence when our real self and our ideal self are in harmony. When they are not – watch out!

Who is your ideal self? Most of us have rarely taken a moment to think about it. While we're regularly implored to find our 'true self', or to unleash our 'inner self', it's infinitely more exciting to think about our ideal self. Who do you wish to become? Consider for a moment how you envisage your ideal self – what do you do for work, and for pleasure? What do you wear? If you were to draw this ideal self on a blank sheet of paper, or to pencil in a few descriptive notes, what would you note down? More importantly, how far are you from this person right now? It's an interesting thought experiment for two reasons. First, it gives you an insight into who you ideally want to become; and second, it gives you a sense of the gap between who you are and who you want to become – that is, of the state of incongruence in which you presently find yourself.

When James Olds finished his dissertation on operant learning in children at Harvard University, he was convinced that the secret to motivation could be located within the brain. But Olds, a psychology graduate, knew very little about how the brain functioned, so he took up a postdoctoral fellowship at the Montreal Neurological Institute under the renowned psychologist Donald Hebb. There, at the Hebb laboratory at McGill University, situated on the second floor of the starkly modernist Donner Building, Olds and fellow graduate Peter Milner undertook one of the most shocking and revelatory experiments in the history of behavioural neuroscience.

James Olds was curious and experimental, and the young graduate didn't take long to make inroads in his chosen field. However, he had little medical know-how, so he was assigned to Milner, a trained neuroscientist three years his senior, assisting him with anaesthetizing the first rat in their pioneering experiment on positive reinforcement (in other words, can you change behaviour by the application of a positive stimulus?). The rat was laid out on a table top and a pair of electrodes half a millimetre deep were implanted into its skull. The target brain region was the midbrain reticular system, a region known for controlling sleeping and waking cycles, but, unknown to Olds and Milner, the electrodes shifted during surgery, and missed the original target. The implantation of the electrode was indeed successful, but the renegade scientists were unwittingly about to explore a part of the rat's brain – a mammalian brain with uncanny similarities to the human brain – that hadn't been mapped before.

The rat recovered from the surgery and was transferred to a rectangular box with the corners marked A, B, C and D. Spindly wires attached to electrodes in the rat's brain were plugged into an electrical stimulator at the other end. The rat moved to corner A, and Olds pressed a button that delivered a mild electric shock to the rat's brain tissue. While the shock did not cause the rat any pain, it did elicit brain activity, and it was predicted that the rat would avoid any further stimulation to the reticular formation. But when the rat was zapped in corner A, it returned to corner A again and again, before eventually falling asleep in a different corner.

When Olds and Milner, feverish with excitement, resumed their work at the laboratory the following day, the rat's curiosity for corner A had blossomed even further. As though it were part of a macabre puppet show, the rat marched to corner A to be zapped, and consistently preferred corner A to other corners, except for sleeping. Olds and Milner then switched corners, now delivering an electric shock when the rat moved in the direction of corner B. Tellingly, within five minutes, the rat altered its course from corner A to corner B. While brief shocks could coax the rat towards specific corners, more sustained zaps could retain the rat in a set corner once it had been relocated there.

Famous for his landmark experiments in the 1930s, psychologist B. F. Skinner had placed rats in an operant conditioning chamber known as a Skinner box, engineered with levers to deliver rewards such as food and water, or punishment by electric shock. Skinner demonstrated that rats could be conditioned to press the lever for food and water, and to avoid the lever that administered pain. Humans, like rats, Skinner surmised, are motivated to seek rewards and avoid punishments, and this small fact can aptly explain much of our day-to-day behaviour.

Hebb's laboratory didn't have a Skinner box at the time, so Olds built one. He and Milner then placed the rat in the chamber, which had a lever that the rat could press to zap itself at will. The first rat in the Skinner box, as Olds later wrote, 'ended all doubts in our minds' that electric stimulation applied to some parts of the brain acted as a reward for behaviour. After two to five minutes of learning, the rat started to zap itself with the lever once every five seconds, the stimulation lasting for a second or so each time. 'After thirty minutes the experimenter turned off the current, so that the animal's pressing of the lever no longer stimulated the brain,' wrote Olds. 'Under these conditions the animal pressed it about seven times and then went to sleep. We found that the test was repeatable as often as we cared to apply it. When the current was turned on and the animal was given one shock as an hors d'ouevre it would begin stimulating its brain again. When the electricity was turned off, it would try a few times and then go to sleep.'

Olds and Milner had hit upon the brain's pleasure circuit, a region so 'electrifying' and pleasurable that any mammal would find it hard to resist a zap, or two, or three, or – as the two researchers discovered – when brain stimulation was targeted at the septum and nucleus accumbens brain regions, some pleasure-seeking rats zapped as often as 7,000 times an hour.

The macabre puppet show played out as rats self-stimulated to the point of exhaustion, shunning food, even when they were hungry, and water, even when they were thirsty. Self-stimulating male rats ignored females in heat, and female rats abandoned their nursing pups, opting to press the lever instead. Some rats self-stimulated up to 2,000 times an hour for 24 hours, prompting the experimenters to forcibly cut them off from the power supply to prevent death from starvation. All the while, Olds and Milner busily mapped the brain's pleasure circuit, something that, in the future, would prove to be an enormous boon for companies, governments, organizations, and anyone else interested in mind control and manipulation, as well as, of course, habit creation.

Neuroscientists have since discovered that these hedonic brain circuits are activated not just by electrodes plugged deep in the brain, but also by everyday pleasures such as food, sex, shopping, learning, gambling, dancing, internet searching, social media, gaming, and artificial stimulators such as cocaine and alcohol. Even higher-order artistic, aesthetic, musical, altruistic, or transcendent pleasures are generated by this tiny gathering of interconnected brain areas called the medial pleasure circuit. Pleasure is our motivator, or stimulator, for choosing one path over another.

Once the brain's pleasure circuit had been mapped, media and technology companies spent decades trialling, testing and fine-tuning habit-forming technologies. The potent cocktail of neurological studies mixed with cold, hard cash has unlocked the holy grail to how humans can start a habit and continue to repeat this behaviour day after day after day.

I estimate that if the woman beside me taps on her phone at the same rate as Olds and Milner's rat – once every five seconds – she's tapped well over 600 times since take-off. Had I told her as a child that, come adulthood, she'd spend hours each day scanning a row of images on a screen and clicking a button if she liked, loved, or hated it, she'd have thought she'd been transported into some bizarre psychology experiment in a university lab. I peer over her shoulder at her screen and spot a square photograph of a couple posing on a golden sand beach. Like, love, or whatever. She presses like.

Today, more than half of the world's population uses social media, with the average person investing two hours and 27 minutes of their time in social media each day. Of course, social media is only one offering in today's smorgasbord of blissful fabrications, which includes watching movies and television, listening to the radio, using smartphones and tablets, and playing on the internet and on games consoles.

Ex-Google executives Jake Knapp and John Zeratsky, who now write about addictive technologies, describe the wizardry within Silicon Valley. 'At Google, we didn't have to trust our hunches about what people wanted; we could run experiments and get quantitative answers,' they write in their book *Make Time: How to Focus on What Matters Every Day*. 'Were people spending more time watching *these* kinds of videos or *those* kinds of videos? Were they coming back to Gmail day after day after day? If the numbers were up, the improvements were working and our customers were happy. If not, we could try something else. Redesigning and relaunching software isn't exactly easy, but it's a heck of a lot faster than, say, manufacturing a new model of car. So the... secret ingredient is evolution: Tech products improve dramatically from one year to the next.'

Developers are continually fine-tuning their offerings with the pointed aim of getting people texting, gaming, liking, tweeting, swiping, uploading, downloading, sharing more often . . . And if people don't get hooked on the activity, if the product just isn't 'sticky' enough, then it's relegated to the dustbin of yet another failed prototype, labelled a failure simply because it didn't manage to take over people's lives.

Ask any tech company who its competitors are, and they'll reply that they're up against all companies competing for limited time resources. 'YouTube doesn't just compete with other video websites: it competes for your time against music, movies, video games, Twitter, Facebook, and Instagram. And, of course, it competes with television . . . Far from fading away, television shows keep getting better, the result of a constant race to crank out the best, most binge-worthy series,' write Knapp and Zeratsky. In other words, a new product launch or improvement must be not only instantly appealing in order to create fast user-engagement, it must also bring the user back the next day, and the following one as well. 'Each time one service rolls out an irresistible new feature or improvement, it ups the ante for its competitors,' the authors write. 'If one app or site or game doesn't keep you riveted, you've got an infinite number of options two taps away. Everything is up against everything else all the time. It's survival of the fittest, and the survivors are damn good.'

I surmise that the lever-pressing rat in the Skinner box would prefer eating a tasty and nutritious meal, exercising daily on a wheel, caring for its pups, grooming and socializing, to receiving an empty zap. But due to the subtle wiring of their brain, rats, like humans, can't control their own behaviour at times, particularly if someone is plugging into their pleasure circuit. But this isn't all bad news. Armed with this knowledge, you can learn to better navigate your way in the world. You can use technology rather than allowing it to use you. And if empty zaps are getting in the way of you finding your purpose, of closing the gap between who you are today and who you ideally wish to become; if empty zaps are preventing you from self-actualizing, or from gaining a state of congruence, then simply acknowledging all of this is, indeed, a revolutionary first step on the road to flourishing.

CHAPTER 3

Buenos Aires, Argentina

'I know well what I am fleeing from but not what I am in search of.'

—Michel de Montaigne

T HE FRENCH EXISTENTIALIST PHILOSOPHER Jean-Paul Sartre was not one to clothe life in a snuggly blanket. We are alone, he declared, abandoned on earth in the midst of infinite responsibilities. You have no other purpose than the one you set. No other destiny than the one you forge. Yet Sartre thinks that most of us remain in denial of our responsibilities. We fall into what he called 'bad faith', deceiving ourselves about this radical freedom.

In *Existentialism Is a Humanism*, Sartre is blunt and unforgiving. 'Our doctrine horrifies people,' he asserts. 'They have no other way of putting up with their misery than to think: "Circumstances have been against me, I deserve a much better life than the one I have. Admittedly, I have never experienced a great love or extraordinary friendship; but that is because I never met a man or woman worthy of it; if I have written no great books, it is because I never had the leisure to do so; if I have had no children to whom I could devote myself, it is because I did not find a man with whom I could share my life. So I have within me a host of untried but perfectly viable attributes, inclinations and possibilities that endow me with worthiness not evident from examination of any of my past actions."' For existentialists, there is no genius other than that which is expressed in output, whether that's art, or music, or scientific or literary accomplishments of some sort. 'The genius of Proust resides in the totality of his works . . . outside of which there is nothing,' he writes. 'No doubt this thought may seem harsh to someone who has not made a success out of his life. But on the other hand, it helps people to understand that reality alone counts, and that dreams, expectations and hopes only serve to define a man as a broken dream, aborted hopes and futile expectations; in other words, they define him negatively, not positively.' For Sartre, we are nothing other than the sum of our actions.

The first principle of existentialism is that existence precedes essence, meaning that unlike an egg timer that's created for the purpose of cooking an egg, human beings have no particular purpose. It is only through our actions that we later start defining what our purpose in life is going to be. 'Man is nothing other than his own project,' writes Sartre. Yet, humans deceive themselves into thinking that, like mere physical objects, they are predestined to be what they are, shifting the responsibility of their actions onto others or onto a moral code. But, according to Sartre, reality exists only in action. In life, we commit ourselves and draw our own portrait, outside of which there is nothing.

———

We exit the car showroom at dusk. Without a map or a phone, and in a country where we don't speak the language, all navigational systems have been switched off. But that's the point. We are fleeing from ourselves, that's for sure, fleeing from the television programmes, the radio and the news; the rules, beliefs, stereotypes and assumptions of a society which had moulded us from birth. No computer, no phone, no social media, no camera, no compass, no internet. These are the rules. But more importantly, no plans. As Nietzsche said, if you continue to be a product of your culture, you can't rise above its values.

It was a brand-new van bought off the dealer's lot, and we paid for it with the contents of 50 assorted containers stuffed full of pesos. It had been weeks of extracting pesos from automatic teller machines, *barrio* by *barrio*, returning to our apartment in Buenos Aires, shoving more notes into another jar, or cereal box, or tea tin, like money launderers, nervously hopping about in the kitchen, counting the containers and the days, until the time came when we had enough money to buy the van in cash, and to drive out the same day.

Our rented half-bedroom apartment in Buenos Aires had the bathroom and bedroom lodged into the ceiling, too low to walk through without bending in half. Zan knocked his head with regularity, cursing each time. It was our ceiling cave from where we watched Spanish telenovelas on midday television, and from where we walked at night, punctually at dusk, and mostly in a straight line. We'd saunter down the grid-like maze of Buenos Aires, along *avenidas* smelling of *locro* and *empanadas*. And if we'd kept on walking, days could have passed, dusk turning to night turning to dawn repeatedly, two diminutive shadows hemmed between a walled garden of apartment blocks. Eventually, instead, we'd grab a beer at a bar and resume our walk, but now in the opposite direction.

There's something unnerving about the infinite. The city streets in Buenos Aires never seem to reach a conclusion of any sort, like the pull-to-refresh slot machine in the casino, the infinite scrolling on social media. Often, we wouldn't find anything of interest on our walks, but occasionally there'd be something gratifying – a cool bar, or a corner art gallery set up by some obscure couple in the *barrios*.

A person who wanders aimlessly through a city with no set agenda, other than to observe, is called a *flâneur* in French. Interestingly, there is no English equivalent. Aimlessly walking the streets in Paris, doing little other than observing the crowd frequenting the boulevards, cafés, parks and arcades, is elevated to an art form there. A *flâneur* is engaged in a philosophical sport, where the purpose of the activity is its sheer futility – no point of interest, no goal in mind, neither going anywhere nor doing anything, but simply walking. While it may appear to some as a complete waste of time, the French literary critic

Charles Augustin Sainte-Beuve thought the act of walking with no destination in mind, and for no particular purpose, was the 'very opposite of doing nothing'.

The philosophy professor Kieran Setiya, too, thought it wise to adopt the mindset of the *flâneur*. Aimless pursuits, like walking to nowhere, can be particularly useful for combating ennui, that debilitating boredom that can strike at any moment. When Setiya hit midlife, happily married with a child, and a tenured professor at a university, he suddenly felt the full force of ennui. As he describes it, 'I felt a sense of repetition and futility, of projects completed just to be replaced by more.' Setiya was suffering a similar plight to Sisyphus, who was condemned by the Greek gods to push a boulder up a mountain, only to watch it tumble back down again, and to return to the bottom to push it up once more. French philosopher Albert Camus writes in *The Myth of Sisyphus*, 'The workman of today works every day in his life at the same tasks, and this fate is no less absurd. But it is tragic only at the rare moments when it becomes conscious.'

Once it becomes conscious, like it did for Setiya, it can become unbearable. For me, I can't remember if ennui came on like a jolt, or if it slowly dimmed the foreground like a lengthening shadow. Whatever the case, I felt like a prisoner caught within a circuit, jogging in my lunch break, snacking in underground troughs, clocking in and out of turnstiles, security passes timing my coffee breaks and my Friday-afternoon getaways. I felt tracked, timed and herded. I was living Friedrich Nietzsche's version of the eternal return, the days unfolding endlessly, and my activities timed to the working cycle. My future was unravelling before me, as though everything was already set in motion.

Immersed in 'everydayness', we can suddenly find ourselves trapped within habitual routines and obligations. And when one's 'stock of knowledge', as the Austrian philosopher Alfred Schütz puts it, is limited to that which is socially derived, coming at us from the news, the television set, the internet, funnelled through the structures of our social world, our 'thinking as usual' can prevent us from coming up with an exit plan. While 'everydayness' may ease life by reducing its complexity, norms can start to determine the layout of one's days. The German philosopher Martin Heidegger sees 'everydayness' as a limitation, as inauthentic; he sees it as a fallen state in which we blunderingly go through life questioning little, other than which brand of cereal to buy for breakfast, or what brand of car to purchase next. For Heidegger, 'everydayness' is a barrier between us and our realization of our self and the world.

For Setiya, I suppose, come midlife, he'd accomplished most of what he'd set out to achieve in his earlier years. Many career goals had been met. He'd read and written a lot. And, having come to some sort of closure, he'd lost the thrill of the chase. His hunting sack was full of rabbits, as it were. What next?

For some, a midlife crisis will often culminate in overhauling the lot – career, house, car, partner – all tossed out in a maddening purge. But, as Setiya learned through studying the nineteenth-century philosopher Arthur Schopenhauer, tossing out to start anew puts the midlifer at the beginning of the road again – a sudden novice, a midlife failure. On the flipside, however, when continuing to tread the same path as before reeks of normalcy, what is one to do?

Engage in goalless activities, declared Setiya: adopt the spirit of the *flâneur*.

We started with the nouns first – *puerta, refrigerador, cama, ventana, silla* – and sticky-taped handwritten notes to items around the apartment. When we opened the fridge, we said *refrigerador*, until that became too simple, and the next thing was to sticky-tape the names of the contents too – *mantequilla, mermelada, leche, salsa de tomate*. When nouns had been exhausted, we started on phrases, scribbling them out and sticky-taping them first to the glass door of the bathroom cabinet, then to all the other vertical surfaces too: *Disculpe, ¿sabe dónde está la oficina de correos?* The walls quickly filled with written text, and then we'd test each other, replacing known words with unknown ones. Meanwhile, Spanish radio boomed from the kitchen, a static mess mixed in with the occasional recognized word or phrase. 'I understood that!' We were codebreakers.

In the early afternoons, we'd cross the city for Spanish lessons in an airtight apartment block, the city traffic bellowing through the thin walls, the summer sun heating up the window panes. The conjugation of 'to be' was set out on a papery-thin school workbook, and taught by the girlfriend of George, an American about the same age as us. Here he was, set up in Buenos Aires, talking Spanish with his thick American twang, running a language school with his Argentinian girlfriend. They'd talk marriage and children and renting more space beyond their apartment for privacy and distance between work and home life. He fascinated us, this brave soul who decided to say to hell with his destiny in Texas, instead setting up his life ten metres above the roaring traffic in Buenos Aires. This wasn't written in his stars. It wasn't found on the life line on his palm. He'd stepped off the path.

'Hola,' George says as we enter the apartment, and gives Zan an awkward kiss on both cheeks as is customary between Argentinean friends. He moves between English and Spanish with effortful abandon.

'We are heading south,' says Zan.

'Ah, where to?' George asks.

'No plan, just south,' replies Zan.

'But we're not sure if we should leave our apartment and the school,' I add. 'We like it here and are almost set up. Leaving is a death in a way, and we've really only just arrived.'

George sits down on a chair and closes the window behind him. He pauses to greet an older student who exits from one of the rooms. '*Estaré contigo dentro de un momento.*'

'I think, in life,' he says, 'as you get older, you don't regret what you did so much as what you didn't do. I think, when you have a choice between to do or not to do, you are better placed to do it, even if it doesn't turn out quite the way you want it to. Because to not do, well, that's when you will have regrets.'

'Or', says Zan, 'as Kierkegaard says, do it or don't do it, you will regret it either way.'

Our backpacks are almost too heavy to lift, but inside them is little to sustain us – physically, that is. No head torches, sleeping bags or wet-weather gear; no maps or guidebooks; no mobile phones or spare batteries; no watches or cameras. Instead, we haul dozens of books, mostly on philosophy, like *The Art of Happiness*, by Epicurus, and *Conversations of Socrates*, and some odd sprinklings of sociology and psychology texts. The question as to how to live was once the focus of philosophical thought, foremost on the minds of ancient philosophers such as Epicurus, Socrates, Plato and Aristotle. What can we learn from them?

But we want to absorb these ancient ideas in a place of no past. Stripped of our ordinary surroundings, we will hear these ancient voices, we surmise, unfiltered, untrammelled by such domestic trivialities as the sea of unwashed laundry or the car registration that has lapsed. We must do away with domesticity at least for a while. Like monks, we must remove ourselves from the clatter of intervening voices blocking our way to true experiences. We even carry in our bags many books on subjects that we have little interest in, because, well, who knows what changes the journey could bring? As intrepid travellers of the self, we must have an open and flexible itinerary.

We use the sun to navigate south. And as soon as we exit Buenos Aires, the traffic thins, until it is just us and the trucks passing south. The land gradually flattens to yellow plains. The Fiat panel van, brand new off the lot, purrs with the energy of a child, its tinny wheels spinning with delight. We head straight. We debate whether we can listen to the music of our past. But music has power over the subconscious to jog memory, to rekindle past selves. Instead, we listen to Argentinian tunes and talkback radio.

As dusk arrives, we start to look for somewhere to stay. With no guidebook or internet, we're weaving blindly through alleyways to find lodgings. But the clock, like the computer, and the GPS, and the media, and the internet, is an insistent voice keeping us on track, and we want none of that.

'It's pitch-black and we're still driving,' I say, hitting my fists upon the dashboard. 'We've been down this street a thousand times.'

It must be past midnight when we finally drop our bags upon a tiled floor. From the street, the house is but a door with a sign, *cabañas*. We drove along the street several times before Zan spotted the hanging sign from a window, obscured by shadows. We are led inside, and down a narrow corridor. The buckles on our backpacks scrape the walls. Zan's head collides into an overhanging plant. The *señora* abruptly stops at an internal door, and for a second it is just the three of us and two backpacks the size of large adults sandwiched within a low-ceilinged space. She fiddles with the keys and opens the door.

We enter an oversized courtyard dotted with pot plants, sleeping cats and the twinkling lights of stars overhead. We climb a stairwell to the rooms above, splayed out like box seats overlooking the courtyard below. Our square room is sparsely furnished.

In the morning, from our window we glimpse a view of a single mountain peak. This austere setting, we feel, is perfect for the brewing of a new self.

Breakfast in the courtyard is shared with a Dutch couple, Maria and Henk, who no longer speak Dutch, German or English, the three languages they've already acquired. Instead, the couple pull out flash cards with Spanish words blazoned afront, and repeat to each other: *planta, piedra, pintura*. By mid-morning the couple converse with the *señora's* four-year-old son, whose Spanish-language skills they're keen to acquire by lunchtime. '*El gato es muy muy lindo*,' says Maria, hammering the accent on the *muy, muy.* Meanwhile, more complicated activities between the couple are performed with gesticulating hands, as though they are playing charades – such as spooning the air (the sign to eat), or motioning to leave (a pointed finger at the door).

It reminds me of the American author Jhumpa Lahiri, whose love for Italian was ignited on a trip to Florence just after college. Although Lahiri had gone on to study Italian for many years after her first trip to the romantic city, true mastery had eluded her. But the yearning for it never did. So, seeking full immersion, Lahiri finally made up her mind to move to Rome with her family, for 'a trial by fire, a sort of baptism' into a new language. There, she began to read and write – initially in her journal, and solely in Italian. Her endeavours culminated in a book, written in Italian, which investigates the process of learning to express oneself in another language, the journey of a writer seeking a new voice. In her book she cites the writer Domenico Starnone: 'A new language is almost a new life, grammar and syntax recast you, you slip into another logic and another sensibility.'

Lahiri abandoned writing in English, the language which won her a Pulitzer Prize. Instead, she chose to subject herself as a writer 'to a metamorphosis'. And, unlike her Indian-born mother, who continued to dress, eat and live as if she'd never left Calcutta, Lahiri, who had emigrated to the USA as a child, wanted to do just the opposite. 'While the refusal to change was my mother's rebellion, the insistence on transforming myself is mine,' she writes, beginning her first story in Italian with the sentence, 'There was a woman . . . who wanted to be another person.'

At night, we share dinner in the tiled courtyard with cats sleeping under the stars. The *señora's* son is perched at the head of the table, leading the conversation in Spanish.

'*Esta comida es muy muy buena.*'

'*Si, si, si.*'

'*¿Más comida para ti?*'

'*Si, si, si.*'

Silence and chewing reign, and the four-year-old is king.

'Mamá, mamá, ¿dónde está mi carro? No, no, no me gusta el azul. ¡Quiero el verde!'

I think about what it would be like if we decided to stay here – all four of us, along with the *señora's* son – in this safe and secluded courtyard, refusing to speak our native Dutch or English, but rather, to slowly acquire the new sounds and syllables of Spanish. As days and weeks passed, we'd learn more words, of course, and would be able to express ourselves better. Within a year or so, we'd have mastered the language further, beyond that of even the four-year-old with his temporary head start. However, would we slowly become the people we were before, just replacing Dutch or English words with the Spanish equivalents? Or would our old selves die, never to resurface in our newfound lexicon? I've heard that, often, people who stutter do not stutter in another tongue. So perhaps we, too, would find a new voice, new thoughts, a new self. I imagine the four of us growing old here in this courtyard, newly born into a new language, metamorphosing into new adults. Who would we become?

It was this that got us pondering a place referred to between ourselves as *Flourish*, naming it as we would an unborn child. It was a space to contain a dream much like a house contains a growing family. If, for Carl Rogers, self-actualization is one of the principal goals of life, then this important life step could not be attained within an ordinary setting. Addicts won't overcome addiction from the confines of their home. They must be removed from their territory and taken afar, cut off and sent adrift. Our memories and habits are tied to the fabric of our ordinary lives – the food in our fridge, the timing and click of the kettle boiling. Self-actualization, we surmise, has to be a process done 'away' from all of this, and we decide we want to find it – the home for *Flourish*.

Outside the Athens city walls, in a sacred grove, Plato set up the Academy, a school where philosophers and sophists came for intellectual discussion, for exercise, and for religious activities. It was in the early decades of the fourth century BCE that Plato led discussions in the Academy's grounds and in his nearby garden.

Epicurus, too, fled from city chaos in Athens to pursue a life of quiet simplicity and reflection with friends, establishing the Garden, one of the world's first philosophical communes. The group of retreating philosophers kept to a diet of bread, olives and water, and occasionally cheese. It was a private space amid trees and plants where ideas could flourish under the guidance of nature. We think: could *Flourish* be modelled on an ancient philosophical commune?

The days pass in our courtyard, and the Dutch couple leap ahead with their Spanish skills. '*Mi madre solía agregar cúrcuma a esta receta. ¡Sí, sí, es un ingrediente secreto!*' laughs Henk. At night, Zan and Henk speak about life at home, while Maria tries to put up with my lagging skills, leaning across to add something in Henk's ear in Spanish, the three of them rollicking with laughter. I, meanwhile, speak to the *señora*'s son about his ginger cat, still struggling to quite comprehend what he means when he says, '*¿Sabes que los gatos pelirrojos son realmente gatos grises bañados en pintura?*'

The *señora*'s mother, *la abuela*, slips around the mansion like a ghost, silent, at times appearing as if out of thin air, lost behind doors. Every ten minutes or so, '*¿Mama, Mama, dónde estás?*', and the *señora* sighs, wipes her hands on her apron, and begins the search for *la abuela*, who is often found conversing with dead relatives in other rooms, the past and present intertwined. Not only are we embedded to the infrastructure of our lives, our past selves are too – captive to them, enslaved to them.

***

One morning, we wake to voices yelping, feet slapping upon patterned tiles, fists banging on empty doors. Shoeless, I burst out of my room and peer over the balcony – at a tide of schoolchildren lugging school bags and carrying lunches. Older schoolteacher types follow the throng with briefcases and notebooks, and the onslaught continues through the undersized internal door, with no end in sight. We pack in a frenzy, stuffing clothes and books into bags, shoving our feet into thongs outside our room, lurching our bags upon our backs, and keeping our heads low. We go searching for the *señora*, who, we discover, has left, and the Dutch couple, too, the doors to their empty room swung wide open, the space devoid of life. We push through the internal door, to be ambushed by midgets clanking their small heads on the underbellies of our bags, and go looking for our van, which we haven't seen in weeks, or has it been months? Released into the shrill daylight, disorientated and groggy, we zigzag across streets and fall into a café for coffee and *medialunas*. It seems our place has become an academy after all, just not quite as we had intended.

CHAPTER 4

Bariloche, Argentina

'To live only for some future goal is shallow. It's the sides of the mountain that sustain life, not the top.'

—Robert M. Pirsig

W E HEAD SOUTH. THE land is so flat a spirit level would measure perfect horizontality. My eyes trail along a line of wire a metre or so from the roadway. I watch the intermittent tail lights of a truck before us flash on, flash off. Occasionally, a guanaco bounds across the road. Every moment of this trip south, I know I'll never see these vistas again as they disappear rapidly, with fleeting points of interest, a continual death. Although change is one of the few things in life that we can depend on, we humans seem to deny its consequences.

Harvard University psychologists Jordi Quoidbach, Daniel Gilbert and Timothy Wilson asked over 19,000 adults varying in age from 18 to 68 how much they thought they would change over the course of the next ten years: 'Will your ideals, principles, your likes and dislikes, will your behaviour change much, if at all, over the coming ten years?' These same adults were then asked to measure how much they'd changed over the past ten years: 'Are you the same person you were ten years ago?'

The psychologists discovered that, strangely enough, most of us think we'll change very little in the future. 'People, it seems, regard the present as a watershed moment at which they have finally become the person they will be for the rest of their lives,' the psychologists discovered, labelling this phenomenon the 'end of history illusion'. The study, published in 2013, found that this illusion was most pronounced in teenagers and grandparents, who seemed to 'believe that the pace of personal change has slowed to a crawl and that they have recently become the people they will remain. History, it seems, is always ending today.'

On the other hand, most people acknowledge how much they've transformed over the past ten years. 'Young people, middle-aged people, and older people all believed they had changed a lot in the past,' the psychologists reported. They noted, 'At every stage of life, people make decisions that profoundly influence the lives of the people they will become.' A teenager drills tattoos into her skin, confident that the body markings she wants today will be welcomed by her older self in ten or twenty years' time – which may or may not be the case. This erroneous belief in a rather static self affects our decision-making, our goals, and how we plan out the course of our lives. As we project into the future, we base our projections on the person we are today – but this isn't necessarily the best course of action. Just hark back ten years to the person you were – your clothes, your hobbies, your eating preferences, where you were living, your friends, your favourite weekend activities, and so on – and you can safely project a similar barrage of change, if not more, in the coming years.

But change is a scary thought for many. If change is inevitable – if we are guaranteed to be a different person in two, five and ten years' time – then we might as well put in place some plans as to how that 'future self' might turn out. Such knowledge of inevitable self-change can be just the impetus we need to do something new. But if we wrongly insist that we have reached the 'end of history', then we are stifling the opportunity to embrace the change that can and will happen.

By dusk, we haven't encountered a township, and the road is patchy. It's dark, and ahead appears the spectre of a flame in the middle of the road. Zan slows the van to a crawl, and we expect to see an overturned truck, or roadworks, or some frenetic person waving an emergency warning, but as we get closer, all we can still make out is the flame, like a giant-sized candle, marking what seems to be a gaping pit in the road. We circle the pit, expecting to encounter the torchbearer, living somewhere within the dark plains. But it is cavernous and black and empty, a blank slate, and the road beyond is relentlessly straight. We accelerate, driving slowly, our eyes peeled.

On this journey, I don't have a goal and there's no destination, which is not what self-help books advise you to do. They say that you need to have a clear idea of where you are heading. And, preferably, to set it all out on paper. 'Don't be modest,' motivational speakers shriek, the type who buy islands in the Caribbean, private jets and fast cars, all on the back of goal setting. Not their own goals, mind you – they charge you to write out *your* goals. 'Think big. Think crazy. You want a convertible? Write it down. You want to make a million bucks a year? Then write that down too.' Goal setting is like conversing with a magic genie who can grant you every wish you've ever wanted. 'The man of my dreams.' 'Black belt in karate.' 'Chalet in the Swiss Alps.'

The trouble with goal setting is that it forces you to spell out your deficiencies, or what you lack in life, and this breeds negativity. Our brain's nervous system takes a beating. Our 'ideal life' or 'ideal self' – laid bare in our list of goals – may also feel somewhat unattainable from where we stand today. And this can breed a sense of hopelessness. Studies have shown that failure to meet goals can be demotivating, ultimately leading to impaired performance.

Motivational speakers are unlikely to mention the opportunity cost of goal setting – the opportunities we forgo when we relentlessly pursue our goals, the price we pay. And in our culture of more, more, more, we're likely to prioritize more money and more status over values or goodwill or creative endeavours, such as learning to repair furniture or fix vintage cars. Few will list 'to become a better person' on their goal-setting sheet. If we must set goals, then studies suggest we should set modest goals that are easily achieved, because small achievements are motivating.

The American psychologist Tim Kasser asked university students to write down their goals for the months ahead. They were also asked to rate how happy they'd feel on attaining these goals. Their progress towards these goals and their current feelings of well-being were tracked in student diaries. Interestingly, students who pursued materialistic goals – like money or fame – tracked absolutely no gains in happiness after progressing towards these goals. In fact, their sense of well-being was no higher than it was in those who failed to make any progress at all. 'The implications of this for a materialistic orientation are deep,' writes Kasser. 'First, when people follow materialistic values and organize their lives around attaining wealth and possessions, they are essentially wasting their time as far as well-being is concerned. By concentrating on such a profitless style of life, they leave themselves little opportunity to pursue goals that could fulfill their needs and improve the quality of their lives.' Kasser found that students who sought non-materialistic goals like personal growth, close relationships and community contribution displayed very steep gains in well-being as they progressed towards these goals. Kasser is in good company here: the Greek philosopher Aristotle also stressed that a happy life must involve engagement with others, not just with the self.

Removing the goal on the horizon means we're forced to confront the countryside we're passing through rather than musing about some distant vista. By removing a goal, time expands. Storm clouds pass, to be followed by clear skies. The mind scans the environment for immediate possibilities. The ephemeral movie of the mind is lulled. But to remove a future is unsettling, as it forces you to own up to the fairy-tale castles you've concocted in the sky.

We stop on the roadside, and I plunder books from the van's floor in desperate search of ideas to fill the recesses of my mind. As I read them within the emptiness of a day, the authors shout upon the roadside where I huddle, knees to chin, my head buried; and then we're off – again, alone with our thoughts – mulling over ideas, letting them sink and ignite with other thoughts and life experiences, a process of mental digestion that needs time and space. These thinkers whose books I read are the lone voice of reason within this maddening trip, and I like to think we are following in the footsteps of Henry David Thoreau, the American philosopher who set himself up in a hut in a forest to live in a simple, humble way, or in those of the Japanese Buddhist monk Kamo Chōmei, who left his life as a court poet and musician in Kyōto to enter monastic seclusion at the age of 60. Chōmei built himself a hut on Mount Hino, south-west of the capital, surviving on nuts, and weaving his own clothes from arrowroot. It was here he wrote on the vanity of human endeavours and the impermanence of all things: 'Nor it is clear to me, as people are born and die, where they are coming from and where they are going.' Indeed, as we head south at speed, I ask myself the question: what exactly are we seeking? Even without a goal or a destination, why are we in a rush? What is it about humans that compels us so?

It was a gradual turning off. First it was the television at home, and then it was the daily news grind, and then we switched off movies in our apartment in Buenos Aires, and finally documentaries, and then all that was left was the swish, swish of the wheels on the bitumen, and the spiralling mental symbols from our intellectuals on the van's floor: Neil Postman, Bertrand Russell, Iris Murdoch. I read Murdoch's *The Sea, The Sea* one night before a window, open to the sea: 'Decide what you want and go for it, Fred, it's just a matter of willpower!' Switching off was a moment-by-moment tumbling into an information void, and it unnerved people that I wasn't engaged with politics, that I didn't know the latest movie or the outcome of some sporting event. But it left space for other things. As Lev S. Vygotsky says, 'Through others we become ourselves,' and so we must be diligent as to who these *others* are. By switching off, we had become gatekeepers to our minds, determining who entered and who was barred. Whereas once our mental stage was a disco parlour of bleating tunes and drunken louts, now it was a concert hall of strictly curated sounds. And turning off meant no more TV hosts, no more brutes talking sport as though it were as compelling as the discovery of some new solar system. We turned off the strobing lights of the entertainment and media complex, and replaced them with the ordinary, humdrum, banal sounds of a motor, the cracking of dry grass, the shrill hum of air in the midday sun.

And so into the void fell an equation, one which I've always treasured. Can you fall for an equation? If you can, Kurt Lewin's behaviour equation has always been the object of my affection. It was brought to my attention by Shush, an American MBA teacher. Blonde fringe circling a heavily made-up face, the glamorous and intelligent Shush's words were a revelation for me – a prophecy of what could be. Lewin's little equation asserts that change is possible – you can become something 'other'; you can shape things, and great things can happen – you just need to tamper with the variables. Not everything is a constant.

Lewin's equation is $B = f(P,E)$, which states that our behaviour (B) is a function (f) of our personality (P) in the environment (E). The way we behave – the things we do – is influenced by our environment, what Lewin likes to call our 'life space'. When we alter our life space, our behaviour (B) will shift accordingly, eventually affecting our underlying personality, or P. Therefore, if you seek fundamental change, you can start by shifting your behaviour, or habits – but this isn't an easy task for habit-forming humans. Alternatively, you can seek change by altering your environment, or E – that which you allow yourself to see and hear on a daily basis. It's up to you which variable you choose to tweak. I chose E.

At the hotel, there's chanting, and it seems like the township is engaged in some sort of uprising. It's my birthday, and I'm oddly contemplative, restless, disgruntled – dissatisfied, as though I wish I were travelling upon a different road. 'I want,' I say to Zan, 'to be engaged fully in my passion, to be pursuing it with vigour, but for starters I can't work out exactly what that passion is, nor where I start to find it. How lovely it must be for those who "always know" what it is that they wish to do in life? Wouldn't then the seeking stop? Ah, the bliss of coming to a halt and knowing – *this* is what I am going to do with my life, and *this* is how I am going to do it'.

At university I had such a friend. Red-headed and straight backed, ironed and buttoned up, Reece got the top mark in every economics class, always finished his homework on time, and handed in his assignments well before the due date. Reece would explain the Phillips curve better than any lecturer, holding the floor as though he were delivering a presidential address, replete with humour. In comparison, I rarely, if ever, spoke in class, was perpetually late and dishevelled, and would often find myself creeping through university corridors late at night trying to stuff assignments under my tutor's door. One time Reece and I went to the movies in town; he liked American gangster movies, whereas I preferred the art-house ones. It was before graduation, and Reece had already been offered a scholarship at a prestigious management consulting firm. In contrast, I hadn't been offered anything, nor did I know what I wanted to be offered, even if I'd had the good fortune of being offered anything, which, of course, I hadn't. I had an economics degree but no direction whatsoever. 'What about working in philanthropy at a bank?' Reece kindly suggested. I distinctly remember standing in the movie theatre café with a choc-top in one hand and suddenly realizing: 'Reece is already on a path, and I'm not. What does that mean to not have a path?'

The chanting townsfolk seem to be moving down the hill towards the town centre, and, peering out of the window between the blinds, I note a group of mainly men and boys in matching blue and white, with flags, cheerfully chanting, some coming up the rear bashing drums, and someone on the periphery of the group, somewhat oblivious to the inner circle, strumming a guitar with abandon under the starry night. 'See him,' I point him out to Zan, 'the one with the guitar? Look how happy he is. Ah, to have a passion and strum it with abandon – how lucky he is!'

The chanting reaches a crescendo under our window and recedes as the group retreats down the hill towards a pub, where, I imagine, they will now cheer on their much-loved soccer heroes on the screen, praying for a victory. I think about the oft-quoted rules for happiness: 'something to do, someone to love, and something to hope for'.

———

It'd be a macabre experience to read your own obituary, as happened to the famous American writer Ernest Hemingway, who survived two plane crashes in two days before discovering that in the meantime news reporters had been covering his tragic 'death'. Apparently, the obituaries provided Hemingway with much reading pleasure over breakfast (with champagne). Self-help courses often involve drafting an early obituary of one's life and times. The practice isn't meant to be macabre, but rather is used to outline what it is you've contributed thus far, and subsequently revealing what it is you still have left to accomplish. If you've always wanted to set up a bakery and still don't even know the elementary steps to baking, then the obituary exercise is meant to make you get a move on: hurry up – time is short! Another approach to the obituary, without the somewhat depressing side effects, is to write a story about yourself in the future tense – filled with characters and exciting plot lines. You write a fantasy story with you as the central character. The benefit of this exercise, apparently, is that you're free to explore, to go wild, to go out there. Because who knows what adventures you could pursue when you're not hemmed in by the fences of reality?

In the 1940s, Hemingway, who was born and raised in Illinois, rented a 15-acre farm outside Havana, Cuba, where he would live on and off for some twenty years. In Cuba, Hemingway took up fishing from his boat, an experience reflected in his novel *The Old Man and the Sea*, which won the Pulitzer Prize for Fiction, and years later, helped him win the Nobel Prize in Literature. The story is about an old Cuban fisherman who lands the biggest fish of his life, a marlin, which is so powerful that it pulls the fisherman and his boat through the seas over several days and nights. While the fisherman puts up a heroic fight, he ultimately loses everything: he fails to catch the marlin and never secures the fame from having slain the fish. It's a good lesson on being mindful about what you aim for, because goals can pull you far from shore.

Indeed, when projecting into the future, it's worthwhile to (at least momentarily) remove success, fame and money from the projection, and to then ask yourself if the goal is still worth striving for. Because if the motivation is money and fame, then, like the old Cuban fisherman, these rewards are certainly not guaranteed, nor are they under your control. It could so happen that your big goal or dream – which pulls you this way and that throughout your life – lands you back on the shore empty-handed.

In his book *Changeology*, John Norcross, a clinical psychologist and professor of psychology at the University of Scranton, recommends writing the tale of your future self: 'Psychologists have long known that the stories we tell ourselves impact our intentions and moods. Depressing tales leave us feeling discouraged and weak, whereas inspiring stories prompt us to be active and successful. We can alter our self-image by rewriting our own stories and narratives with better endings. Instead of listening to those who don't believe that we can change, we can weave a compelling tale of self-improvement and transformation. It's just like imagery but with words.'

While it's unlikely we'll get the chance to read our own obituary – Hemingway could never have predicted the tragic news article that accompanied his *real* death on 2 July 1961 – we do have a certain level of control over the narrative underpinning our day-to-day lives. So, as Norcross suggests, it's important to journal your future narrative with a high degree of optimism. 'There is nothing noble in being superior to your fellow man,' Hemingway once wrote. Instead, he argued, 'true nobility is being superior to your former self'. And this is indeed something worth striving for.

We are traipsing through snow with a real-estate agent, the wet grass squelching underfoot. The agent, a sullen brute in his mid-50s, manhandles a collection of keys in his pocket and picks out one, before returning it to the pit of his pocket, the next key shoved into the lock and returned in the same manner, while our feet sink further into the white slush. Once we are inside the house, the cold hits us, but it has a cosy cabin charm and woody smell – I picture a couple drinking Argentinean hot chocolate and reading *Labyrinths* by Borges before an open fire. I can see it here, our place to flourish, a white house by the lake, its central room jutting out over the lake floor. From almost all angles the lake can be glimpsed, obscured only by a single cupboard door in the hallway when opened. I stare at the lake from the kitchen, the bathroom, even the shower, like a smitten lover, gazing at its form, its shape, its hidden glories – watching the subtle shift in colour as the sun slides silently overhead.

Most of us would regard a peak experience as mountainous – like reaching the crest of Everest after many arduous days of hiking, or diving with whales, or making a million dollars on a stock-market trade – the euphoria, the euphoria – or, for some, riding the wave of some drug-induced high. But for Abraham Maslow, a peak experience was something that could happen to you within the everyday. You are driving the kids to work, and you see something exquisite, or hear a piece of music on the radio that turns your banal trip into something 'oh, so much more'. Maslow taught his patients how to recognize peak experiences. He trained them to stare intently at a flower for hours and watch how their perception began to shift. 'Find your peak in the everyday' seemed to be his mantra – and, of course, what a gift to possess if you can master it. I watch the clouds overhead alter in colour by the millisecond, not wishing to miss a single hue as I take milk out of the fridge and make a cup of tea.

We are frustrated with the people who don't go along with our attempts at conversational Spanish. Are we not in Latin America? '*¿Donde está el banco?*' I ask. 'The bank is in town, you walk this way,' they inevitably reply in English. Our attempts at Spanish immersion are falling short due to the ever-present code of English, which we cannot shake. We realize that our own language has been commoditized, sold off – no longer a secret code but a public infrastructure for the distribution of messages, like a free public train.

We decide to tell people we are Russian. Who speaks Russian here? We think it is the least likely language to be spoken in the southern tip of Latin America. With no English to get between us and our desire to speak Spanish, people are forced to speak to us in the local dialect instead. Our cunning plan works well until locals start to enquire, with sudden interest in our life in Russia, where we live, what it's like, how we compare Russia with Argentina. I hastily practise a few Russian sayings that we mutter to each other when others are present before laughing hysterically back inside our lake house.

It is here in the lake house with the white snow garden that I mull over the idea of doing something drastic, like taking out a five-year lease on it. There's nothing like forcing destiny by fixing in. If we take out a lease then we'll be forced to stay, and the white lake house could become our philosopher's commune.

What are the ethics in life of 'fixing in', sticking a flag in the ground and saying to destiny, 'Stuff you, work around this one!'? The flow of life is forever redirected. By signing a five-year lease on the white house, we can, in one impulsive moment, drastically shift our future selves. Is this permissible? Shouldn't there be some sort of meeting between the current and future selves as to whether this decision is the correct one?

This is common when people marry, have children, get a tattoo on their neck – they, too, are fixing in. Every decision we make over the course of the day could be 'fixing in', like a mountain climber who hammers a peg into the rock face. It's the next step. What we eat, how we move, what we buy, how we think, they're each another peg locked in on the slow climb to our future self. But it's often only the big moments in life we think about – like taking out a fixed-term lease on a remote house in Argentina

– not decisions such as whether to spend a day in front of the television or to answer emails.

Days disappear with our heads in Spanish-language books, listening to Spanish talkback radio, and walking the streets, terrorized by pent-up domestic dogs. I envisage ageing here together in this white lake house. Over time, the foreign feel of Spanish would become more familiar; we'd understand more on the radio – but with this, would normality descend upon us, and boredom too?

One Saturday night we enter a bar to find the answer. If the meaning of life is out there, then it will come from outside ourselves; it won't miraculously appear in our thoughts. We decide to leave our fate in the hands of a stranger, someone who will tell us the next part of our journey. 'Hah, take that one, determinists!' we symbolically gesture.

The free-will-versus-determinism debate has been raging since the time of Aristotle. Some philosophers, like the existentialists, argue that we have the power to create our lives minute by minute, to steer our own destiny by the choices we make. But determinists disagree, instead believing that our life is predetermined – like an orbiting spacecraft set on a loop. We have been conditioned by our genes, our childhood and our society to be a certain person, and off we go, living out our life as best as we can within the circle of our own orbit. The determinists argue that everything we have done up to now is nothing special, nothing other than what we were always going to do when we reached a set age. It was already coded in the neurons in our brain. Determinists think that decisions are not in fact freely made choices but rather are simply us following what had already been set in motion. For determinists, radical and absolute self-transformation is not possible.

But what about handing over our destiny to a stranger? Wouldn't that throw a spanner into the determinists' works?

We happen upon a local bar, a wooden hut built on stilts stationed just out of town. Barricaded by bodies, the bar is clearly a local favourite. I push my way through the throng and look about, spotting the barman tucked far in the corner. I muscle on, and then stand, waiting to be served, brushing arms with a dishevelled white-haired man, late twenties, unnaturally thin, with piercings in his eyebrows, nose and cheek. He speaks a mix of English and Spanish. I don't mention the Russian thing.

He tells me he's heading next week on a spiritual trip to a place in the mountains. It's a regular journey he makes, and its purpose is to digest a kind of Peruvian tonic called ayahuasca, a blend of the ayahuasca vine and the chacruna shrub. He tells me it has the rather unsavoury effect of violent purging, followed by a mind-bending trance which can last for days. 'We have decided that you will tell us the next part of our journey,' I shout over the din of the bar. 'Where should we go next?'

The white-haired man doesn't seem perplexed by such a suggestion, as though it were not at all an uncommon request on a Friday night. He stares into the middle distance as though conjuring up some mystical thought. I wait as he ponders with a furrowed brow. And then he tells me he needs to give it some more thought.

The following day we visit our destiny guide at his place of work, a local restaurant holed up in an out-of-the-way mall. We sit on plastic chairs in the car park. He appears later, pattering over with a tray of bean tortillas and soft drinks, framed from behind by his boss's gaze. 'He's understanding,' he says, motioning his hand backwards towards the kitchen. 'He knows it's my religion.' We wave at his boss, who glares and slips from view.

That night we wander back to our van parked in a vacant lot. The window is smashed in. Our books are safe, but our money and clothes have been stolen. Three days later we're driving south through Patagonia, along empty back roads to the end of the world. We're excited, but at the same time we are worried about what it might mean to come to the end of the line.

CHAPTER 5

Ushuaia, Argentina

'Action may not always bring happiness; but there is no happiness without action.'

—Benjamin Disraeli

'WANDERER,' WROTE SPANISH POET Antonio Machado, 'your footsteps are the path, and nothing else.' One of Spain's most celebrated poets, Machado implies that our destiny happens only in motion. 'Wanderer, there is no path, the path is made by walking.'

We are so governed by our minds that we can fool ourselves into believing that self-change comes from thinking about it. It'll happen, we assume, as a light-bulb moment. We will be driving along in the car, or we'll be walking in a city park at dusk, and the idea will hit, bang. 'Of course, this is what I will do with my life. This is who I am. This is my true self. This is the path that I must take.' We fool ourselves into thinking that we just need a little time, some space, and then, once all the receptors are open, the voice within will tell us the way. That the key lies within our mind somewhere, and one day the answer to the meaning of our life, and our purpose, will explode forth. But this is not how self-change happens. Your footsteps are the road and nothing more.

On our way south, we find lodgings at a horse homestead, and the owners are insistent that we take their horses up the mountain pass. It's part of the daily rent. We load books into small backpacks, along with water and food – and clamber on. The horses don't move, as though indifferent to our weight upon them, and it's not until we've been immobile for some minutes that the owner claps and smacks them on the rump. They shudder to life and sprint though the sunlit door.

We pad up a dirt track in a line, one horse behind the other, and at the crest of the hill I encounter something unexpected. The *señor* hadn't told us exactly which direction to take, and here is a junction with three possible paths outlined on a wooden sign, a veritable fork in the road. Zan dismounts from his horse and peers at a glass-cased sign half-hidden within the rubble. The horses drop their heads and chew the grass.

In medieval times, crossroads – the intersections of ancient highways and byways – were places to fear, to move through quickly, to not linger at for too long. In Irish folklore, crossroads were between-worlds, no-places, where witches met and spirits passed. Fear of making the wrong decision can, indeed, keep us at crossroads for longer than we need to be. We hesitate. We weigh up the options. But too much time thinking or analysing whether one path is better than the next can be detrimental to progress. We need to make a choice. We need to act. Don't fritter away your life in thinking, warns Kierkegaard – instead, take action.

Kierkegaard called his time one of 'reflection', but 'devoid of passion'. He writes: 'Thus our own age is essentially one of understanding, and on the average, perhaps, more knowledgeable than any former generation, but it is without passion. Everyone knows a great deal, we all know which way we ought to go and all the different ways we can go, but nobody is willing to move.' Too much weighing up, thinks the philosopher, can make us mad and depressed, or can incite laziness. Many, having so beautifully cultivated the habit of reflection, conjure up some illusory project to think about before deciding – after considerable deliberation – that it's probably best to do nothing at all.

I continue to sit motionless on the horse, undecided and unmoving, as Zan carries on investigating the paths. Without our input, the horses will happily laze about in the shade, perhaps for hours.

We choose a route and pad along the track. After a few minutes, the horses seem to relax into their stride, one foot in front of the other, plod, plod, plod. From atop the horse, it feels like a rhythmic beat, tap, tap, tap, and I think if I had musical neurons in my brain, then I'd come up with a song to sing – the ascending song as we steadily climb the hill, or the shortened staccato song to accompany the descending drop. It's odd to be so elevated, floating above the ground. I touch a leaf on a tree, and search for birds or insects on a branch. But after a while, this odd floating sensation, too, becomes normalized.

One way to view your life is as a rider seated upon a horse. While the rider makes plans and comes up with ideas, the horse acts. Problems occur when either one is dormant. If you're the thinking type, then the rider will be in charge most of the time. You like to research things, to write lists; you like to come up with options. You like to discuss the risks and rewards, the pros and cons. 'What are my passions? What am I good at?' And this rumination can go on for a while, sometimes for a lifetime, while you continue to think things through and write lists. And as the years pass, you start to notice that the same list may appear year after year, and you take some solace in that, as though you're on to something. But this is the rider in action, while the horse is still in its stable, waiting for direction. 'Once I know for sure, there will be no stopping me.'

But if you're the doing type, then the horse is probably the one in charge. You're always *doing* – working in your job, studying, seeing friends and remembering birthdays. You keep things routine and fairly on schedule. You'd like to move to your favourite suburb one day, or change careers, but you just don't know how this could happen. You'd like to spend less time working and more time on creative endeavours, but there are never enough hours in the day. Lacking direction from the rider, the horse will continue to trot along the path it knows best. 'Oh yes, we will get onto that next year.' But inevitably, when confronted with change, the horse will put its nose forward and insist that the well-worn path is the best one to take.

Existentialist philosophers think you are nothing more than what you do. The rider atop the horse, with grand plans and many tremendous ideas, is nothing if the horse remains in its stall all day and night and does not venture out. He is only what he achieves on the horse. On the other hand, the rider on a horse that keeps plodding along with no plan or goal in mind is at risk of living a life that, at the end of the day, is a bit of a disappointment. As the American poet Bill Copeland once said, 'The trouble with not having a goal is that you can spend your life running up and down the field and never score.'

A listless rider and horse can cause frustration and apathy. The Hungarian-American psychologist Mihaly Csikszentmihalyi calls this 'psychic entropy'. It's that boredom that hits you on a Sunday afternoon. Lead weight in your feet. Marbles in your brain. Psychic entropy can feel a lot like depression: you wander from room to room in your house and nothing grabs you. But once you decide to walk the dog, or go for a swim, or bake a cake, you find that this cloud inevitably lifts, and time passes smoothly once more. When the horse is moving, it's no longer kicking up a fuss in the stall, trapped and stultified by its own inaction; it has freed itself – the gate has opened. By taking action, new vistas open. By inching forward, you are exercising the horse, keeping it agile, so when the time comes it can gallop. As American painter, visual artist and photographer Chuck Close once said: 'Amateurs sit and wait for inspiration, the rest of us just get up and go to work.'

Some life coaches insist that real change only comes from within – that it's not until we dig deep into the recesses of who we are that we can locate our true self; it is not until we can somehow locate this inner self that we can start to live authentically. There are seminars and courses to help people discover who they really are, involving questionnaires and quiet thinking time to rationally work through all the options. Questions like: What sort of person am I? What are my strengths and weaknesses? And it's through such rational deliberation that the outlines of a quasi-roadmap of life will begin to emerge, or so the theory goes. Some say that once we discover our authentic self, we can begin to live up to the self we were meant to be. Like finding the career that will make us fulfilled and happy, or the partner who will both reflect and complement us.

This thinking, surprisingly, has its origins in religious doctrine, which has underpinned philosophical thought in the west for centuries. The idea that we are predestined – that our roadmap of life is more or less laid out for us by some higher being – is central, in fact, to Protestant thinking. But many life coaches rip out the religious part, leaving the doctrine of 'predestination' intact, but understood in a radically different way.

'The danger of this lies in believing that we will all know our "truth" when we see it, and then limiting our lives according to that truth,' writes the Harvard philosophy professor Michael Puett in *The Path* (co-written with Christine Gross-Loh). 'We're taking a limited number of our emotional dispositions during a certain time and place, and allowing those to define us forever.' Furthermore, these serious life plans are often not based on rational consideration. To make plans for some imagined future self, founded on a belief in who you think you are today, is an exercise in fortune telling, an utter abstraction. 'You, the world, and your circumstances will change,' insists Puett. And you are limiting your future potential to 'what is in the best interests of the person you happen to be right now and not the person you will become'.

I'm not a creative person . . . I'm often pessimistic, looking out for what could go wrong . . . I'm a loner . . . I don't take criticism well . . . I find it difficult to make friends . . . I am competitive and don't work well in teams . . . I am introverted and shy . . . I need to be busy and don't enjoy downtime . . .

The trouble with writing out personal statements is that we tend to believe the manner in which we describe ourselves. Labelling has a tendency to fix or cement such attributes, to make them harden. Furthermore, who we think we are today is mostly a combination of habits and patterns acquired over the course of our lives. You say, 'I'm an early riser and fitness junkie' because you got into the habit of running in the early hours of the morning; or, 'I'm a loner and depressive' because you habitually avoid social engagements and have a patterned tendency to think negatively about stuff. You might say, 'I'm musically inclined' because you play the piano and have done so since childhood. This is not you, but simply a description of your habits, which are always open to change, every moment of the day. 'Some patterns are good, and some are less so,' writes Puett.

As a child, Emma Stone suffered from severe anxiety. 'The first time I had a panic attack I was sitting in my friend's house, and I thought the house was burning down,' she recalls. 'I called my mom and she brought me home, and for the next three years it just would not stop. I would go to the nurse at lunch most days and just wring my hands. I would ask my mom to tell me exactly how the day was going to be, then ask again 30 seconds later. I just needed to know that no one was going to die and nothing was going to change.' Stone's parents sent her to therapy, but it was, ironically, acting classes – being on stage, remembering lines to say in front of an audience, and making people laugh – that provided the cure. 'It gave me a sense of purpose,' she recalls. Today, when she experiences that pang of tightening, of anxiety, she takes action – doing something like baking. Would Stone, one of the highest-paid actresses in the world today, and the recipient of an Academy Award, be labelled 'anxious and shy' by psychologists? Probably not.

The danger of finding yourself and living some sort of authentic life based on a so-called inner self is that perhaps you'd like to change a few things about the 'you' that you've found. Perhaps you'd like to be more artistic, active, musical or assertive. The spectrum of who you are, or could be, is almost limitless. The question then becomes: How do you tap into these dormant aspects of yourself?

Professor Puett's students in Chinese philosophy at Harvard University rarely miss a class. Not because Chinese philosophy is integral to vocational success, but because Puett's teachings challenge students' assumptions about themselves and what makes for a meaningful life. Puett instructs his students to look outward for transformation and growth. Unsurprisingly, the curriculum doesn't entail withdrawing into the mountains or woods to find yourself; nor is it about teaching the all-popular 'mindfulness' of detachment and non-judgement ('observe your feelings, accept them and just let them go'). On the contrary, students are taught to bring about transformation via the trivial, mundane habits and patterns in their daily lives, which might include the ritual of bed-making, for instance, or placing fresh flowers on the table, or sweeping the floor after meals. 'In order to help ourselves change,' writes Puett, 'we must become aware that breaking from our normal ways of being is what makes it possible to develop different sides of ourselves. Rituals . . . are transformative because they allow us to become a different person for a moment. They create a short-lived alternative reality that returns us to our regular life slightly altered.'

To abandon tightly held plans about your future and face up, instead, to the unnerving – but exhilarating – sensation that you don't actually know what the future has in store for you is the message Puett likes to preach. 'When you hold too tightly to a plan, you risk missing out,' he insists. Unexpected opportunities, unforeseen changes, serendipitous encounters – these are the moments that can radically alter the trajectory of your life. It's an appealing thought: that you have not yet met the person you will become.

The past few weeks have been sucked into a void. We reach the end of the world – a township, Ushuaia, on the far reaches of the Argentinean coastline, beyond it a restless ocean at the foot of snow-capped peaks. We find the cabin upon the shore, third in line. And we knock at the green door.

After some minutes, there's a sound within, and the door opens. A man in his mid-twenties looks us over, yells something to someone inside, tells us to wait a second, then closes the door. I stand on the snow-covered ground and observe a row of unpainted wooden cabins bleakly facing the waves, no fences, no letter boxes, no cars – nothing to signal any form of habitable living. The owners, I think, must ride their bikes or walk to town for supplies – surely a 35-minute walk at least.

Every second the sea wind picks up and snow-filled air batters against the cabin's exterior. The door opens again, and a dog with a bend in his trunk, his head cocked sideways, speeds out, and the man reappears in the half-light with a key in one hand and a cigarette in the other. He takes a drag and peers at us suspiciously through half-closed eyes. 'You are friends of Ignacio,' he says in Spanish, referring to the white-headed man at the bar several hundred kilometres back, our destiny guide. In fact, we'd never actually asked his name. I nod and say, '*Si, somos amigos de Ignacio.*'

Some philosophers have said that *Homo sapiens*, man the thinker, should be *Homo faber*, man the maker, because a defining characteristic of humans is the need to work, create, innovate and build. The things we make are externalizations of our existence. When we create the world around us, we create ourselves. A meaningful life therefore entails having meaningful work, or something to do.

But here we find ourselves within a subculture of people whose life is based on having no work. Life is what happens in the between moments, when the rest of the world's population is filing, fixing, lifting, teaching, writing emails and scoring goals. For the no-worker, this is a time gift from the heavens.

We dump our bags on the floor. Even with the cabin door shut, the roar of the ocean is unsettling. We lock up and return to the van. As the motor shakes into life, a curtain moves from a neighbouring window, a cabin door opens, and a woman and three men tumble out upon the snow, shoeless, gesticulating. The van's back door opens, and they pile in, uninvited, seating themselves upon our philosophy books, picking them up quizzically, flicking through the pages. The girl's hair is blue. *La chica fria*, or the cold girl, she's called. Her wrists are adorned with woven bracelets, an E-shaped tattoo on her finger. She carries pois – cloth wicks on the end of two long chains that become flaming torches she swings about her head at night. '*Ella es una experta*,' Juan tells us, still dragging on the same cigarette.

As we patter along the back roads of Ushuaia, the Argentinian crowd talk among themselves in cheery tones. I can't help but think that perhaps the meaning of life is not to find one's purpose in work, but instead, to find one's purpose in no work. To live simply, cheaply, and to expand the hours to their daily limit. Couldn't the meaning of life be to find some cheap idyll, and not demand more than a beautiful sunrise, a dirt track to wander and time to gaze at the starry night sky? Why can't we put up our hammock and be done with it?

The Spanish philosopher José Ortega y Gasset splits humanity into two classes of people. The first class is made up of people 'who make great demands on themselves, piling up difficulties and duties,' he writes in *The Revolt of the Masses*. And the second lot are those who 'demand nothing special of themselves, but for whom to live is to be every moment what they already are, without imposing on themselves any effort . . . mere buoys that float on the waves'. The philosopher's division hinged on which road was travelled: either the more rigorous and difficult path or the easier and more pleasant path. 'The decisive matter is whether we attach our life to one or the other vehicle, to a maximum or a minimum of demands upon ourselves,' he adds.

That night, as I read Bertrand Russell on a window seat, the rhythmic ocean beat is offset by the deep bass percussion of techno music pounding against the shore. The cabin floor vibrates. I think about this community of no-workers and their friends – there is a regular stream of bikes and motorbikes – a faceless community sounded by the bell of electronic beats at nightfall.

'What do you do?' It's a question we often ask of others when we first meet them. 'I'm a mechanic.' 'I'm a horticulturalist.' It's the way we often define ourselves. What's your job? But are we our jobs? Is our identity in life tied to how we earn our keep, whether we add up numbers, stack bricks, dig holes or fly planes? And if we aren't our jobs, then who are we?

British-born Samuel Smiles was one of the first self-help gurus, back in the mid-1800s. Smiles, a government reformer, used self-help – and in particular, the 'rags-to-riches' narrative – for the purpose of rallying the working and middle classes in support of industry. Smiles' book *Self-Help*, published in 1859, was replete with examples of poor people from humble origins who were propelled to success through hard work, diligence and a commitment to the work ethic. Smiles' advice was clear for those seeking a clear path up the social order: rise early, keep your head down and work, work, work. *Self-Help* sold over a quarter of a million copies.

From the 1800s, newspaper columns, books, magazines and pamphlets started dedicating space to the virtue of hard work, listing successful go-getters whose lives were shaped by work. These virtues were promoted in books for children, 'which drove home the point that hard work would allow a person to be the author of his destiny', history professor Peter Stearns notes in *From Alienation to Addiction*. 'It was hard to escape their influence.'

Smiles referred to workers as 'noble soldiers', whose work contributed to the well-being and progress of a nation in equal measure to the contributions of the great men of history. 'National progress is the sum of individual industry, energy, and uprightness, as national decay is of individual idleness, selfishness, and vice,' he wrote. Industry is righteous, idleness is evil and selfish. A new reverence for industry and work was born.

Smiles wasn't alone in pushing a reverence for work. Around the same time that Smiles' book came out, newspapers were on board with the industry line. 'Idle men and women are the bane of any community,' a journalist wrote in a Massachusetts newspaper. 'They are not simply clogs upon society, but become, sooner or later, the causes of its crime and poverty . . . Every family motto should read: "Be something. Do something. Bear your own load."'

The views of Smiles and other publicists in the early days of the Industrial Revolution (a time when workers were very much needed in factories) contrasted markedly with those of philosophers in classical Greece and Rome, who advised avoiding 'work' at all costs. For Greek philosophers, idleness, not work, was a virtue. The aim of life was to employ leisure time for self-development activities such as learning, the arts and political activity. In fact, the Greek word for leisure, *skholē*, is the root for the English word 'school'. Leisure time was time to discuss, time to study.

Although the English-speaking world has rallied behind the industry line that hard work can propel one up the social ladder, Europeans are less convinced. 'By the late nineteenth century, and still today, Americans were far more likely than Europeans to exaggerate opportunities for upward mobility based on diligence and efficiency,' writes Stearns. Many Europeans continue to believe that social barriers cannot be overcome by individual effort alone.

While it's true that longer hours at the factory, laboratory, office floor or studio don't grant you social power of any sort – such as influence on society's values, wars, infrastructure, schooling and so forth – they do offer a kind of pseudo-social power, or prestige, through the mass-produced items that you are able to buy as a result. More hours on the job mean more consumer items, and some of that stuff – like expensive cars or inner-city pads – can make someone appear more socially powerful, even when they're not. And for most people in modern society, this seems to be a good enough trade-off. It's called 'instrumentalism' when, rather than defining life, work becomes an instrument with which to achieve a better life. Work may no longer have a point, it may not develop you personally, it may not be useful, you may not even know exactly what you are doing, but that's not the issue at hand. Work means money, and money can be spent on acquiring stuff.

For many today, a job is chosen not by careful analysis of the specific features of the working day (what exactly will I be doing?), but on the basis of the salary and the perks. It's commonplace to hear the statement, 'I would have taken the job, but they didn't pay any more than what I'm getting now.' But does work really have to 'do it' for us? William Morris, an

English textile designer and author, seemed to think it does. Just because work provides a livelihood, argued Morris in a lecture entitled 'Useful Work versus Useless Toil', it's not necessarily good or worth doing. 'In short,' he went on, 'it has become an article of the creed of modern morality that all labour is good in itself – a convenient belief to those who live on the labour of others. But as to those on whom they live, I recommend them not to take it on trust, but to look into the matter a little deeper.'

———

Way past midnight, a group huddles against the shoreline, wrapped in blankets. We turn out the lamp in our room and track the shadows. A car boot opens, and in the greenish glare, Juan's face is set in concentration. He pulls out a box and lugs it into a far cabin. Morning threatens to break around him.

By dawn, the cabins, four battered huts upon the shore, appear deserted. But we know Juan, the cold girl, and the perhaps six or more others are inside, unconscious, like vampires, cocooned inside hammocks hanging from rafters in the hallway and the loft. And, not expecting to see anyone until midday or later, we use the quiet of the morning to go snowboarding on fresh snow. We glide down mountains, exhilarated by speed, whipping across feathery fields, triumphant.

Days pass. Early rising, snowboarding, and at night fitful sleep amid techno beats, except on weekends, when it's just us and the ocean hum. I think to myself: When life is a ticking clock towards death, why would anyone work? Why would anyone think, 'You know, I only have four thousand weeks here on this glorious earth, and I'm going to use those God-given hours to drive a forklift, nurse the sick, drive a bus, or teach a class. I'm going to limit my holidays to four to six weeks a year, and the rest of the time, I'm on task.'

I do, indeed, understand these cabin dwellers, who share shelter, stitch their clothes, make bulk food with water and stock, all in the spirit of no work. But, having observed the spirt of no work over the past few weeks, to me this lot don't seem all that spirited – unless, wildly inebriated, they're setting up an elaborate ski jump off a cabin roof or snowboarding over parked cars. Among themselves, they're forever planning the next novelty, never satiated by a big night, always seeking an even bigger one. And come afternoon, they're listless – too bored to go snowboarding proper, sometimes too dulled out to even bother getting anything to eat. The enormity of having to choose what to do at every point in a day seems almost too much to bear. And, so, when one person suggests, 'Let's go into town to see a *pelicula*,' they're all in – relieved at having had their day worked out for them.

'Most of the work that most people have to do is not in itself interesting,' writes Russell, 'but even such work has certain great advantages. To begin with, it fills a good many hours of the day without the need of deciding what one shall do. Most people, when they are left free to fill their own time according to their own choice are at a loss to think of anything sufficiently pleasant to be worth doing. And whatever they decide on, they are troubled by the feeling that something else would have been pleasanter. To be able to fill leisure intelligently is the last product of civilization, and at present very few people have reached this level.'

Russell outlines two reasons why work is good for us. The first is that we can exercise our skill at something and, in turn, improve, much like we gain pleasure from getting better at sport or a musical instrument. When we work, we naturally get better at it – whether that's the skill involved in operating on a human eye or pulling off a smooth plane landing in a snowstorm. Provided that our skills can continue to improve, we gain monumental satisfaction. And second, work's constructiveness is good for us. In other words, work allows us to build on something, which becomes a monument when the work is completed. When the novelist finishes her novel, it's a delight to contemplate – all that hard work manifested in tangible form. So, too, does the architect delight at the sight of a house on a hill, painstakingly designed by him over many late nights, or a school principal beam at the sight of tiny hands plucking strings in a new purpose-built music hall. 'The satisfaction to be derived from success in a great constructive enterprise is one of the most massive that life has to offer,' continues Russell.

For these no-workers, each day unfolds in much the same manner as the last, and with nothing to build on, they are simply passing time, neither improving, nor building, nor constructing; in fact, they are in stasis.

In *Why is Economics Not an Evolutionary Science?*, Thorstein Veblen writes: 'It is characteristic of man to do something . . . He is not simply a bundle of desires that are to be saturated by being placed in the path of the forces of the environment, but rather a coherent structure of propensities and habits which seek realization and expression in an unfolding activity.' It's true, we all need something to do with our time. Even the ultra-wealthy, freed from economic need, continue to work, engaged in various projects at the same time. Without projects to occupy their time, the comfortably rich can fast turn into neurotics, the smallest worries snowballing into monumental concerns. 'Most of the idle rich suffer unspeakable boredom as the price of their freedom from drudgery,' writes Russell. 'The satisfaction of killing time and of affording some outlet, however modest, for ambition, belongs to most work, and is sufficient to make even a man whose work is dull happier on the average than a man who has no work at all.'

It takes but a quick glance at the physical and mental health statistics of unemployed people, typically afflicted with bouts of depression, obesity and low self-esteem, to realize the importance of work in life. The Russian novelist Fyodor Dostoevsky writes: 'Deprived of meaningful work, men and women lose their reason for existence; they go stark, raving mad.' Abraham Maslow too would think that by not working we were not taking advantage of our life, writing that the desire for self-fulfilment is 'the desire to become more and more what one idiosyncratically is, to become everything that one is capable of becoming'. If we want to be more than hammock dwellers, then we need to stand up and find out what that is.

CHAPTER 6

The Atacama Desert, Chile

'The highest and most beautiful things in life are not
to be heard about, nor read about, nor seen but, if one
will, are to be lived.'

—Søren Kierkegaard

I N MY FINAL YEAR in high school, a career adviser sat inside
a makeshift cabin for a full day waiting for students to file in,
one by one. 'What is your passion?' he asked us in turn. 'What are
your goals? What are your strengths and weaknesses? What,' he
asked, 'is success for you?'

Back in high school I liked reading a lot and playing sport, so
the career adviser plugged these words into his computer and
out spat an answer. Apparently, I should pursue a career in sports
journalism, not that I had any interest whatsoever in writing
about sport. 'Careers Day' was an attempt to match our skills
and desires with the job market.

Millions of students today enrol at universities to engage in
all sorts of individualistic pursuits. And then there are millions of
others at home alone, or isolated in studios, pursuing their dream
of making it in the business world, the lone entrepreneurs in dim
garages dreaming of start-ups that will make a squillion. These
lonely automatons are hard at work in the suburbs, eschewing
other opportunities because nothing should get in the way of
their dream.

A basic feature of Western thought, writes Edward
Slingerland, a professor of Asian studies, in his book *Trying Not
to Try*, is 'extreme individualism'. The ideal person in Western

society is radically alone. 'For the past couple hundred years in the west, the dominant view of human nature has been that we are all individual agents pursuing our own self-interest.' And this dominant view has trickled down. It has influenced how people relate to one other, the attention they devote to their own individualistic cares in comparison with activities that benefit the common good, or other people. 'As economists and political scientists have only recently begun to realise,' writes Slingerland, the extreme individualism of the West is a 'fairy tale cooked up over the last century or two by a bunch of elite, landowning males – what the philosopher Annette Baier has scathingly referred to as "a collection of clerics, misogynists, and puritan bachelors".'

Slingerland contrasts this lonely Western mindset with ancient Chinese thinking during the Warring States period (the fifth to the third century BCE), a time of exceptional philosophical creativity. Central to theories relating to the pursuit of the good life was a concept called *wu-wei* (pronounced 'ooo-way'), best translated as 'spontaneous action'. The good life was about cultivating the art of spontaneity and living an effortless, harmonious existence. A person in *wu-wei* operates in a dynamic, unselfconscious and effortless fashion, writes Slingerland. 'It feels good to be in *wu-wei*,' he states. 'We're also attracted to effectiveness, and people in *wu-wei* tend to be socially competent as they move through life.' By embracing spontaneity, according to ancient thinkers, we can make better sense of our work and our goals.

Wu-wei is similar in theory to the highly popular 'flow' concept in the West, touted by psychologist Mihaly Csikszentmihalyi. Like flow, *wu-wei* is a desirous state for humans to be in; great leaps in creativity and insight happen when people are in flow. But while Western flow tends to relate to people pursuing individualistic activities – the lone concert pianist, the tortured artist, the hard-working manager – Eastern *wu-wei* places this concept in a social realm. '*Wu-wei* is about more than isolated individuals incrementally improving their personal bests in the Ironman Triathlon or mastering a new level of Tetris,' writes

Slingerland. '*Wu-wei* involves giving yourself up to something that, because it is bigger than you, can be shared by others,' he writes. 'An essential fact about *wu-wei* is that it's not just about the experience unfolding within the mind of an isolated individual but also about social connections between people.' It's this 'social' aspect of *wu-wei* that western approaches tend to overlook.

What's also overlooked in the west is that success is not an isolated case. Take the talented tennis player, the upcoming talent on the courts who's destined for greatness. While those in the West call attention to her individual talents, what's conveniently forgotten is that her father got her to the courts each day, her mother paid for her lessons and equipment, and her coach taught her everything she knows; and that's not to mention her ancestors who passed on their incredible tennis-playing genes. Nothing exists in isolation.

The most poignant thing is that our life becomes significant only when it's shared. The great novelist requires readers, just as the tennis player requires an opponent to knock the ball back across the net. 'We have been taught to believe that the best way to achieve our goals is to reason about them carefully and strive consciously to reach them,' Slingerland writes. 'Unfortunately, in many areas of life this is terrible advice. Many desirable states – happiness, attractiveness, spontaneity – are pursued indirectly, and conscious thought and effortful striving can actually interfere with their attainment,' he concludes.

Had we been taught at school to consider dreams as a group, or collective, endeavour, what would have changed? Had we been taught to seek out a network of like-minded people to pursue something that none of us could have achieved alone, would we be happier? Would we, in fact, be more successful?

The border crossing is perched somewhere in the mountains between Argentina and Chile and our van is circled by customs police. Dogs sniff the books and I'm breathing frantically, in, out, in, out, in a manner that seems maddeningly out of control. Customs police talk among themselves in muted voices, muffled and indistinct. We are led into a rectangular office and stand there, helpless, as official books are opened and shut and a line of uniformed men add our details, such as car registration, visas and passport numbers, into dust-worn notebooks. They search our coats and inspect our shoes. A younger police officer gets under the car with a flashlight.

Through a long-unwashed window, a customs officer and his dog appear, stepping out and heading inside the open back door of our van. I think about Juan and the cold girl, who, by early afternoon, will be emerging into daylight, the cold girl in her fake fur cooking toast on the outside barbecue. Juan will emerge later, blowing about in the kitchen, his pants dragging from his undernourished hips.

It's the high altitude, I realize, the fall in oxygen levels, that I'm mistaking for nervousness. I pant, my lungs gulping back oxygen, gills flailing like a fish out of water. But when my heart races, I instantly relate it to what my mind perceives, forgetting that my body too is adjusting and readjusting to the ever-altering conditions. Our rigid views on mind and body can be traced to the seventeenth-century French philosopher René Descartes, who theorized that the mind and the body are separate entities. This thinking is called dualism. In his *Meditations on First Philosophy*, Descartes argues that while you can exist without your body, you can't exist without thinking. In other words, he suggests that we are 'thinking beings' and that thinking is the activity of an immaterial soul, not a physical body.

But in his book *Phenomenology of Perception*, the French philosopher Maurice Merleau-Ponty took dualism to task. When we perceive the world around us, he argued, we do so as a 'lived body'. When I stand at a border crossing panting nervously, I do so with mind and body. We are not just minds and spirits, we are embodied beings, and both have something to say if we care to listen. Interestingly, we never refer to the body as intelligent or knowledgeable. 'Oh, what an insightful body you have. It is so wise, so clever, so enlightened!' Instead, we tend to focus on the mind. Or, when we do focus on the body, it's solely for it to be exercised or stretched. But in doing so, we are effectively limiting our perception, or awareness, of the world around us. 'The body is our general medium for having a world,' Merleau-Ponty writes.

Once our passports are returned and the customs police head back inside, the border gates open and we enter Chile. We continue onwards, this time due west. It is mountainous on the border with Argentina, but this soon falls away into fertile wine-growing regions, and after hitting the coastline, we aim north, beyond Santiago, and still further north. Days pass.

Eventually the land turns from farming soil to arid parched earth, and eventually sand. We pass mining towns and gaping pits in the earth where multinational corporations dig for copper and gold. At one point the bitumen road fades, but we don't think much of it as we continue in a northern trajectory. The traffic thins to a solitary truck every hour or so; before long it is just us, the sand and the setting sun.

I'm mesmerized by the monotone colour and the blue-white sky as we drift across this blank sandy canvas. There's nothing to jog memory, nothing to distract. We are birds on northern migration. Without a map, we use the sun to navigate, keeping an eye on the shadows it casts. There's a wondrous freedom in not knowing the way exactly, but it's infinitely more comforting to follow a route, using a GPS. You plug in your destination and wait for a voice to tell you where to go. We do the same with authority figures, parents, partners and friends.

Eventually my body calls for water, and I swallow hard, and before I say anything, I'm scrambling about on the floor of the car looking for water bottles, and it's at that moment that Zan says, 'Where's the road?' I peer above the dashboard to see flat dirt to the left and to the right, sand in the middle distance. I can't distinguish between the road and the roadside, it's all one stretch of yellow dirt. Zan slows the van to a stop and we get out. We find ourselves in a desert, without a map, compass, computer or phone, and now without water. What does it mean to come to a place with no road?

We sit next to the car and wait for we know not what. We listen for an engine. The last truck passed about 40 minutes ago, we assess, although time seems to have been lost at the same point as the road. We think of all the things that have kept us safe in the past: the phone, the internet, the roads, all these pointers that kept us on track, like little toy trains going around in circles. Here we are, free from all that, perhaps freer than almost everyone. And now, we are two of the few people who don't have a clue where they are.

Soon the stars appear in an arc above our heads, and they are brighter than city lights. We look skyward, realizing that in some small way, even if we perish in the desert, we've done it, we've lost ourselves completely, and wasn't that the point? Zan turns on the music in the car, and the beat cheers us up. Instantly we dance, our faces lit up by stars, and it's at this point that it comes to us that in this little flicker of existence, so tiny in the scheme of things, this little jewel of life that we've been granted, so fleeting and so precious – shouldn't we always be dancing?

Then Zan suddenly stops and starts to walk towards elevated ground. 'Is that a road?' I follow his shadow into the darkness, and up ahead, like a mirage, I too think I see a ribboned line over a hill. We are on track, but not quite. Zan tracks the road on foot, while I return to the car and start the engine. I fear going off course, desperate now to keep to a path. I collect him about 100 metres on, and he leaps, clearly relieved, into the passenger seat.

Twenty minutes later, we pull up beside a swanky new hotel, like some steel growth emerging from the desert floor, a hotel for miners, smelling of plastic and paint. The fluent English of the hotel staff is suddenly reassuring. Sitting on the bed facing the window, I down a chilled drink from the minibar and look out through the cinema-sized window that faces the desert, now shrouded in darkness – still out there, and forever embedded in my consciousness.

———

The next morning, we wait at reception for so long the morning sky tilts backwards. At one point, a figure appears, beady eyes framed by brown glasses, her desk toppling with books, notepads, newspaper clippings and printed sheets of A4 paper. The woman is in her late forties, her hair bunched in a bun on the crown of her head. She wears a beige jacket over corduroy pants.

She asks for our passport, and writes our names in a book, which she takes some time to find within the mess of objects on her desk. Her phone goes off and she forgets our presence.

'What are you reading?' Zan asks when she gets off the phone.

'Oh,' she replies, as though in fright at the prospect of answering. 'What, now?'

'Yes, now.'

She fiddles with a pen and drops it onto the floor, disappearing again, and suddenly reappearing, red-faced, with the pen in her hand.

'Oh, news on the internet.'

Carla is a mother of three who works at the hotel desk during the day while her children are at school. 'School hours are precious,' she says, and with these hours she reads – newspapers, books, the internet – always immersed, her head bowed like a devotee. At times, she circles a newspaper story with a red pen and violently cuts out a snippet. These clippings are transported to a corkboard that leans back against the wall. Beside her, a leather satchel bulges, threatening to vomit out its contents of books.

Periodically, the automatic door opens to the desert, and sand enters like an unwanted guest, piling along the skirting boards and turning the white tiles a subtle beige. But Carla is rarely out of her chair, seemingly unable to wrest herself away from her reading material.

She has so many ideas she needs the corkboard for laying them flat. She employs a notepad for jotting them down, dot points, 'things to do'. With so many ideas, I imagine they must become jumbled up in the neurons of her brain, much like her corkboard, a collage of interweaving pictures, like signposts pointing every which way. But then comes the time when the children are to be collected, and Carla reluctantly picks them up and heads home. Perhaps she'd like to change jobs one day, or move her children to a different school, or learn a new skill, but instead she reads, circles, pins and reads on. She is the potter without clay, the painter without paints.

The neuroscientist Jaak Panksepp, who spent many decades mapping the emotional system of the brain, tries to put this into a name we can understand. That name might be curiosity, interest, foraging, anticipation, craving, expectancy, but he thinks the word 'seeking' best explains it. Panksepp has identified seven core emotional systems that he thinks drive humans. These instincts are embedded in the ancient regions of our brain and are essential to our survival. He lists them as seeking, rage, fear, lust, care, grief and play. But it is seeking that Panksepp argues is the most important: 'Seeking is the granddaddy of the systems.' It is the mammalian motivational engine. We love, more than anything, to be in a state of eager, directed purpose. It's what compelled us as ancient people to dash about seeking food and shelter; it drives our foraging behaviour, our curiosity about our environment; it propels us to create networks, to investigate and to seek meaning. In a sense, it's the energy source that makes things happen.

Panksepp notes that humans are happiest when in search mode, seeking rewards of some description. Very few of us can happily sit on the front porch and watch the world go by. Before long, we're off, seeking something new. Our need to seek explains many of our behaviours, which at times are perplexing even to us. We find ourselves foraging with an unexplained ferocity, planning the next big thing, the latest business idea, money-making scheme, dinner party, overseas trip or property purchase; we seek newness in news, in people, in connections; we seek new weather, new disasters, new ideas, new inspiration. The more novel and unexpected it is, the bigger the hit we get from it.

Panksepp says we get off on all this seeking. The seeking itself is our reward. This explains why our seeking has a sense of being insatiable (like a conveyer belt that's forever moving onward), and although we may convince ourselves that finding a partner, having a family or buying the mansion with the pool will see an end to our seeking – that it'll be the day when we can put up the hammock and happily look at the sky – neuroscientists give us the unfortunate verdict that no, we'll simply replace the completed search with yet another one.

Our ancient brains are constantly seeking because in the past, survival – which hinged on finding food and water – was a full-time occupation. Never quite satiated enough – almost always on the point of starvation – we had to keep grazing, just like the donkey in the field, in order to get our fill. But today, with most of our food and shelter needs met within modern society, the stimulation we get from seeking is channelled elsewhere.

The internet provides an artificial outlet for this kind of seeking activity. When online, we are in complete and utter search mode – seeking new ideas, images, messages, connections. Our seeking pathways, called dopamine transmitters, which energize us while seeking, are firing when we're in search mode.

Panksepp says animals can be driven into a frenzy when rewards for search are dished out in minuscule chunks; unable to be satisfied, they continue their search at a more frantic pace. The 'ding' announcing a new text or email message is akin to the bell Pavlov rang for his dogs. When we log on to read the news or open up our social media account, we become sweating rats in the laboratory, pressing the lever to get our fix: refresh, refresh, refresh. Our search may take us to property websites, online shopping sites, films or talks; whatever it is, it is grounded in the addiction for newness. In short, we are seeking a hit – a fix – of dopamine. A high.

Not surprisingly, drugs like cocaine and amphetamines also fuel the dopamine system. Drug users can get to the point where they can't stop seeking drugs, even as the rewards for using decline over time. Our internet usage, similarly, is typically less rewarding as news sites begin to bore us and internet research leads us nowhere. However, according to Panksepp, the problem for both rats and larger mammals like us is that we can get caught in a loop where 'each stimulation evokes a reinvigorated search strategy', a form of positive reinforcement. We keep clicking links because we have no choice – we're caught in a loop. We've developed a pattern, or habit, and as we all know, habits are hard to break.

Our need to seek could be put to good use if we did not live in a time of distraction. Our insatiable curiosity and directed purpose could be harnessed to write operas, learn languages, paint and sing – like the aristocrats of the past, who, like us, were spared the trouble of locating food and water to survive. Seeking is a motivating force that can move mountains. It is rather unfortunate for us, however, that our society has set up a range of activities to direct this seeking behaviour – to take it in, to set it on loop, to use it up.

The desert wind picks up, and with it comes a whistling down the lift well so intense that residents on the third floor complain. 'We can't speak to each other,' they say, 'the whistling is so loud.' The automatic door opens, and the wind sends Carla's papers into a corner. She darts around grasping at pages and cradling the crumpled heap like a baby. Then, resuming her position without so much as a pause for breath, she returns to reading the screen.

In our room, I sit on the crisp-sheeted bed and stare blankly ahead. For some reason I am thinking about Carla downstairs. If she is 46 now, and if she has been working at the hotel for 12 years, she must have commenced work there when she was 34.

I think about those years. I think, what actually has she done with them?

If I were to ask Carla to relate what she'd read or watched or seen over the past month, or even just over the course of the last few days, I'm sure she'd struggle to remember much at all. The screen is an information well, like a darkened pit devouring conscious thought. Carla has been pressing levers on the internet to give herself a dopamine high. But I'm sure she'd convinced herself that her search had meaning – that it was an instrumental search for knowledge, for life direction and for inspiration.

The economist Thomas Schelling calls the mind a 'consuming organ'. We are built to consume. While our ancestors spent the bulk of their day gathering and preparing food, today supermarket chains and food outlets meet these basic needs for us. So, having freed up time, we've moved into consuming other things – and a large part of this consumption is conceptual. Today, we spend the bulk of our time consuming concepts and information to meet psychological needs. 'People have switched from consuming food (foraging for nuts) to consuming ideas (foraging for information in blogs),' write Dan Ariely and Michael Norton in their paper 'Conceptual Consumption'.

I think about what Carla is searching for – and come to the conclusion that she doesn't actually know, nor even perhaps care. Her mind is set on seeking the novel, the new and unexpected, and when something piques her interest, she gets a dopamine high, which sets her off on a new search.

'We are driven to fill our lives with the quest to "access" information,' writes communications theorist Neil Postman in the prescient 1992 book *Technopoly: The Surrender of Culture to Technology*. 'For what purpose or with what limitations, it is not for us to ask; and we are not accustomed to asking, since the problem is unprecedented. The world has never before been confronted with information glut and has hardly had time to reflect on its consequences.'

The vast amount of information consumed in western society comes from myriad technologies foisted on the populace, starting with the printed word, the photograph, the typewriter, transatlantic cable, motion pictures and wireless telegraphy, and, more recently, moving into computer technology and the internet. Globally, the average internet user spends around seven hours online each day. Since the advent of the internet, the amount of information available for consumption has mushroomed; according to Robert McChesney's *Digital Disconnect*, by 2010 the amount of data created on the internet every two days was equivalent to all extant human cultural artefacts and information created from the dawn of time until 2003. We're awash in information, so much so that we can't quite remember what we've seen, read or heard.

The Roman Stoic philosopher Seneca believed that memory is the essence of self. Our memories of what we do in a lifetime – whether we climb mountains barefoot or sit in an ergonomic chair at a desk – become the scaffolding of our unique self. 'As individuals express their life, so they are,' write Friedrich Engels and Karl Marx in *The German Ideology*.

But not all memories stick. Most sit in our short-term memory for just a few seconds, never to be recalled again. It's our long-term memory that we rely upon for reflection, for deep understanding, and it's here that we develop an idea of self. We're defined by the moment when we saved a child from drowning; by the fact that we speak French as well as English; by the literary mind that we possess from reading Proust at home.

Cognitive scientists point to long-term memory as the powerhouse of the brain. It is a vast reservoir with almost limitless capacity. With each expansion of our long-term memory comes an enlargement of our intelligence, writes Nicholas Carr in *The Shallows: What the Internet Is Doing to Our Brains*. The very act of remembering, he writes, modifies the brain in a way that can make it easier to learn ideas and skills in the future. Carr mentions a study conducted by the German psychologists Georg Müller and Alfons Pilzecker in which they estimated that it takes an hour or so for memories to become fixed, or consolidated, in the brain. 'Short-term memories don't become long-term memories immediately, and the process of their consolidation is delicate. Any disruption, whether a jab to the head or a simple distraction, can sweep the nascent memories from the mind,' writes Carr.

The Australian educational psychologist John Sweller is an expert in cognitive overload. Sweller believes that when too much is going on in our working memory, the successful transfer of information from working memory to long-term memory just doesn't happen. Eastern philosophers might liken it to the cup that's already full, so that more water poured on top simply cascades over the edge. To prevent cognitive overload, no more than four pieces of information should be processed at any given time – though the optimal number is probably less, at two, thinks Sweller. Less is more when it comes to memory retention.

The glaring problem for educational theorists is that distraction is the enemy of learning, and most technologies are what Carr refers to as interruption machines. Reading online comes complete with hyperlinks, banners and images; we encounter constant updates from feeds, posts, instant messaging and notifications. If, as Sweller advises, we optimize learning by limiting our input to some two pieces of information, then what do we make of the technological disco parlours that civilization has invented over the last few decades? What are the consequences for our long-term memory? What are the consequences for our sense of self?

When the key to memory is attentiveness and deep concentration, giving ourselves time to form connections with periods of rest and contemplation, what do we make of the internet, the television, the radio, and all these other forms of technology that have been thrust upon us with no thought to the human being at the helm? Postman argues that the tie between information and human purpose has been severed. We live in an age of technological progress, but no longer human progress. 'Information appears indiscriminately, directed at no one in particular, in enormous volume and at high speeds, and disconnected from theory, meaning, or purpose . . . Information is dangerous when it has no place to go, when there is no theory to which it applies, no pattern in which it fits, when there is no higher purpose that it serves.'

As a curious and conscientious type, Carla, seated at hotel reception, had accommodated herself to the various technologies at her disposal. She had watched television, made and received calls on her mobile phone, worked on her desktop computer, surfed the net on her laptop, texted on her smartphone; she had uploaded and downloaded photos and videos, cut and pasted, friended, followed, liked, pinned, and she had experienced rich media. But while Carla worked with all of her twenty-first century tools, what had become of her? If the art of remembering is the art of thinking, as the philosopher William James once said, then what happens when our memory becomes so sorely impaired by information overload that we can't remember a thing? After 12 years on the information front line, what had become of Carla?

CHAPTER 7

Cusco, Peru

'No good work whatever can be perfect, and the demand
for perfection is always a sign of a misunderstanding of
the ends of art.'

—John Ruskin

W E SPIRAL EVER UPWARD, the van's motor at full
throttle. As I gulp water, a headache sets in like a giant
passenger in the cabin. We have been driving up a sharp elevation
for most of the day, winding heavenward into the dispersed air
of the Andes.

When we arrive at the hotel, a woman is lying flat on its tiled
floor, vomiting. A Peruvian receptionist is on the phone. My head
is a tomato, rounded, soft at the edges. A tourist tells me it'll go
in a few days. 'You shouldn't have driven so quickly. You've got
to do it slowly over days, never in a single day, what were you
thinking?' At night, I pant in bed, my brain exchanging flash
cards of tunnels, tongues and glittering teeth. The walls sway
and beat, perception shifting to a wide-angle focus.

By morning my head feels like a turnip. We leave the hotel early
and return to dirt roads. We continue to drive, hoping I'll shake
the headache, and arrive in Cusco, suddenly among westerners
with monstrous prams, bags hanging every which way, cameras
choking necks – walking shopping malls.

We find ourselves in the old town, still searching for
accommodation, when we spot a *hotel privado*. A stylish Spanish
señora speaks on the phone, effortlessly beckoning us to come
in. She is seated on a sixteenth-century sofa, surrounded by

antiques, baroque armchairs and candelabras. At the far corner of her store, we are led into a tiny makeshift bedroom which she rents out, with an antique double bed, a Biedermeier side table and a writing desk. Beyond, through the window, we glimpse her mansion, an exquisite colonial home, a courtyard of fountains. She places a miniature key in our hand and tells us not to disturb the customers in the daytime when we enter and exit. But at night, we are welcome to open the door to the store for more air, as the room can become hot and stuffy. 'Wander about,' she says with a wink. 'But do not touch anything! These pieces are precious, and my husband will know if you've moved anything.'

A Persian cat slinks about and sits on the throne of a Victorian chaise longue like a renaissance poet, its yellow eyes fixed upon us as we unpack our desert clothes into the cupboard. The bedside lamp is made of what could possibly be a mix of gold and marble, a cornflower Persian carpet lies conspicuously upon the floor. Airtight and dusty, two grandfather clocks compete with each other against time.

I ask the *señora* how she chooses what to buy for her store. All purchases, she says without hesitation, must be linked with meaning. The embroidered bergère chair was purchased to symbolize meeting up with her best friend from school whom she'd not seen for some 30 years. An emerald ring was purchased as a gift to herself when she sold her first painting. Purchases tied to experiences, or goals in life, it seems. Out goes shopping therapy and in comes something more meaningful. 'This way,' she says, 'the things will have more meaning for you, plus you've accomplished something.'

'But why are you selling your precious things?' Zan asks.

'Oh,' she says, 'my husband is sick. And I will be moving into an apartment soon – selling the house, selling it all.'

I think we've moved onto an uncomfortable subject, but the *señora* seems to take it all in her stride. In the dusky afternoon, she paints with an erect back by a window. She wears a long silk gown and fur collar, jewels upon every second finger.

I sit alongside her to watch her paint. She is tackling a scene directly from a photograph. It's in the realist style, and the subject is an outside feast – children and adults sit before an oversized table under the midday sun. Her work is almost photographic in detail. She speaks in English, in full flowing sentences melding Spanish words within. With no regard for an English accent, she lilts the words until they droop with heavy Spanish intonation.

At one point she grabs a jar of light blue paint and heaves it onto the canvas.

'Why did you do that?' I stammer. 'You were almost finished.'

'Ah,' she says, 'that's my little act of rebellion. Who wants a perfect painting? Life is not perfect. We will die one day – that is not perfect. Our whole life is towards death – the imperfect state. Painting too must be imperfect. I like to add the imperfect mark at the end, to show that I don't care for its perfection.'

I agree with her, but I don't know why the painting must suffer this philosophical blow, particularly as it was quite beautiful and almost finished.

'You are a perfectionist?' she asks, turning her dark eyes to my stunned face. She holds her brush mid-air, waving it as she speaks, and I am concerned for her gown, the lace of which seems perilously close to the paint.

'Oh, I suppose at times I am. I like to do my best, and I know when something is not right,' I reply.

'Ah, nonsense,' she says, whipping more blue paint onto the palate and smearing it almost in rage. 'As a perfectionist, you live an insane life, trying to get everything right.'

She points to the birds on the rooftops of the building before us, taking flight and landing, squabbling and pecking. 'Animals don't seek perfection. They just do what they do and get what they get. We are animals too,' she says. 'This perfectionism stuff,' she says, her voice rising, 'I tell my daughter, what nonsense, trying to get everything right all the time. It's too much. It drive you crazy.'

'Yes, I think you are right,' I reply. 'But how,' I continue, 'do you stop yourself from fixing it again?'

'When I first started to paint, it was like that,' she says. 'I was in my forties, I'd always wanted to paint, it was the start of a new romance for me. But within 20 minutes, I'd be cursing myself, "You can't paint. That looks like a big blob, a mess. What are you thinking!" It got so bad I almost quit. "Never again," I said, "it's too horrid." And so, instead, I decided to just say – well, I'm going to put a big blotch on it at the end, so of course it's bad – but I'm not doing it to make it perfect, I am painting because I want to paint. So, I have much more freedom than other painters who are always wanting to be perfect. And I improve faster. I am much better because I am not aiming for perfection – I am aiming for nothing, I just do because I want to do.'

One night the *señora* arrives home flushed and plainly unsettled. She throws her shawl upon a daybed in the store and plonks herself down, grabbing a decanter and filling a glass.

We are both seated on the window side of the store, reading under lamps.

'How do you know that you are living your life?' she asks. 'How do you know you that you are not borrowing someone else's dreams?'

'Whose dreams would they be?' I ask.

'Someone else's,' she says. 'I am having this conversation with my son,' she continues. 'He tells me he wants to do this or that, or be this kind of person when he grows up, but it's always the same thing that his friends are doing, or someone on television, or someone he has read about in a book. It's always borrowed, never his own.'

'But how do you know it's not his own?'

'Well, that would be a coincidence,' she says. 'But I know my son, all these things are not him.'

I do often think about goals that I haven't pursued and wonder why they are goals at all. It makes sense to have a goal for something that you've already started – you like running and your next goal is a marathon, for instance. But some goals seem to have no beginning point, like dropping a tack onto a board and saying, 'That's where I want to be' or, 'That's what I want to do or have.' Where do these goals come from? And what is their point? Are they simply there to taunt you each New Year for not having accomplished them, yet again? People who want to write novels often have such goals on their list. Writing a novel takes time, effort and sacrifice – and I suppose not everyone has this as a bundle. But I find it odd that some people can have the goal of writing a book, yet they don't write at all; it's akin to wanting to be a tennis champion but not playing tennis.

Can goals be unwittingly implanted into our brains by someone else? Is it possible that many of the goals and dreams we carry around in our heads are not our own, but have been picked up along the way like dust on the back of a truck?

Psychology professor Kenneth Gergen thinks so. In postmodern society, we are exposed not just to the ideas conjured up in our own head, to the sights and sounds directly experienced, but to a multifaceted plethora of voices and ideas from the digital realm, from social media, the internet, digital videos and so forth. 'Emerging technologies saturate us with the voices of humankind – both harmonious and alien,' writes Gergen. 'These relationships pull us in myriad directions, inviting us to play such a variety of roles that the very concept of an "authentic self" with knowable characteristics recedes from view. The fully saturated self becomes no self at all.'

Gergen argues that with social saturation each of us comes to harbour a vast population of hidden potentials: 'All the selves lie latent, and under the right conditions may spring to life.' But how instrumental are these 'others' in shaping the self? Can news hounds, celebrities and the axe murderer in last night's movie really affect the self? Gergen's wife, the social psychologist Mary Gergen, asked a group of college students to complete a survey entitled 'Remembering Persons'. The questionnaire asked students to name three people who entered their thoughts during day-to-day activities – in other words, three real or fictitious people with whom they had an imagined interaction, a concept Mary Gergen terms 'social ghosts'. 'Many developmental and clinical psychologists have suggested that only people with very unsatisfactory social lives and those who are mentally or emotionally disabled or immature would report experiences of interaction with absent social figures,' Mary Gergen writes in *Feminist Reconstructions in Psychology*. Normal people just don't carry out imagined relationships and interactions with internal voices – or so it was believed.

However, the survey found evidence to the contrary: out of 76 college students, all respondents bar one admitted to having imagined interactions with at least one person. 'The majority of respondents wrote about three relationships . . . although some people added more experiences,' Mary Gergen writes. So, who are these social ghosts populating the inner worlds of college students? According to the survey, past friends, family members and former teachers are often present. But in 29 per cent of cases, so are people the students had never actually met, such as celebrities, fictitious characters and religious figures. 'Among the famous social ghosts unknown to the respondent, entertainers were chosen over 80 per cent of the time,' she writes. Students revealed that continuous imagined interactions with rock stars or celebrities led to changes in their existing beliefs and values. The findings suggest that personalities from books, movies and television and figures from the internet can populate the self in profound ways. As movie and television stars titillate, novelists inspire and media personalities reveal all, we are wrenched from familiar patterns of existence. As philosopher José Ortega y Gasset once said: 'Tell me to what you pay attention and I will tell you who you are.'

We search for conversational Spanish lessons in the old town, but without any success. Without a guidebook or any sort of information about town life, some things – we realize – just won't happen. If it's not in our path, it's not in our path.

Instead, we spend time at the parks – watching the 'park boys', as we call them, a group of charismatic local boys who woo the tourist girls. As the tourists hunt for *chullo* hats and *zampoñas* at park stores, comparing Peruvian textiles on everything from backpacks to blankets, the boys pick them off one by one, like shooting fish in a barrel. We watch the courting process and listen to their conversations as they relay the hunt, as well as the occasional conquest.

Follow your bliss, it certainly has a ring to it. But many will denounce such a glib self-help-sounding motto. When it comes to finding our true purpose in life, we want something more rigorous and scientific, something imbued with both algorithmic complexity and mystical connotations. But Aristotle saw pleasure as the gold standard for finding one's true path. What is it that gives you pleasure? What is it that you do effortlessly, without prompting? What is it that doesn't need to appear on your 'to do' list because, well, you'd probably do it anyway if you could – if you had more time?

Happiness is a signal, like a bell ringing, alerting us to our path, thought Aristotle. When we are happy, what are we doing? What is it that gives us pleasure? We need to notice it, feel it, sense it and note it. The pleasure and happiness we experience in our lives have important implications. Taking Aristotle's sage advice, during the day I begin to write down the times when I feel the happiest. With pen and paper at the ready, I stop and think, 'What am I doing right now?' Nietzsche tells us to be curious and mindful of moments in the journey that elevate and inspire us. 'What have you truly loved? What has drawn you upward?' He impels us to acknowledge the things we love, or honour, as these are keys to the 'fundamental law' of our self. If it were at all possible to do so, Nietzsche urges us to set our loves before us, as though we were laying them out on a table, in order to compare them like objects. 'Consider how one completes and broadens and transcends and explains another: how they form a ladder on which you have all the time been climbing to find your true self,' he writes in his essay *Schopenhauer as Educator*. 'For your true self does not lie deeply hidden within you. It is at an infinite height above you, or at least, above what you commonly take to be yourself.' Follow your happy moments – for these are the pebbles that lead you to your life's quest.

For some reason, I feel an uncanny familiarity in the antique store, surrounded by artefacts, chatting to the *señora*: the warm glow of inspiration. Why do we have such moments? Why do certain people stand tall in our memory while others disappear into the dark recesses of our mind?

Some people reflect the person we wish to be – we may think of them as representing an ideal self, or more simply as a source of inspiration. This helps explain why we remember movie scenes more vividly when we've identified with a certain character. If you leap back into your memory banks and recall some early figures in your life, did someone in particular – a person who stands out in your memory more than others – hold a quality or trait that you admire?

A dreamlike painting by the surrealist artist Remedios Varo is hanging above the *señora*'s desk. It's exquisite, and it reminds me of the *señora* – so I can see why she treasures it. Varo left Spain to journey to Latin America, to Mexico. Painting, for Varo, just like for the *señora*, was not just about colour and composition, it was a means of gaining self-awareness, of exploring inner thoughts and feelings. For surrealists such as Varo, identity starts and finishes within, in our dreams, thoughts and imagination. We are our consciousness and our subconscious. Of course, I think, this is at odds with the thinking of existentialists, who argue that we are only what we do, what we make. We are not our dreams, our wishes, our intentions; we are not what we could be, only what we are. But if we are to meld the two ideas a touch, perhaps Varo's nascent ideas are like the rider – our bubbling inspiration is what ignites the fire – while the existentialist views are the horse, who eventually takes these ideas by the reins and takes action. The rider and the horse need each other. We need our dreams and inspiration, just as we need to get up one day and 'bloody well do something' with our life. But as Varo insisted, those otherworldly thoughts, dreams and ideas that often can't manifest in 'this' world also count.

———

'He wants to do something creative,' the *señora* tells me days later, still speaking about her son. She is hand-stitching a hem of a skirt, while mixing a drink for her husband, who we haven't seen for days. 'But he thinks he has to be a film director, or a poet, or a musician, or an actor – those are creative,' she adds. 'Only those things, nothing else. But I say, that is rubbish. Life is creative. Making a fine home is creative. Decoration, love, friendship is creative. We can live a creative life – not just a job. Plus, I say to him, he is so talented at inspiring people – so talented at negotiation, all those things – he should have a business, but he just wants to do what his friends are doing.'

Maslow, too, at one point thought that creativity was limited to those studying or working in the 'creative fields'. 'Unconsciously,' he wrote in *Toward a Psychology of Being*, 'I had assumed that creativeness was the prerogative solely of certain professionals . . . Theorists, artists, scientists, inventors, writers could be creative. Nobody else could be.' But in his decades-long study into creativity, Maslow concluded that creativity is not something unique to certain professions but is universal to every human who's born. 'I learned,' he wrote, 'that a first-rate soup is more creative than a second-rate painting, and that, generally, cooking or parenthood or making a home could be creative while poetry need not be; it could be uncreative.'

What makes a person creative? Maslow describes a woman who helped the downtrodden. 'One of her "creations",' he writes, 'is an organisation which helps many more people than she could individually.' He mentions a psychiatrist who 'never wrote anything or created any theories or research but who delighted in his everyday job of helping people to create themselves . . . Each patient was a unique human being and therefore a completely new problem to be understood and solved in a completely novel way.' From another man he learns that constructing a business could be a creative activity. 'From a young athlete, I learned that a perfect tackle could be as aesthetic a product as a sonnet and could be approached in the same creative spirit.' Maslow comes to apply the word 'creative' not just to works of art or snippets of writing, but to activities, processes, and even attitudes. He believes that people can be creative in housekeeping, in parenthood, teaching and coaching; in designing a garden bed, or a feast for the family. Even one's approach or attitude to life can be 'creative', he thinks. Spontaneous, expressive, natural, free-flowing individuals live creatively in their approach to life, with 'less blocking and self-criticism', less fear of ridicule, more childlike in their approach. Maslow thinks that this childlike, creative self is inherent in all of us – from birth – but for many people, it 'most often is lost or buried or inhibited as the person gets enculturated'.

Maslow calls creative people 'integrators' who bring separates, even opposites, together. The painter will 'bring together clashing colours, forms that fight each other, dissonances of all kinds, into a unity'. And so too does the parent or teacher who somehow manages to integrate the unruly demands of children to bring out their best, or the plumber who comes up with a creative solution to a dripping pipe that's flooding the basement of a house. In summary, a creative life is expansive and can integrate all of a person's myriad loves and passions – and it needn't be constrained to the few pursuits we've traditionally deemed to be 'creative'. You needn't drop everything to become 'creative'. Just look at what you do best, what you do naturally, what pesters you, what gives you bliss, and then pursue this with all the creative vigour you can muster.

Days unfold in a semblance of normality. We leave before the store opens and return when it closes to help the *señora* sweep the floors. We make ourselves quiet, like mice, although the cat is forever watchful. From antique row, life seems almost complete.

Here amid luxury, swimming between our miniature room and the antique store, we watch the rich clientele of the *señora*'s store wander in and out, touching fabrics and passing a relaxing hand over beadings and cornices.

The *señora* lets her clientele swim about in silence, not wishing to disturb their meditative turns about the labyrinthine aisles. All the while, she sketches imaginary scenes in a small notepad or reads under a yellow lamp at her desk.

'Wanted objects,' says anthropologist Grant McCracken, 'tell us not who we are, but who we wish to be.' These objects in the store give the *señora*'s patrons a bridge between the present reality and their ideal future, as they imagine 'the possession of certain ideal circumstances that exist now only in a distant location'. In this sense, we use objects to project outwards, to experiment with identities. It goes some way to explaining why city streets are a house of objects – tiny stores showcasing objects from luxury fashion, to jewellery, to watches, shoppers moving from one house of objects to the next, seeking with the same relish with which we traditionally sought food for survival.

The cultural theorist Jean Baudrillard spent much of his life studying objects. In *The System of Objects*, he examined why we surround ourselves with objects. While some may be useful, such as a refrigerator for cooling food or a pen for writing, many, such as antique busts and French Aubusson tapestries, are not. When objects have no use in our lives, why are they present at all?

We value objects in different ways, writes Baudrillard. A wedding ring has symbolic value for us. An investment property can be exchanged in the marketplace for money, and therefore has economic value. But in our commoditized world, we also buy and store objects for their sign value, to inform others and remind ourselves of our own identity, and to differentiate ourselves from others. It is through our objects that we hope to become ourselves, who we really wish to be.

The Frankfurt School, a German philosophical movement, has a lovely word for it: reification, or, in German, *Verdinglichung* – 'making into a thing', or 'objectification'. We are dominated by things, and over time have become more 'thinglike'. It helps explain why some people own multiple cars: one car for the corporate self during the week and another for the adventurer during leisure time. We also buy objects in a system, notes Baudrillard. For instance, our enlightened self buys a range of bamboo linen towels, yoga paraphernalia, organic hair products, and a yurt for the backyard – a series of possible purchases that knows no limits. The adventurer in us buys a distinctly different system of objects: a road bike, camping equipment and associated clothes, a four-wheel drive, fishing gear, climbing equipment, a kayak – the list goes on and on. 'The fulfilment of the project of possession always means a succession or even a complete series of objects,' writes Baudrillard. 'This is why owning absolutely any object is always so satisfying and so disappointing at the same time: a whole series lies behind any single object, and makes it into a source of anxiety.'

Baudrillard argues that we can possess expensive artwork and seemingly worthless objects with the same fanaticism. 'This fanaticism is identical whether it characterises a rich connoisseur of Persian miniatures or a collector of matchboxes,' he writes. 'Collectors are forever saying that they are "crazy about" this or that object, and they all without exception ... cloak their collection in an atmosphere of clandestineness and concealment ... which in every way suggests a feeling of guilt.'

The patrons in the *señora's* store delight in their finds – a gold renaissance enamel ring is held up to the light as though Sirius were being viewed through a telescope. 'The beauty, the beauty' – and it is here, watching and listening from our room, or sitting reading on the window ledge, that I sympathize a little more with the love of stuff. These women, I note, are in a state of ecstasy – aestheticism gives them a thrill in no unequal measure to soccer fans anticipating a game on Friday night. Pleasure, bliss, zest for life – if a rare ormolu jewellery box sends you to heaven and back, then this is your pleasure.

What's so meaningful about delight is that it comes upon us unawares – we become a breathless, squealing child again. We cannot plan for it, nor coax it to happen. Unlike forcing yourself to study, or work, or eat, you can't make yourself delight in something. Delight is spontaneous and unpredictable, and utterly unique to the person who experiences it. These precious 'delights' in life need to be acknowledged. Because sometimes they are telling us something we need to know about ourselves, and our purpose.

———

One day the daughter returns from Spain. She has the familial accent with the almost lisp-like 'th'. Unlike her mother, though, she is less open and more suspicious, having lost the provincial trustworthiness of town life after living in New York and Berlin, and within a day we are moved out of the store to dusty quarters out the back of the mansion, where antiques are replaced by rotting wood. Indignant, we leave the following day without saying goodbye, just a note to the *señora* sending her our love.

CHAPTER 8

Baños, Ecuador

'If the doors of perception were cleansed everything would appear to man as it is, infinite.'

—William Blake

W E ARE WINDING INTO Baños, Ecuador, a town known for its hot springs, sitting at the foot of an active volcano. Every so often, Tungurahua – one of eight active volcanoes in Ecuador on the Pacific Ring of Fire – erupts, throwing ash plumes several kilometres into the air and altering the landscape, a gradual cycle of decay and repair, of renewal and change, much like our own transformation.

In town, we follow a group of well-worn travellers into a dog-kennel structure behind steel fencing. We are allocated a boarding room adjacent to the communal bathroom. We throw backpacks onto steel bunk beds, well away from the floor. A small window, shut with rusting nails, offers some form of security, beyond which the owner, a balding man in his late sixties, patrols the grounds like a security guard, filling up buckets of water and taking them around the back.

That night we are bitten in rows, tiny red lumps so straight you could put a ruler underneath and draw a line as though they were a mystical star constellation. The lumps flare up and itch like crazy. But the well-worn travellers, immune to discomfort, are awake before dawn, noisily washing in the loo outside, sharing *maté* from a single gourd. Awake and unsettled, Zan asks in Spanish where they are heading next, and they laugh at the suggestion they are heading anywhere. Like us, they have lost their sense of direction, and of time, too, as the town quietly slumbers.

In my corporate job, the turnstile was my timestamp. Morning, 8 a.m. sharp; and if I were to grab a coffee at 9 a.m., the sensor would unlock the barrier, clocking me out. The clock kept me to a punctual timetable, a consistency as regular as a heartbeat. The clock meant that I did more or less the same thing at the same time every day, tiny repetitive moments that over time became as effortless as breathing. This is the key to habit formation: repetition, over and over again, day in, day out. 'All our life,' writes William James, 'so far as it has a definite form, is but a mass of habits – practical, emotional, and intellectual – systematically organized for our weal or woe, and bearing us irresistibly toward our destiny, whatever the latter may be.'

Since the late 1700s, when the first recorded system of clocking on was imposed in the cotton mills, the clock has regulated the rhythms of working people. The clock is a symbol of discipline and exactitude. The office worker is employed on company time. Time is money, and time wasted is money wasted.

There are endless books that teach us how to use our time wisely: techniques to get more done in less time; how to build effective time-management habits; how to defeat procrastination; or how to multitask by doing more things at the same time, like eating on the way to work, or working while waiting for a plane.

In 1755, Reverend John Clayton's pamphlet entitled 'Friendly Advice to the Poor' noted the importance in industrial life of being thrifty with time. 'If the sluggard hides his hands in his bosom, rather than applies them to work; if he spends his Time in Sauntring, impairs his Constitution by Laziness, and dulls his Spirit by Indolence' then he can expect only poverty as his reward. Clayton complained that labourers waste the best hours of the day for the sake of observing the world around them, that the tea table is a 'shameful devourer of Time and Money', and that so too are wakes, holidays and annual feasts. Clayton strictly advised against 'slothful spending the Morning in Bed'. Rising early, he claimed, introduces an exact regularity into families, a wonderful order into 'their economy'.

Homilies to humble workers rising early and working hard have been common for centuries now. 'In mature capitalist society all time must be consumed, marketed, put to use; it is offensive for the labour force merely to "pass the time",' writes E. P. Thompson in the paper 'Time, Work-Discipline, and Industrial Capitalism'. Mature industrial societies of all varieties are 'marked by time-thrift and by a clear demarcation between "work" and "life".'

Thompson notes that the years between 1300 and 1650 saw important changes in the understanding of time. From the fourteenth century, many cities and market towns in Europe installed a public or church clock that chimed on the hour. In the early nineteenth century, clockmakers attempted to bring clocks nearer 'to the truth', or to near-perfect accuracy; successfully made clocks would seldom skip a second over a year or longer. The acceptance or even reverence for timekeeping devices was integral to the industrial age, when disciplined workers were needed on deck at the same time to perform synchronized tasks.

The clock or watch, a mechanized instrument with two hands, has become our timekeeper and informer. It can insist on a 6 a.m. start at the gym; it can ensure that children are behind the school gates by 9 a.m. sharp to avoid a late slip being meted out; it means our work output can be quantified by the minute to measure our productivity and efficiency.

Before the mechanized clock, the measurement of time was related to daily goings-on. Fishermen and seafaring people lived their lives according to the tides and were often up all hours of the night. 'The patterning of social time in the seaport follows upon the rhythms of the sea,' writes Thompson. 'And this appears to be natural and comprehensible to fishermen or seamen: the compulsion is nature's own.'

Before the clock, work and life intermixed – the working day lengthened or contracted according to seasonal fluctuations or the task at hand. In places such as Madagascar, writes Thompson, time might be measured by the time it takes for rice to cook (about half an hour) or for the frying of a locust (a moment). In

Burma, monks were said to rise when there was enough light to see the veins in their hands.

Before the coming of age of large-scale machine-powered industry, work was irregular, tasks were varied, and work and idleness intertwined – much like the behaviour of university students today, or artists and writers, who have spells of light work followed by times of almost complete engagement in the work process. Thompson argues that this pattern is characteristic of people who have control over their working lives; it's our 'natural' human work rhythm.

In our natural work rhythm, we work according to observed necessities. 'There is a sense in which it is more humanly comprehensible than timed labour,' writes Thompson. But for those accustomed to labour timed by the clock, this attitude to work appears wasteful and lacking in urgency, he explains.

Ironically, an engraved gold watch after five decades of disciplined service to a firm has been a common gift to employees. The small mechanized instrument with its reliable metronome that never lost a second was shackled around the worker's tired wrist. The gold watch was a symbol – and a dark reminder – of those 50 years of madcap mornings when much of that time was spent dashing around, years spent racing against the manic ticking of a clock – a gadget that could measure, record, timestamp, push, push, faster, faster, harder, harder, tick, tick, tick, go, go, go . . . right until the end.

———

There is something about the hot-spring town that holds us, and so we rent a room above a gymnasium. I organize daily Spanish lessons, timed for sunrise. I wander through sleepy, misty streets lit up by the green of the Amazon, a colour Van Gogh would have devoured.

My wizened teacher waits for me at the front door of his colonial home. He bars entry until I say the customary '*Buenos días,*' and then we climb the stairs to his study, where he seats himself behind his walnut desk and his steaming coffee, and enquires, 'You have your notebook? Good. No computer, not good for memory.'

It's true: if you want to remember something, write it out by hand. When we write, the small muscles in our hands are employed to physically move the nib of the pen across the paper. When writing by hand, these tiny movements leave a motor memory in Broca's area – the sensorimotor part of the brain – which helps us remember. This sensorimotor system also helps us to recognize letters when reading. Anne Mangen, a professor in literacy at Norway's University of Stavanger, paired up with the neurophysiologist Jean-Luc Velay at the French National Centre for Scientific Research in Marseille to compare keyboard typing and handwriting. Two groups of adults were asked to learn an unknown alphabet consisting of some twenty letters. One group was taught to write them by hand, while the other group used a keyboard. Three and six weeks into the experiment, the groups were tested on their recollection of the letters and on the speed with which they could distinguish the correct letters from those appearing in reverse. The verdict: those who had learned the letters by writing them out by hand came out best in all tests, and what's more, fMRI brain scans indicated activation of Broca's area within the handwriting group. Keyboard users, in comparison, showed little or no activation of this area of the brain. Mangen concluded that the sensorimotor component of our brain helps us to learn and remember, and that this brain function is activated most when writing by hand.

———

The gymnasium wants a yoga teacher and Zan tells the owners I can do it. But I am hesitant. I started a training course once, but never finished. And having attempted so many yoga styles over the years, I never know exactly what I am doing. But the young couple at the gymnasium are excited by the idea of yoga classes, and so we decide on Iyengar every Tuesday and Thursday, from 4.30 to 5.30 p.m. – locals free, tourists pay ten pesos. I demonstrate and Zan translates. We print off advertisements and sticky-tape the posters to poles around town. And the marketing pays off – dozens of locals and tourists turn up at the gymnasium door.

I run through the yoga technique directly from a book I've stored in the van. 'Inhale,' I say, tilting my head towards the open page at my right. But the next sequence of moves comes with a lengthy description, and I forget where on the page I left off – and the class bursts into laughter as a Dutch tourist tumbles sideways onto the floor from feigned asphyxiation. But at the end, we sit crossed-legged, sip herbal tea and look at each other in bemusement as Zan boils more water in the kitchen. I nod politely and say '*Sí*' too many times, mostly as the incorrect response to the question being asked.

It seems like the perfect arrangement – Spanish lessons in the morning, followed by yoga twice a week at the gymnasium – and the centre booms with our marketing blitz. We are thinking that we, too, could stay here in Baños, move our yoga studio closer into town, where the tourist action is. This could be it, we think, as we wash dishes from the gymnasium, sharing a kitchen with the owners, listening to Spanish radio. This could be our place, near the warm-water springs, a place where we could find ourselves, a place where we could flourish.

That weekend, we take a quick trip to Cuenca by bus and find accommodation nine floors high in the city centre. It's cold, and the old hotel has outside seating, set up with kitchen facilities. I hastily boil a kettle for tea, and we sit sipping with roaring traffic below.

Cuenca is 2,560 metres above sea level, and water boils fast – but that's because it 'boils' at a lower temperature. The better-prepared would have known to wait. Boil the kettle for three minutes longer, perhaps ten minutes, even more.

That night, I don't think too much about it as I watch Zan make a track between bed and bathroom and back again. And come morning, I'm keen to leave the hotel and see the sights. I urge him to get out of bed, to buy lemonade from a corner store. But as we leave, he is dragging his legs, not speaking. I try to take it all in, the clanking of roller shutters as owners open their stores in the walled medieval city, the motorbikes and trucks making deliveries, and I find an old bookstore, but it's closed until midday. We turn into a busy road, two-lane traffic, and I dodge business people in jackets carrying briefcases, with files stacked under their arms, women with plastic shopping bags full of vegetables and warm soda, and I try to occupy my thoughts, a lone traveller, trailed by Zan's shadow long lost within his ailment, and then suddenly the street empties of sound. Silent. Motorbikes glide past. Cars float. Footsteps fall silent.

I am on Zan's back, as he climbs a winding stairwell – up, up. Four flights, five flights. Zan's legs buckle underneath him. He puts me on a plastic seat, and I stare ahead – blankly, and then directly into the colossal head of Elvis, thick sideburns, an opened white shirt trimmed by black chest hair, a dancing gold chain. The room is cut in two by a light blue curtain, pulled shut, and Elvis moves between his desk at the window to the curtain and beyond, and I find Zan nodding, and there's a grabbing of cords, and I turn to Zan's face – up close, peering into it – and he tells me with a gaping mouth that I need to be put on a drip. 'A drip,' I say, terrified, terrified of being pinned down and injected by Elvis. With desperate pleas, I say I'd rather die.

Back in the hotel, I lie flat on the bed. A French couple place water bottles at the door. Days pass. We move from the bed to the bathroom and back. At night my stomach lurches with sea snakes, my organs vibrate, sewage stink in my mouth. I think about Baños, our small utopian town, now a million miles away.

It is a common regret of the dying. 'I wish I had let myself be happier.' When nurse Bronnie Ware spoke with terminally ill patients in the final weeks of their lives, she listened to many of their regrets. 'Many did not realise until the end that happiness is a choice,' she says. But many important life moments had been wasted in worry, stress and distraction.

James Hollis, a Jungian analyst who works in private practice, identifies two common threats that steal many a happy moment in our lives. 'Every morning we rise to find two gremlins at the foot of the bed,' he writes in *Living an Examined Life*. The first threat is fear, identified by that consistent voice in your head stressing that the world is too big for you. 'You are not up for it. Find a way to slip-slide away again today,' this voice insists. And the second threat, according to Hollis, is lethargy, which repeatedly reminds you to take it easy, there's no rush, life can wait. 'Hey, chill out. You've had a hard day. Turn on the telly, surf the internet, have some chocolate. Tomorrow's another day.'

Hollis believes that these 'perverse twins munch on our souls every day,' and 'over time, they usurp more days of our lives than those to which we may lay fair claim. More energy is spent in any given day on managing fear through unreflective compliance, or avoidance, than any other value. While it is natural to expend energy managing our fears, the magnitude of this effort on a daily basis cannot be overemphasized.'

Lethargy takes many seductive forms too. We avoid tasks, we stay away from that which is difficult, we numb our days with social media distraction or screen entertainment. 'We have a vast wired culture to help us in this task, a connected twenty-four-hour distraction . . . we can sleep our life away and never awaken to the summons of the soul that resounds within each of us.' Hollis says that the task of each of us is to recognize and stand up to these twin threats. 'The task of the hero within is to overthrow the powers of darkness, namely, fear and lethargy... Sooner or later, we are each called to face what we fear, respond to our summons to show up, and overcome the vast lethargic powers within us.'

When we decide to leave the hotel, we don't return to Baños. We head south to a cabin on a mountainside, like dogs finding a place to die, out of sight. Most of the cabins are empty, except for one in which an Italian trio drink on the porch from morning 'til night – rising late, retiring later. 'We come here every year,' they say in Spanish or Italian, I'm not sure which. Zan is now just 64 kilograms – at over six feet tall, he is a skeletal frame, barely walking. Locals step aside on the streets, not wishing to interact, fearing contamination. Wild dogs track us from our cabin on the hillside to the town and back again, smelling death.

Just out of town I read signs for bowel treatments, colon flushing done behind curtained doors in suburban homes. Instead, I buy water at the store and retreat. Zan lies on a hammock in the sun, unable to read, his eyes fixed skyward.

Beyond the window, from my bed I study the fields where human traffic still meanders at its own pace – free of footpaths and streets set down in concrete by urban planners. Some call these paths 'desire lines' – meandering trails, the natural pathways that humans walk. When I take a closer look, I behold that they are not straight, but drift, snake and wind all over the place. I think about life as a series of circles, spanning outwards – we push out and double back, a circular journey – not linear.

We're often misled into thinking that life needs to be linear, that we need to select early on what it is we wish to do and then follow the chosen path relentlessly. But nature isn't linear, and often successful lives aren't either. In a study of winding career paths, Todd Rose, at the time the director of Harvard's Mind, Brain, and Education Program, and the computational neuroscientist Ogi Ogas rounded up people who were successful and fulfilled in their careers, from architects to engineers to animal trainers. But when interviewed, the vast majority were a little sheepish about their career history, relaying with some embarrassment that they had done a lot of job-hopping in the past, jumping from one thing to the next. The researchers named the study the Dark Horse Project because most taking part in it erroneously believed they were the 'dark horse' – the odd one out who had pursued a winding career path, as opposed to choosing one career and sticking with it. Dark horses, note the researchers, 'never look around and say, "Oh, I'm going to fall behind, these people started earlier and have more than me at a younger age."' Instead, they say, 'Here's who I am at the moment, here are my motivations, here's what I've found I like to do, here's what I'd like to learn, and here are the opportunities. Which of these is the best match *right* now? And maybe a year from now I'll switch because I'll find something better.' Each dark horse practised short-term planning and shunned long-term planning. In his book *Range*, David Epstein describes the career history of Nike co-founder Phil Knight, who wasn't really into setting goals, but was more one for failing fast so he could quickly reassess and apply the lessons learned to his next venture. In the early days, Knight wanted to be a professional athlete, but he wasn't good enough, so he started selling running shoes just to stay involved in the sport. 'I feel sorry for the people who know exactly what they're going to do from the time they're sophomores in high school,' he said.

As soon as we have gathered strength, we return to Baños and look up the number of a local doctor, originally from Russia. He urgently sends us to a roadside cabin for a range of blood tests, and then gives us the news: typhoid. He hands over a box of endless orange pills and tells us not to drink juice. 'Introduce foods slowly . . . really slowly.'

We leave our lodgings at the gymnasium, instead renting out a small room in a field with a family and a dog. We lie in bed, eyes to the ceiling, still too ill to read.

One day the local school's marching band begins practising for an upcoming festival, and an army of children march around the field outside our room, blowing trumpets and horns, and the assault on our ears becomes too much. I try to do my philosophical exercises and practise what the French philosopher Pierre Hadot calls the 'view from above'.

Hadot spent a lifetime studying ancient Greek and Latin philosophical texts, obsessed with putting philosophy into practice, with treating ancient philosophy as a way of life. In his book *Philosophy as a Way of Life*, he devotes an entire essay to the practice of 'view from above', a visualization technique that teaches one to zoom out from one's life to gain some perspective. From my single bed in this single room in Baños, I zoom above the ceiling and look down on the building in the field from up high. I see myself lying flat on the bed, with Zan on the other side of the room, two flat figures staring at the ceiling. I zoom further out and see us within Ecuador, bordered by the Amazon on one side and the desert on the other, and then zoom further out still and see us as a single light, a tiny sparkle on a moving, rotating planet, and I think how sweet it is to be that single light, even as I regurgitate.

The manager of the hostel where we're convalescing has a pedigree dog, which she takes on weekends to dog shows, where it wins ribbons and has its photograph taken for the newspaper. By Thursday night she is preparing for the weekend; the dog gets a bath from a purpose-built tub in the backyard, shampooed and scrubbed, cut and styled, his fur blow-dried with a hair dryer.

The manager's weekend dog duties are her escape from the reality of running a hostel, a means of forgetting the busted hot-water system, the leaking roof and the last-minute cancellations. At dog shows, I imagine, she takes a keen interest in other dog enthusiasts, expecting neither their admiration nor their affection, but rather, just enjoying the company of others who share the same hobby as her.

The wonderful thing about securing a hobby is that the choice of what to do needn't be restricted to what's cool or trendy, or what's respected; it needn't be limited to what pays well in the market or garners a certain degree of respect from peers; a hobby needn't be connected to what our parents expect from us, nor to what we dreamed as youngsters of being when we grew up. In fact, a hobby is not tethered to anything – and that's precisely what makes it so appealing.

The Greek philosopher Antisthenes once said that you need to furnish yourself with unsinkable goods that can float out of a shipwreck with you. In the dark times, that will be your hobby – let's refer to it in the French, your *passe-temps*, literally meaning 'pass the time' – that you will turn to. We need to find ourselves our treasures, as the French philosopher Michel de Montaigne calls them, that no harm can corrupt: 'We should set aside a room, just for ourselves,' he says, 'at the back of the shop, keeping it entirely free and establishing there our true liberty, our principal solitude and asylum. Within it our normal conversation should be of ourselves, with ourselves, so private that no commerce or communication with the outside world should find a place there; there we should talk and laugh as though we had no wife, no children, no possessions, no followers, no menservants, so that when the occasion arises that we must lose them it should not be a new experience to do without them.' In other words, we should keep ourselves company, and a *passe-temps* is the best way to do that. As Epicurus says, 'Not what we have, but what we enjoy, constitutes our abundance.'

CHAPTER 9

Bocas del Toro, Panama

'In soul time, time can creep or fly or even seem to move
backward depending on one's mood.'
—Gary Eberle

W E'VE WASHED, SPRAYED, SCORCHED our bags and
clothes in the midday sun, but nothing will destroy them.
The bugs have been attached to us for months now. We're defeated
and exhausted. We want to go home. But at the travel centre,
we read a sign for cheap flights to Panama and book, leaving the
car with our well-travelled companions, organizing something or
other for its return. We don't care, we just want out.

On the plane to Panama, I itch in straight lines, invisible
predators attached to my arms like unwanted guests. We often
think that the best way to change who we are is to pick up and
leave – almost like treating our current self as someone we wish to
avoid. But as Montaigne said, the problem with moving elsewhere
is that you take yourself with you. Simply getting on a plane and
taking off doesn't mean that a 'new you' will disembark on the
other side. On the contrary, it's likely that once you find your feet
in your new locale, most of your old habits and behaviours will
emerge again, like weeds under the soil. Our bad habits, invisible
predators like bedbugs, are hard to shake.

On the flight, I drink a glass of juice without retching. And as
I look out across the clouds, I envisage the yoga couple in Baños
dispersing into air.

We are at the docks, and nobody will take us. It's too dark, too windy, and all the boats are finished for the evening – the owners eating dinner or watching television. But we can't stay. The only hotel in town feels like a brothel, labyrinthine corridors around surgical ward rooms, the carpet reeking of dead fish. When we offer three times the normal price for a trip on a speedboat, there's a sudden surge of energy and talking, and within minutes our bags are packed into the stern of a speedboat, and a local leaps in with a torch.

We launch into the waves. It's pitch black. The driver hits full throttle, and we're off, too fast, his torch giving a mere metre of light ahead at most. I peer into the blackness, expecting to hit a sailing boat, or ferry, or some monstrous barricade in the water, but the driver seems content to rip it at full speed into the inky blackness. It's windy, but we skim across the water – gripping the edge of the boat with both hands, seeking light or some outline of the shore on the other side; seeing nothing. As for how far away this island sits, I am at a loss. But soon enough, the motor slows, and even before I see moored boats, the driver has released the engine into a putter. We clamber out and enter the first hotel we see, nothing but mere wooden planks above water, and that's where we sleep, on wooden rafters with the ocean sweeping below our resting bodies. It's uncomfortable, but it has no bedbugs, and it's not a murderous brothel. We feel strangely elated, as though we are sleeping in the Ritz.

The next morning, we wake to sunlight streaming through the wooden planks. There's something noticeably hardened about us. Shoeless, Zan's feet are thick soled, and he walks in straight lines, no longer following paths, or the road, no longer guided by human traffic. He takes the direct route, bare feet on hot gravel or broken glass. He has decided to forge his own path, literally, in the hope it might translate figuratively. For six hours, we sit on the doorstep of a hostel waiting for the owner to return – content, happily spending time together, reading, philosophizing. I compare this with our days in the city, when we'd be frustrated if someone were a mere five minutes late. Here, hours drift – we dance with time.

When the hostel owner fails to show up, we take a boat across to another island, where we meet dreadlocked Ayaan, about the same age as us. He takes us to his 'auntie's' accommodation, the place where he lives full-time, or at least when he's back from the States, his 'other home', as he calls it. Vegan, shoeless, a surfer, Ayaan introduces us to a couple in their late thirties – Liam is American and Raya is Spanish, and they are expecting their first child within months. Upon their shoulders, the couple sport their monkey offspring, one brown and the other black, which eat food from their plates and hang from rafters in their cabin.

We walk with Ayaan to his land on the water. We wander behind as he scampers up trees and hangs upside down, signalling to us like a blond forest goblin, bounding from tree to tree, pointing out their botanical names, and showing us which fruit can be eaten and which will give you a stomach ache, evidently pleased to have an attentive audience. I think about my boss in Brisbane, probably now in a meeting, or in his car, or having his seventh coffee of the day with an adviser who'd prefer to be elsewhere. I think about Kelly in her air-conditioned suite, positioning her prisoners on the run, and I place these images alongside Ayaan in the distance, his hair matted from sea salt.

In the morning, Ayaan wakes early for surfing, and then he heads across to the docks to find tourists who'll stay in his auntie's house for the night. It's a slow, simple existence. I think of my life and its underground current moving me on, from one place to the next, never at rest. Why can't I, too, grab a hammock and watch the waves splash against the shore? There was a time when we were all like Ayaan, climbing trees, swimming in the ocean, tasting the sting of an underripe berry. But they were the days before technology and the infinite pool of wonders in a box. In the days before all possibilities became options. Before we started to seek the intangible.

Ayaan surfs twice a day by taking a small dinghy out to unsettled waters far from the coast. While the world's workers are busy serving coffee, driving forklifts, emailing clients and conducting seminars on workplace practices, he is watching the tail of a dolphin glide effortlessly through the skin of the sea.

Work is our vehicle for self-realization. Work is our clock, compass and itinerary, informing us where to be and what to do when we get there. It's a social-classification system, employed by others to gauge our intelligence, creativity, wealth and likely political leanings.

When someone doesn't have a job, it's disquieting. We can't place them on the radar of industrial society. Work is equally disquieting for philosophers because the topic unleashes a host of unspoken issues around slavery, class inequality and the mass-production economy. Why do we work? And what's the difference between meaningful work and useless toil?

The philosopher Hannah Arendt believed that the modern age had glorified labour to such a degree that we have become a 'labouring society'. No higher or more meaningful activities are actively pursued because work is it – we're either labouring or we are consuming the fruits of other people's labour, otherwise known as leisure. This is life on Factory Earth.

Since Factory Earth spins on the axis of work on one side and consumption on the other, Ayaan – who neither works nor consumes – is what's commonly referred to as a dropout. Ayaan does not contribute to Factory Earth; he does not grease the wheel of the machine and is therefore regarded as useless.

Many anthropologists believe that work can be fulfilling for its own sake. They point to the fact that we've always worked at something. In feudal times we worked on the land to survive. As artisans and craftspeople, we produced all sorts of wares that we utilized in our homes or sold to others at market bazaars. Mother Earth does not just hand life over to us on a platter. We've got to work for the takings.

But something happened to 'work' when Mother Earth became Factory Earth in the 1800s; when work transformed from 'working for yourself' to 'working for someone else'. Indeed, once everyday folk could no longer toil on common land to grow food to survive, and when mass production in factories wiped out home and domestic businesses almost overnight, the masses had to work for someone else (that is, for the factory owners and the land-owning class). The result is that most individuals today are born into serfdom to Factory Earth. In *From Alienation to Addiction*, history professor Peter Stearns writes: 'With factory industry, most people, for the first time in human history outside of some forms of slavery, could never aspire to work without direct supervision.'

The modern workplace today rarely offers workers a sense of the whole. Marketers do the marketing; accounts people do the accounts; salespeople do the selling. Workers are performing parts of the mechanized whole, rather than being, as in the craftsman's time, the sole creators. An accounts person cannot work down in the marketing department, just as most salespeople have little knowledge about the real workings of the products they sell.

Broadly skilled workers require too much training, and therefore become far too valuable. The modern age, just like the products it produces, demands the cheap, throwaway worker. But that takes its toll on us. The so-called father of modern economics, Adam Smith, thought that it would lead to 'mental mutilation' in workers – that this soft process of deskilling would make workers ignorant and dull. It is hardly invigorating to repeat specialized and narrow tasks over and over again. In *The Wealth of Nations*, Smith wrote: 'The man whose whole life is spent in performing a few simple operations, of which the effects too are, perhaps, always the same, or very nearly the same, has no occasion to exert his understanding or to exercise his invention in finding out expedients for removing difficulties which never occur. He naturally loses, therefore, the habit of such exertion, and generally becomes as stupid and ignorant as it is possible for a human creature to become. The torpor of his mind renders him not only incapable of relishing or bearing a part in any rational conversation, but of conceiving any generous, noble or tender sentiment, and consequently of forming any just judgment concerning many even of the ordinary duties of private life.'

The social thinker William Morris, a figure in the English Arts and Crafts movement in the late 1800s, concurred: 'To compel a man to do day after day the same task, without any hope of escape or change, means nothing short of turning his life into a prison-torment.'

The Arts and Crafts movement, in contrast, valued processes that enhanced the life of the worker. Crafts retained the individual stamp and creativity of the maker, garnered through decades of training, a build-up of specialized knowledge. Every handcrafted item was imbued with what the social thinker John Ruskin calls the 'hand and eye' of the worker. The purpose of artisan work was not to maximize profits, but to enrich experience.

Since the 1960s, the consensus among anthropologists, historians and sociologists has been that early hunter-gatherer societies enjoyed more leisure time than later agrarian societies and contemporary industrial society. Aggregated comparisons show that in those early societies, on average the working day was between three and five hours, far shorter than the legal working day of around eight hours in many countries today.

Interestingly, the division of labour, which is the operating system of Factory Earth, is a very recent experiment in the human laboratory. According to the economist Friedrich A. Hayek in his paper 'The Use of Knowledge in Society', it was put in place simply because it was convenient at the time. 'Man has been able to develop that division of labor on which our civilization is based because he happened to stumble upon a method which made it possible. Had he not done so, he might still have developed some other, altogether different, type of civilization, something like the "state" of the termite ants, or some other altogether unimaginable type.'

Work in antiquity, in comparison, was very much integrated into life. There was no sharp distinction between work and non-work hours. People often ate, slept and raised their children in the places where they worked. Work was often performed in groups, mixing labour with community socializing. For artisans in particular, work was wrapped up in their identity, and skills were passed between generations – a source of great pride. 'French peasants,' writes Stearns, 'often conducted *veillées*, or evening gatherings, where by lamplight a group would work together, exchanging conversation, perhaps even songs, and sometimes dining together as well. These occasions drove home the extent to which traditional rural work often – by more-modern standards – mixed experiences, combining sheer labor with family and with social enjoyment.'

And since creative work was time- and energy-consuming for the worker, people only produced what was needed. Today, in contrast, Factory Earth celebrates an embarrassment of riches – we have slushy makers, egg-white separators, electronic jewellery cleaners, T-Rex dinosaur bedroom table lamps and giant-hand stubby holders. We luxuriate in the glory of shower caddies, fridge magnets and snow globes. Morris compared the condition of Factory Earth to the house of a rich man. 'If such a man were to allow the cinders to be raked all over his drawing-room, and a privy to be established in each corner of his dining-room, if he habitually made a dust and refuse heap of his once beautiful garden, never washed his sheets or changed his tablecloth, and made his family sleep five in a bed, he would surely find himself in the claws of a commission de lunatico. But such acts of miserly folly are just what our present society is doing daily under the compulsion of a supposed necessity, which is nothing short of madness.'

Indeed, it could be argued that this elaborate system of work that we all labour under is largely unnecessary. Just look back in time and you'll find humans surviving and flourishing under very different work conditions. But, of course, back then we didn't have the luxury of owning slushy makers or snow globes.

Raya is a yoga teacher from Spain, with the customary Spanish lisp which is difficult to understand. I follow her along a dirt path circling an estuary.

'We meditate now,' she orders.

'What, now?' I ask.

'Yes. Right now.'

She falls into silence, and I watch her long legs trot along at the same pace. She doesn't seem to be doing anything, other than being quiet.

'Are we going to go somewhere to meditate? Like under this tree?' I ask.

'No, I don't like to sit. I'm too busy for that. And anyway,' she explains, 'life is too short to sit around staring into space. When I say, "State shift," then you just meditate as you go.'

'What do I do when I state shift?'

She is talking ahead of me, and it's hard to hear her voice against the wind. 'You just don't think about anything and just look around and see things and hear things and touch things. See the wind. Hear the sun. Feel the sparkles of light. Just say yes to everything. And then when you feel that you've entered the door, then you can go back if you like. You don't have to be there all day. We're not monks.'

I am a little confused, but I nod in silence.

'It's a memory photo – snap,' she continues. 'It's a photo of the mind. And you can think about it later, one day, and all the colours and sounds will still be there. In your mind.' She turns to me and smiles. 'So are you ready to take a memory photo?'

I nod and frown.

We return to her cabin, where she has her home altar. It's in a spare room in the far corner. On a small, elevated table lies a collection of her personal objects: a feather, a shell, a photograph of her and Liam, a scarf and some flowers picked from the estuary. She lights a candle and asks me to join her to sit before it, enveloped by the vanilla and lavender scent of the melting wax. We listen to the leaden weight of raindrops on the roof as her monkey taunts us from above.

Raya has come to Panama to withdraw from life, to find herself. Days of meditation and yoga, mostly done alone, long solitary walks by the water's edge, cooking food and retiring early. Her life here, an absorption in self, is almost complete, and she desires as few distractions as possible. Nothing should get between her and her inner world.

Like Raya, the Cynics retreated, shunning comforts, seeking space. The Greek philosopher Diogenes of Sinope lit a lamp in broad daylight and said to passers-by, 'I am searching for a human being.' The human he was seeking was one unburdened by the folly, vanity, pretence and self-deception so characteristic of humans. No doubt, the search was long.

Cynic philosophers regard life as a training ground for the self. Much of this training involves seeing societal conventions and customs — such as wealth, power, fame and reputation — for what they really are: rather silly. The Cynics believed that these societal values lead us up the garden path, creating unnatural desires and a vicious character. Rather, Cynics say, we should live in accordance with nature, and the simpler the better. Diogenes renounced the desire for property and comfort. He slept in a tub belonging to a temple, and after seeing a peasant boy drink from the hollow of his hands he destroyed his single wooden bowl. If prestige no longer matters, then one's abode — its size and location — ceases to matter too, as does one's pay packet. In fact, when we think about the areas of our life that cause pain, the great bulk of them come from societal standards of success, appearance, dress and so forth.

The couple do seem intent on keeping their emotions in check, almost contorting with the effort — no frustration, no ill will, no gossip. How to look pleased rather than elated by good news. How to keep a face of equanimity when the supermarket shelves are bare, or when Ayaan brings a girl around without warning them first. Emotions are viewed like a galloping horse in constant need of reining in.

But some scientists who study the brain and emotions seem to take a different approach, seeing emotions as an essential component of our intelligence, tied in with decision-making. The neuroscientist Antonio Damasio asserts that to make wise judgements we must employ both intelligence and emotion.

'We're trained to regard emotions as irrational impulses that are likely to lead us astray,' he writes. 'When we describe someone as "emotional", it's usually a criticism that suggests that they lack good judgement. And the most logical and intelligent figures in popular culture are those who exert the greatest control over their emotions – or who seem to feel no emotions at all.' However, brain scientists now believe that emotions are integral to decision-making. To make good decisions in life, we must tap into our feelings and harness our emotions. When we ignore our emotions, we do so at our own peril. 'Emotions are profoundly smart,' writes Jonah Lehrer in *How We Decide*. 'They are not simply animal instincts that must be tamed.'

There is something disconcerting about Raya and Liam. For all their effort to be freed from superficiality – to not be pulled by the allure of wealth or fame, or any other such banal frivolities – there's something self-serving about them. Far from being indifferent, it's all about them – their food, their yoga, their meditation. They are the centre of their own world, and at times I wonder if they even realize that I – or Zan, or Ayaan, or anyone at all for that matter – exist when outside their orbit.

The problem with utter fixation on self is that the self is always going to be deficient in some way. The meditation practice this morning is plagued by random thoughts and worries. 'Is there gluten in this sandwich I just ate?' enquires Raya. And then there are the moments of disgust with self, the bloated belly, the limp hair, the skin crinkles from sand and sea that mark the face no matter how much one stands on one's head; or the lapses into concern about the lack of care that other people show for one's impeccable lifestyle and eating habits.

And without anything really to do with their time – neither work nor commitments – they idle about. What's so apparent is that there are no bright spots on the horizon for Raya and Liam, no opportunities for change as their world shrinks in size to their yoga mat, the vegetable markets and the odd tourist who wades into shore, but most days they are too lethargic to notice who arrives and who doesn't. They slip into a deadening ennui, especially come mid-afternoon.

Their world has narrowed to a cabin, with all the doors shut. They needn't enquire into the hearts of others because others should be interested in them. But without enquiry, or curiosity, it is as though they set out to write the great novel without a single character in their book: having taken no pains to find out what others are like, they have no characters to draw upon. They are limited to their own self-centred passions, each day taking a walk inside the poisoned garden where nothing is in bloom. 'One of the great drawbacks to self-centred passions is that they afford so little variety in life,' writes Bertrand Russell. 'The man who loves only himself . . . is bound in the end to suffer intolerable boredom from the invariable sameness of the object of his devotion.'

Russell thought that we should avoid self-centred passions and instead acquire interests that help prevent us from dwelling on ourselves. 'It is not the nature of most men to be happy in a prison, and the passions which shut us up in ourselves constitute one of the worst kinds of prisons. Among such passions some of the commonest are fear, envy, the sense of sin, self-pity and self-admiration. In all these our desires are centred upon ourselves: there is no genuine interest in the outer world, but only a concern lest it should in some way injure us or fail to feed our ego.'

It's often said that a sure-fire way to go insane is to self-obsess. There's ample evidence to suggest that the more you cut yourself off from the world, thinking only of your own needs, the more miserable you will become. Child psychologists often look for cues to assess a child's development: sharing, acknowledging others and forfeiting things to attend to another's more pressing concerns are signs of a flourishing human being. To stay selfish one's whole life is to stay developmentally stunted.

What's more, in place of moral norms, I find that Raya and Liam are governed by medical and psychological norms telling them what to eat and drink and how to think. They seem perpetually worried about their health and can spend hours analyzing the ingredients on a tin can or pack of noodles, as though they were peering into the dust clouds of an advancing typhoon.

This is a result of what the historian Christopher Lasch refers to as the 'therapeutic state', run by an army of well-intentioned professionals, including social workers, psychologists, dieticians, marriage counsellors, sex therapists and child-development experts. These practitioners govern not by law but by technique and normalization, offering step-by-step instructions on just about everything – how to relate to our partner; how to quell disputes in the home; what not to eat during pregnancy; how to raise children; how to be a good mother; how to be tidier, neater, calmer, smarter. And the bookshelves, too, overflow with well-meaning advice on grains, wheat, gluten, fat, starch, salt – all put under scientific analysis alongside children who won't sit still, bank accounts that won't grow, partners who won't listen and entrepreneurial careers that won't flourish.

The rationalization of daily life as carried out by the new sciences and pseudosciences subjects everything to a rigorous list of dos and don'ts. 'I know those pastries look good, but just think about the sugar!' But it has the unsavoury effect, according to Lasch, of draining the joy out of work and play. It's fuelled by fear – particularly when it comes to food – of diseases and death. Or, in the wider social realm, fear of being unsuccessful or unloved, or of somehow not living up to some societal standard.

Lasch argues that the rationalization of life has caused a 'drastic shrinkage of our imaginative and emotional horizon'. We no longer turn to Tolstoy's *Anna Karenina*, for instance, as a guide to human nature, or visit art galleries for some much-needed respite; the literary and artistic are brushed aside for the *Beginner's Guide to Cognitive Behavioural Therapy* and a remedial massage. It is little wonder that modern life seems 'too highly organised, too self-conscious, too predictable,' Lasch adds. He argues that the intrusion of experts into family life undermines our own authority, will and self-respect. No longer responsible for our own lives, no longer keyed into our natural instincts or our own ways of doing things, we become dependent on professional services, mere consumers of 'expert' information and advice. What's more, so stressed about bagels, almond milk and pastries, how can we ever transcend self-interest? How can we serve others, nature or the planet, when everything we eat, drink or think has to be put to some gruelling standardized pseudo-scientific test?

I think Raya needs to embark on a project to escape her windowless prison of the self. By peeking outside the windowless self, she will behold a marvellous place. As Robert G. Ingersoll, known as 'the Great Agnostic', once said, 'Reason, Observation and Experience – the Holy Trinity of Science – have taught us that happiness is the only good; that the time to be happy is now, and the way to be happy is to make others so.'

CHAPTER 10

Isla de Ometepe, Nicaragua

'The more side roads you stop to explore, the less likely that life will pass you by.'
—Robert Breault

T HERE'S A RUMOUR SWIRLING that the hotel only has room for a dozen people, and the bus has twice that number. When we come to a stop, panic erupts and travellers run, jovially at first, but then with quickening urgency, down the dirt road. Some climb fences, others take shortcuts through the scrub, while I crawl along bearing our heavy load, peering into dirt paddocks in this empty part of Nicaragua, my eyes like marbles in my skull. Red dust covers my feet, bags and lungs.

The 'hotel' is 800 metres down the road. It is still in the process of construction, with just the foundations and walls intact. It's a roofless skeleton of a building, empty rooms opening to the void above. Before the building is a lake, where the wind picks up every second and vomits red dirt over the construction site and into our eyes. There is no restaurant, but there is a room where you can buy bottled water, sun cream and salty crackers.

Somehow everyone seems to find a position to sleep for the night, each gravitating to a roofless room like bees in a honeycomb. An oval-faced French girl with dreadlocks sings and strums a guitar. She wears an indigenous Mayan dress, her polished voice trained in Paris. Her song creeps through my skin, invading my body. There are, indeed, music pieces that make us quiver, Rachmaninoff's Piano Concerto No. 3 in D minor, Barber's *Adagio for Strings*. How does music do this to us? Interestingly, when researchers hooked students up to PET and MRI scans to measure body functions – heart rate, respiration depth and skin temperature – they found that the chills experienced from music are accompanied by changes in blood flow to the brain. The areas affected are linked to reward, motivation, emotion and arousal, the same areas that are also activated by stimulants such as food, sex and drugs, explaining the 'high' we get from listening to music.

Part way through the night, the temperature drops. I grab a sheet and pull it about us. The wind picks up, and dust showers the roofless hotel. I grab the edges of our sheet before it lifts skyward like a sail on a boat. It flaps furiously in the wind, my arms locking it down like weights. And there we rest under a billowing sail all night.

When I wake, my eyes are wedged shut, stuck to a white bed of sandpaper, and Zan's eyes are red raw. We wash them, but it hurts to blink, and we go to the shop to ask, 'What's happened?' 'It's an eye infection from the dust,' the owner of the place says in Spanish, giving us ointment.

At breakfast, we stand in line for a photographer from New York. He has been commissioned to take pictures of nomads, or seekers, those people who don't live anywhere fixed, not content to call it quits and put up a flag in one spot. Our arms drag by our sides and we're not allowed to smile. We think about our future image on some gallery wall in New York, two red-eyed, malnourished backpackers on their last legs in Nicaragua. We throw pebbles into the lake and ripples span out in concentric circles towards the lake's edge.

The next day we leave, accompanying a group of Americans on a minibus to their camp, a dirt patch in a field, roadless and forgotten. We find a lodge, across from a larger brick complex where the group hold meetings and discuss plans. Through a missing windowpane, a cow peers in to view the humans at rest, a domestic still life, complete with books and water bottles.

The Americans are recently arrived missionaries. Most will stay for two years. They are open, curious and good listeners, and strangely comforting in this unnerving place. We share lunches at a wooden table in the middle of the patch, and dinners as well. They don't drink alcohol or swear, and when we accompany them to the supermarket, they are profoundly captivated by food items, ingredients, packaging, as though the world were in technicolour. Supermarket excursions span out into hours as the missionaries place coconut water and yuca into trolleys with the relish of children discovering candy canes.

As we drive back to the complex, the missionaries comment on the film unfolding beyond their window. They take a most intense interest in the setting sun, the Spanish word for soap, unfinished second storeys on buildings, poles and wires that stick haphazardly through a roof – what could they be for? – and the patterned colours of parrots and how they compare to the ones in Costa Rica. Would I call it a zest for life, or even joy?

Bertrand Russell calls it zest and argues that it's a distinctive mark of happiness. Strawberries, he writes, are neither good nor bad. But for the man who likes them, he gains pleasure from them that is denied to the man who does not. 'To that extent his life is more enjoyable and he is better adapted to the world in which both must live,' writes Russell. He goes on to say that the man who enjoys football is to that extent superior in zest to the man who does not gain pleasure from the sport. And the woman who loves to read is superior in zest to the woman who does not read for pleasure. The more interests we have in life, the more blessed we are. 'The more things a man is interested in, the more opportunities for happiness he has, and the less he is at the mercy of fate, since if he loses one thing he can fall back upon another. Life is too short,' he continues, 'to be interested in everything, but it is good to be interested in as many things as are necessary to fill our days.'

By nightfall the camp is quiet, the missionaries exhausted by so much stimulation during the day. Early to rest, early to rise makes a person healthy, wealthy and wise. And wise indeed. The early ancients taught that life was a matter of balance, and that an enjoyment of one thing – be that food or good wine – should not be at the expense of other enjoyments. A person whose love of food is so intense they spend most of their day eating is not wise. Nor is the person who loves playing tennis so much that they skip work to hit the courts. Excessive love for one thing is often a form of escape; it must be tempered. Have many interests in life – this seems to be the message.

The missionaries seem to relish discomfort – or, at least, they certainly don't complain about it. There is nothing of comfort here – no soft seating, cushions or sofas, no washing machines or dryers, no televisions or computers. But when they take a ginger biscuit out of a tin for tea, the missionaries chew silently, slowly, savouring the explosion of taste in the mouth. When all is discomfort, small pleasures become euphoric. I think back to the comforts many crave at home, with their underfloor heating, their rain-style showerheads with pulsating massage features, their breathable orthopaedic shoes, their special foam mattresses on beds designed for pressure relief, and their recliners for putting their feet up at night. So much comfort that nothing is comforting any longer.

Haruki Murakami, one of Japan's most successful authors, writes for four hours each day and then runs ten kilometres afterwards. Murakami seems to insist that this daily practice of suffering is part of his success. 'Exerting yourself to the limit over and over again, that is the essence of running,' he says in an interview. 'Running is painful, but the pain doesn't leave me, I can take care of it . . . However it's a toughness I seek out. It is an inevitable torment which I deliberately take upon myself.'

———

There's something intriguing about the missionaries, who are quite unlike anyone I've met before. A man in his twenties nicknamed Sheep, due to his thick, blond, woolly hair, was raised in a commune in America's south. Sheep hasn't watched a movie or any television drama in his life. Instead, he strums expertly on a guitar, writes poetry in a small notebook, and has a keen aptitude for botany. Sheep, too, doesn't seem pulled by myriad desires. Unlike us, he is not a seeker. His pathway is that which he treads today – a singular mission.

As the internet has expanded our world, so our dreams and expectations have bubbled up alongside it. Whereas once it was perfectly normal to hold down a job for life or buy a home in which to live forever, constantly switching careers and locations has become the new norm. And as the internet has spawned endless images of far-flung places, some 281 million people today live in a country other than where they were born, up 84 per cent in 30 years.

Undoubtedly, pretty pictures on the internet have broadened our perspective. Our dreams and expectations are overlaid by fitness retreats in Mallorca and week-long stays in New York. What about doing a degree in English literature at Oxford? We input the search, 'Where is the best place to raise a family?' Ah, the Netherlands. 'Hey, what about taking a year's sabbatical in Amsterdam?'

While there's nothing wrong with broadening one's horizons, can too many choices be bad for you? Behavioural economists describe 'choice overload' as the unhappiness felt when we're overwhelmed by too many options. Rather than presenting us with the possibility of making the 'perfect' decision, too many options on the table can have the opposite effect – we fail to make a choice at all. Paralyzed by information and conflicting ideas, we do nothing other than accumulate more information, or more choices, and any decision is put on hold until another time.

In *The Paradox of Choice: Why More is Less*, the psychologist Barry Schwartz writes, 'choice no longer liberates, but debilitates'. Schwartz argues that 'clinging tenaciously to all the choices available to us contributes to bad decisions, to anxiety, stress, and dissatisfaction – even to clinical depression'. The magic of the internet is that everything seems possible: Danish sabbaticals; the Great Wall marathon; early medieval literature classes. We're awash with possibilities, but not necessarily with realities. Can you really afford to pack up and take the family to Canada? Which of these ideas is actually possible?

In a study of chronic procrastination among Turkish adults, researchers found that most people who procrastinate do so because they are indecisive. Overwhelmed by too many options and unable to make up their mind, indecisive procrastinators choose to do nothing at all. Making a choice limits other potentialities, and making a choice requires action, and the 'indecisive procrastinator' is plagued by fear, and probably also laziness. The Turkish study found that rather than their failure to act being a means of avoidance, which happens when we put things on hold – 'Oh, I'll do that at some point . . .' or, 'Now is not the right time' – more people actually procrastinated due to indecisiveness.

The missionaries leave early and are back at dusk – laden with food and with stories of people they've met, faces beaming. They spend time decorating their brick complex with plants and art prints framed with makeshift frames – hammered together using wood offcuts – and I think, it must be nice to have a time frame, to know that for two years this is where I will be, and this is what I will be doing. Knowing the future means they invest time in meeting the locals, they memorize names of cows in the patch. Rather than, like a perfidious lover, always scanning for the next thing that happens to catch their eye, they limit their expectations to what actually stands before them.

The Spanish philosopher José Ortega y Gasset proposed that 'your life' consists of what you do with your time and energy within the limit of your circumstances. You are presented with a variety of possibilities as to how to live your life, and you are free to choose one activity over another. Of course, not all possibilities are open to all of us. Not many of us, for example, have the option to clamber into a private spaceship and rocket into orbit – not unless you are one of the few billionaires uninhibited by circumstance. Nonetheless, we do all enjoy a certain degree of freedom in how we allot our time and energy, given our particular station in life. 'Fate gives us an inexorable repertory of determinate possibilities, that is, it gives us different destinies. We accept fate and within it we choose one destiny,' writes Ortega y Gasset.

It's common to see people weighed down by this responsibility, however. Some deal with the enormity of it by thinking, 'Should I quit my job, or should I ask for more hours at work? Or I should go back to study, or not study, or move overseas, or return home?' Some deploy much of their allotted time to considering the choices they could make in the future. They weigh up the endless possibilities and before long, a forever shifting future presents even further possibilities to consider, and their rumination sees no end.

Ortega y Gasset doesn't give much weight to the thinking part of all this. 'Man's destiny', he writes, 'is primarily action. We do not live to think, but on the contrary: we think in order that we may succeed in surviving.' If we are, then, what we do, and not what we think we *ought* to do, then it's important at some point to stop contemplating the options and to act.

In *Essentialism*, Greg McKeown describes working with a young and particularly energetic tech executive. He was so clever and enthusiastic that work opportunities just kept getting tossed his way. Young and eager to build on his success, the tech expert pursued every opportunity with gusto. 'By the time I met him he was hyperactive,' writes McKeown, 'he seemed to find a new obsession every day, sometimes every hour. And in the process, he lost his ability to discern the vital few from the trivial many. Everything was important. As a result he was stretched thinner and thinner. He was making a millimetre of progress in a million directions.'

When McKeown sketched out an image for the young executive – a circle surrounded by lines flinging outwards like fireworks, much like a child's drawing of the sun, the image caught the attention of the tech executive, his energy dispersed every which way. 'The story of my life,' he sighed.

But many of us fall victim to this: we start new projects with gusto and determination only to be taken over by some new idea which steals our attention. We attempt to 'straddle' the new activity and the old, like piling up sandbags on a donkey's back, only to become weighed down by too many tasks to do, some of which might be in conflict with each other.

When McKeown's child was born, he excused himself from the bedside of his wife and the beaming face of his newborn child to answer a couple of work emails and to attend a quick client meeting in person. 'To my shame, while my wife lay in hospital with our hours-old baby, I went to the meeting,' he writes. Looking back at his decision to 'straddle' work tasks around family duties on such a day, he is horrified. How could he not see that work was not 'essential' on such a significant day? How could he not see that work emails could just wait?

The client was unimpressed too. 'As it turned out, exactly nothing came out of the client meeting. But even if it had . . . in trying to keep everyone happy I had sacrificed what mattered most.' This got McKeown thinking: 'Why is it that we have so much more ability inside of us than we often choose to utilize?' And: 'How can we make the choices that allow us to tap into more of the potential inside ourselves?'

When McKeown sketched out a second image for the tech executive, the young man started nodding. This image consisted of a circle topped by a single long arrow pointing skywards. 'What would happen,' McKeown asked, pointing to the image, 'if we could figure out the one thing you could do that would make the highest contribution?'

Now we all know that life isn't as simple as deciding to do 'one thing' and pursuing it. Had we been born aristocrats in seventeenth-century Denmark, then this might have been possible. We could have applied our time to painting or, if we were so inclined, to studying the disparate parts of the reflecting telescope. But modern life is nothing like it was for the wealthy in Early Modern Europe. Today, we commute, work, shop, drive to appointments, fill in forms, pay bills, clean, groom, and then it's time to rest so that we can do it all over again tomorrow. And companies have got into the spirit too, by piling on top of these basic human survival tasks a plethora of virtual tasks, a 'second life of tasks': social media, mobile chat, screen entertainment, gaming, and who knows what else?

McKeown suggests that we need to take note of what's taking our time and energy and to decide whether this activity fits into our intentional purpose. Clearly, taking the kids to school is a duty that's firmly entrenched on the 'to do' list; however, do you really need to be checking the news five times a day? 'Without being fully aware,' McKeown writes, 'we can get caught up in non-essential habits – like checking our email the second we get out of bed every morning, or picking up a doughnut on the way home from work each day, or spending our lunch hour trolling the internet instead of using the time to think, reflect, recharge, or connect with friends and colleagues.'

He continues: 'When we try to do it all and have it all, we find ourselves making trade-offs at the margins... When we don't purposefully and deliberately choose where to focus our energies and time, other people . . . will choose for us, and before long we'll have lost sight of everything that is meaningful and important. We can make our choices deliberately or allow other people's agendas to control our lives.'

If you could manufacture more time or energy, then you wouldn't need to worry too much about it. But, as the first law of thermodynamics states, we can neither create energy nor destroy it, but merely transfer it from one place to another. And it's this transference of energy – the decision as to where to channel your finite resources – that determines your destiny. But tarry not – as Benjamin Franklin aptly puts it, 'You may delay, but time will not.'

It's interesting to analyse what happens when choices are restricted. I ponder the missionaries here, content in their dirt plot, mesmerized by the multicolour world of supermarket goods, and immersed in reading the same line once again from their scant collection of books. Rather than witnessing their life as a blur outside the car window as they whizz past on their way to some new destination, they instead take a chair out to the dirt patch and stop, and listen, and discover that much that they didn't know was actually before them – like the orchestral wind whistling over the lake, or the even line of shadow around a palm tree.

Reality television can offer interesting artificial parallels to real life. Like miniature psychological experiments, the contestants on these programmes are often put to the test under restricted conditions. In one show, fashion designers are given a week to design and sew a range of garments for a catwalk show. With almost no resources – denied outside help and the use of books for inspiration, they are frantic. In one challenge, the designers are sent to the local grocery store to buy materials for their garments; in another, they're restricted to designing clothes using apartment furnishings, or the clothes they happen to be wearing at the time. But interestingly, whatever the challenge, the fashion designers somehow manage to 'make it work', as the motto of one of the hosts seems to be. At the end of the challenge, exotic dresses and pantsuits are paraded down the catwalk, constructed from old trouser legs, orchids or curtains. It's a fine example of the merits of cutting back, and it's why psychologists often prompt their patients to stop avoiding and to start seeing opportunities that are before them. What are you avoiding? What can you do with your life right now to make it better? Marathons and overseas jaunts are great, and it is certainly nice to dream, but is there something you've been putting off that's at your fingertips right now, that could change your life for the better? This approach makes us turn to face the life we live and say: If this is it, if this is all I've got to work with, then how can I 'make it work'?

CHAPTER 11

Brisbane, Australia

'Condition, circumstance, is not the thing;
Bliss is the same in subject or in king.'
—Alexander Pope

THE BUILDING IS SO newly constructed, it smells as though it has come out of a packet. The view from the eighteenth floor casts a wide-angle glance across the length of Puerto Madero, where Argentinean locals speak to each other in English over their native Spanish, and where a cup of coffee costs five US dollars. We are shown the kitchen but are not expected to use it, and there's a noticeable lack of cooking equipment, no pots or pans, no knives. Like rich Argentineans, we are expected to frequent restaurants at night, and perhaps skip the intervening meals altogether.

An old friend of Zan's suddenly appears at our door. He's wild-eyed and delirious, a drunk ruled by his passions. He grabs a beer from the fridge, and from the balcony cheers, 'To the good life!' Spinoza would disagree. He would call this drunk a slave to his passions, and would exalt loudly: 'He is not free.' To a live a free life, Spinoza asserts, we must be ruled from within, not whipped about here and there like some wet rag hanging off the back of a truck.

It's here where I find myself purchasing a skillet to cook eggs. I've never liked eggs, especially for breakfast. But I'm also adamant we eat more healthily, and exercise more, and the drunken friend who keeps buzzing from downstairs is left to go his own way.

It's not until we return home to Australia that it's confirmed that I'm pregnant, five months in fact, and the doctor comments on the fact that I don't look pregnant at all. 'It's your first baby,' she says. 'Enjoy it, this won't happen with the next.'

Our baby is born in a hospital a mere walk from the corporate prison in Brisbane. We take her home in our arms, refusing to submit to baby equipment. She's carried 49 floors above the city streets, to a corporate-office-style apartment – a football field of carpet with no furniture, nothing but a cot and an oversized soft cow. The granite kitchen is five metres long, and there are two bathrooms that should be in a nightclub, not in the home of a couple with a newborn.

It's here where I take my daughter, bundled up tight, down 49 floors to the corporate foyer and stand behind office workers for coffee. I'm bedraggled and unsuitably dressed. I pray I don't see my old work colleagues.

Like homing pigeons, we've returned to have our child. From the 49th floor, I watch office workers jog around the perimeter. I watch them eat chicken and cheese focaccias sourced from underground troughs. I hear them bellow on the street on Friday nights. Here, away from domesticity, I fall into domestic life.

In the corporate world, the meaning of life is money, and, pointedly, to make more money than your peers. Life is highly geared towards acquisition: money, promotion, property, cars and other tokens of symbolic success, like Italian hand-stitched shoes and gold-rimmed watches. In contrast, in the eighteenth century, the rich – awash with their love of literature, music, art, fine conversation, even tea ceremonies – looked beyond acquisition. The modern-day executive, however, is often so fixated on drinking the 'success' tonic that, over time, it can become a bitter drink. The trouble is, when the successful executive does eventually 'make it' – securing more money than they'd ever dreamed of making – they lack the knowledge or skills to utilize it properly. They can't, for example, set themselves up in a studio to paint, or compose music, or build furniture, or write poetry, or create a Japanese garden, or breed koi fish, or polish their German. They can't do so because they've spent the bulk of their adult years learning the how and what and where of making money and being a success. So, at the end of the day, all they can do, and all they are left with, is what they've always done – and that's making and spending more money, even though money is now as worthless as toilet paper.

We in the West associate affluence with money. An affluent family is one that's rich. An affluent person has a lot of money, property and material goods. But the word 'affluence' derives from the Latin word *affluere*, which means 'to flow to'. An 'affluent' is an old term for a stream or river flowing into a larger body of water. In *You Can Win*, the Indian self-help author Shiv Khera republishes a list that reportedly includes the eight wealthiest men in the world in 1923, whose combined riches exceeded the wealth of the US government at that time. 'These men certainly knew how to accumulate wealth,' writes Khera. Underneath this list, the author describes the fate of each man. 'The President of the then largest steel company, Charles Schwab, lived on borrowed capital for five years before he died bankrupt' is the first entry. The president of the largest gas company suffered a mental breakdown and ended up in an insane asylum; others went to prison or died penniless, and three ended their own life. 'They all knew very well how to make a living,' Khera writes. 'What they forgot was how to make a life!' These rich men accelerated the 'flow' of money towards themselves, but at the expense of maintaining a 'flow' in other areas of their lives – familial, physical, psychological, spiritual and social. 'They were people who were so engrossed in their professional lives that they neglected their families, health, and social responsibilities,' Khera writes. Over time, these other aspects of their life (which we may liken to the tributary that flows into the larger stream) were starved of water, eventually destroying the whole river.

At a bar, I have a drink with an old colleague, who is dressed in faded grey trackpants with bulging knees and a T-shirt almost enmeshed into the rounded folds of his belly. His wife manages a cosmetic store in town, while he trades the markets at home, chasing stock prices up and down as his bank account swells and recedes as predictably as the tides. He tells me that he's looking to learn to short-sell but can't seem to grasp the concept of seeking opportunities to find companies that lose money, which goes against his life philosophy. Today, he tells me, he has made money but then lost it. I suspect he will experience the same fate tomorrow.

When the domestic markets close for the day, he's either trading stocks on the other side of the world, or reading books on trading, or studying courses online. His friends are names on stock forums who give him stock tips or teach him something about P/E ratios. He is interested only in that which has practical purpose, his thoughts seldom moving beyond anything he deems purposeful, which always has to do with making money. But lacking any irresponsible and irrelevant interests, he has no escape from his pent-up concerns and worries, no respite from his money-making mission.

It brings me to think about a fashion designer from Copenhagen I was once in contact with who divided her day into working on the 'useful' and working on the 'useless'. For her day job, she designed couture bridal and evening wear for women, using fabric sourced from her travels around the world. But her second job, which she labelled as pursuing the 'useless', granted her the freedom to create without any boundaries at all, playing and experimenting with making dresses, shoes, flowers, chairs, bowls and plates, all utterly impractical and pointless creations because they were made from paper. She found that the lightness and fragility of paper gave her a new medium to explore, but also, more importantly, it gave her a sense of play – of working for pure creativity rather than for some more serious business-related goal. Because, as far as I know, no one can wear a miniature paper dress. No doubt, her 'useless' second job had a rather purposeful component in the end, as her discoveries with paper were often reflected back in her couture work – showing that it's often these more 'useless' moments in life that can be the most fruitful.

———

Even though my ex-colleague towers over the bar, well beyond six feet tall, his head the size of a public sculpture, the bar manager seems intent on ignoring the man in casual attire. In his tracksuit – cushioned clothing for long periods at his desk at home – his body seems to contort beneath the cotton, desirous for attention. 'Hey, look at me, you fool! I am a part of your life too.' His face, too, is set in a grimace of dissatisfaction at what he feels is his right to own the same as, or more than, others, which, to date, he thinks has eluded him. Victor, I know, thinks he needs a win. Deep down, he believes that only those born into wealthy families, or the offspring of the famous and well-connected, can flourish. He feels that he has to come up with some clever strategy to bring him up to the bar – to the same height as these luckier ones.

Take Pablo Picasso, for instance, one of the rare painters to amass incredible riches and fame during his lifetime. Picasso's painting of Marie-Thérèse Walter – who was his lover from 1927 to 1936 – fetched $106.5 million at auction in 2010. The indefatigable Picasso whipped up the predominantly blue and white painting *Nude, Green Leaves and Bust* in a single day. Clearly, you'd think, the Picasso clan, connected to one of the most recognized art names in the world, would have a head start in terms of wealth, connections, and therefore opportunities.

In her memoir *Picasso: My Grandfather*, Marina Picasso writes about the legacy of being born into greatness. 'I writhe in pain as I inch my way back in time, reliving the things that had destroyed me; silent, then stammering, then finally expressing all the things that had been buried deep within the little girl and adolescent and had eaten her alive. It takes fourteen years of misery to rectify so many years of misfortune. All because of Picasso.'

It seems that Picasso's luck, or genius – however you like to describe it – did not trickle down to those closest to him. His son, Paulo, died early, 'betrayed, disappointed, demeaned, destroyed', according to his granddaughter, after a lifetime of heavy drinking. Picasso's grandson, Pablito, ended his misery by downing a bottle of bleach. Picasso's mistress, Marie-Thérèse, whose reclining white frame is immortalized in a private collector's home, hanged herself in her garage, while Picasso's second wife, Jacqueline Roque, captured in the painting *Jacqueline sitting with her cat*, ended her life by shooting herself in the head. 'No one in my family ever managed to escape from the stranglehold of his genius,' writes Picasso's granddaughter.

To be born wealthy is not necessarily to be born lucky. As the psychology professor Suniya Luthar discovered in her research into affluent children, it may be disadvantageous to be born into the upper-middle class. In 'Children of the Affluent', Luthar and Shawn J. Latendresse found that so-called privileged or rich kids had higher rates of depression, anxiety and substance abuse problems, and committed more random acts of delinquency, than average, which they put down, among other things, to excessive pressure to succeed and being isolated from their parents. 'Family wealth does not automatically confer either wisdom in parenting or equanimity of spirit,' they write. The children of the wealthy, according to Luthar and Latendresse, seem to feel they have a claim on becoming extraordinary in some way – or at least on 'achieving' something in life, such as wealth, fame or success in a career. They are unlikely to say: 'If I'm a good person, a good mother or friend, then I'm happy.' But success, fame, stellar grades, scholarships, accolades and so on are not entirely under one's control. Such uncertainty breeds fear. They are living in a constant state of tension, stress the psychologists. 'If I don't achieve, who will I be?'

So-called 'privileged' children are often also denied an important motivator, and that's money. If you're already loaded (or are going to be one day), then what's the point of working hard? And if your parents are notoriously brilliant, the steep climb to a similar position at the top of the stairwell will, of course, appear impossibly hard, or futile – particularly if your parents are too preoccupied with their own endeavours to give you a leg up.

In *The Winner Effect*, Ian Robertson argues that it can be a terrible curse to have a 'god' as a parent. The other curse of modern times, he argues, is 'genetic fatalism', or the belief that much of what we are and do – our personal characteristics, personality, behaviour, psychology, happiness, self-control and intelligence – is written in our genes: a form of biological predestination. 'It leaves you, as the human actor in this drama, helpless,' Robertson writes. In the story of genetic fatalism, if you're born to a genius, a business mogul, a world leader or whatnot, that makes you – by dint of genetic makeup – brilliant as well. Intelligence, in this narrative, is not a matter of commitment, dedication, overcoming odds, devising strategies, and plain hard work, but is, instead, a 'thing' that one either has or has not. And if you already have it – as children of the privileged set are told they do – then you needn't chase it.

Marina Picasso describes the Picasso clan as 'stillborn descendants of Picasso, trapped in a spiral of mocked hopes'. Indeed, a similar statement could be said of any child who has descended from greatness. So frightened of failure, many children under the shadow of rich, famous or successful parents struggle to even put a toe on the first rung of the ladder.

In some ways, to expect greatness because of one's upbringing is the antithesis of flourishing, which involves the struggle to become your ideal self. 'Flourish' is a verb, not a noun. One cannot *be* 'flourish', but one flourishes by dint of what one does in life. But for my ex-colleague, this deep-seated hatred of those granted more at birth eats at him and hinders him from seeing the path he can take in his life. In many ways, unlike the descendants of Picasso, he has greater scope to paint the canvas of his life; he doesn't stand under the shadow of a giant. Instead, he stands under the shadow of his own delusion. 'What would happen,' I say, 'if you made a million dollars tomorrow morning? You'd be so enthusiastic, wouldn't you?' Victor nods. 'You'd invest more money, because then you could make five million dollars,' I continue. 'But then if you made five million, it could be fifteen million. But what happens if you made eighty million dollars? Is there a point at which you'd go, "You know, if I made X then I'd be happy, I'd stop trading"?'

I don't think he is listening. He leans across the counter in search of the waiter to get a drink. 'I'm thirsty,' he says.

Why can't we say, well, that's enough. That's great. I'll take this and be done with it. And then I will devote my time to designing tiles, or growing a maze of hedges in my backyard, or breeding alpacas. What stops us? Is it greed? Are we delusional? To realize gains, does that end the dream and commit us to reality? Is it like a small death? Do we lose the potential?

Victor excuses himself to go to the toilet. Should disaster or sickness or bankruptcy happen, he needs subsidiary interests, I think, something he can turn to for respite. Too narrow a focus makes life unbearably hard when things go sour, as they inevitably will. The Danish philosopher Søren Kierkegaard was never fooled by shiny pieces of metal. If you could wish for one thing in your life, what would it be? For Kierkegaard, it wasn't wealth, power or even fame, since such attributes fade over time, and ultimately disappoint. 'Pleasure disappoints, possibility never,' he declared. 'If I were to wish for anything,' he said, it would be 'for the passionate sense of the potential'.

But is this potential that Kierkegaard describes the same potential as that of a stockmarket trader desirous of mega gains? To sell is to end the journey – to not sell is to maintain the illusion of the potential wins down the road. Perhaps the potential that Kierkegaard refers to is the potential within us to self-actualize, to become the best that we can be. 'Who could my old work colleague be?' I think, coming up with a range of possibilities, from turning his wife's cosmetics store into a successful brand, to writing and teaching others about trading, to setting up a trading education website. There are many possibilities.

But what would happen if he made millions overnight? I mean, just think about how money could transform *your* life. Imagine holding in your hand a winning lottery ticket of say five million dollars. This is the ticket that will empower you to live out your dreams. You will be able to buy and do whatever you please. You will be happy forever after. Or will you?

Over the years, psychologists in great numbers have attempted to crack the happiness code. If the code to happiness were exposed, what a jewel of knowledge to behold! We'd know (at last) the answers to those nagging questions: Does money bring happiness? Is perfect health essential for happiness? Are people with children happier than those without? Is winning the lottery the secret to everlasting happiness?

In 1978, the psychologist Philip Brickman and two colleagues published a paper in the *Journal of Personality and Social Psychology*. The paper compared the happiness levels of three groups of people – 22 lottery winners, 29 paralyzed accident victims and a control group of 22 people. The psychologists wanted to find out whether lottery winners were in fact far happier than paralyzed accident victims, a rather odd question to ask, because, well, who would think otherwise?

The psychologists collated the data and compiled the results, and years later, the findings in this infamous paper are still quoted. The paper was a wonderful achievement for Brickman, only soured by the fact that he took his own life four years after it was published. So what did the study discover that was so controversial? That the pursuit of happiness is futile unless one happens to land the jackpot? Not quite. Brickman and his colleagues uncovered that lottery winners were actually no happier than people in the study's control group. What's more, paraplegics were only slightly less happy than the lottery winners.

The findings are a practical example of what psychologists call adaptation – humans' handy knack of adapting to both good and bad events in life. According to adaptation-level theory, a stroke of good fortune, like winning the lottery, brings on such a spike in momentary happiness that everyday events in the proceeding years will feel a tad dull in comparison. 'While winning $1 million can make new pleasures available, it may also make old pleasures seem less enjoyable,' Brickman and his colleagues wrote in 'Lottery Winners and Accident Victims: Is Happiness Relative?' Furthermore, humans habituate to life events – in other words, we become accustomed or used to something, whatever it is. 'Thus lottery winners become accustomed to the additional pleasures made possible by their new wealth,' Brickman writes. Over time, the thrill simply wears off.

Apparently, a similar process happens with accident victims, as incomprehensible as this might seem at first. Following an accident, a victim will experience a small lift in everyday pleasures when contrasted with the 'extreme negative anchor of the accident'. And through the process of habituation, over time the negative effect of the accident on general everyday happiness recedes.

What the researchers concluded was that individuals are born, more or less, with a uniquely personal happiness threshold – what Brickman calls a 'set point'. Whatever life throws at us – both good and bad – we typically gravitate back to this personal happiness set point, which is determined by our personality traits. Personality, it seems, trumps the lottery when it comes to attaining everlasting happiness. The psychologists conclude that for the lucky few born with a 'happy disposition', life will be pretty dandy no matter what happens. As for the rest of us, well, we need to keep working on happiness; it's a commitment. Happiness is something we need to cultivate, much like the fitness junkie cultivates strong abs.

Recent research has been critical of this early study, observing that the sample size of lottery winners was too small to draw meaningful conclusions. Other studies since then, using significantly larger sample sizes of lucky lottery winners, have concluded that lottery wins *do* tend to make people happier (surprise, surprise), at least as far as money worries and life satisfaction are concerned. They mightn't still be sailing high decades later, but they're not beset by money worries either, and this does make them relatively better off than someone who is perennially juggling their finances.

Here's a case in point: Alone in a shoddy motel after a 14-hour shift on a worksite, one Sydney labourer logged into the lottery app on his phone to check the week's Powerball prize. 'Bang,' he said. 'I saw it there, it was just there. I was sitting on my phone, alone, a few beers in, thinking "what's going on?"' As the only Division One winner of the draw, the 30-something labourer was in line for the full $30 million prize. He called his mum, and at 3.30 a.m. – once the beers had kind of worn off – he drove home.

A few years after the experience, the former labourer, who'd long quit his 14-hour days on building sites, and who now worked part-time in the entertainment industry to 'pass the time', was asked the big question: Did the lottery win make him happier? He spoke about odd happenings, mostly of people from his past repeatedly popping out of the woodwork, but seemed to conclude, 'If you're not happy, and you want to win the lottery (to change that) you're going to be terribly mistaken.' His verdict about winning the lottery was that it 'doesn't make you any happier, it just makes life easier'.

Perhaps an important point to draw from this is that happiness is mostly found by looking within ourselves, and that we shouldn't expect money or significant life events to provide happiness for us. And for my old work colleague, he needs to understand that privilege does not guarantee happiness, and neither does it guarantee success.

CHAPTER 12

Paris, France

'Only in growth, reform, and change, paradoxically enough, is true security to be found.'
                                    —Anne Morrow Lindbergh

I S IT POSSIBLE TO wake up one day and say, 'To hell with it, I'm tired of the old me, I demand a new one?' The Dutch philosopher Baruch Spinoza did. He felt that something was missing in his life. Seeking 'some new and different objective', he left the security of his family's importing business and their respectable place in society to 'embark on a new way of life', which, for him, was to devote himself to the study of philosophy. Spinoza set forth to find happiness, or what he called 'the supreme good', a quest shared by many ancient philosophers, from Socrates, Plato and Aristotle, to the Stoics, Sceptics and Cynics.

Spinoza must have had some inkling that his old way of life was at odds with his true nature, his ideal self. He must have felt restless, unsatisfied and hemmed in. He yearned for the 'freedom to philosophize'. In *Ethics*, he writes about the freedom to live the life you deem important, to be a self-governing agent and to take matters into your own hands concerning how you are to live, and what you wish to do with your time. And this was not to be based on fleeting passions but on a deep, rational understanding of your unique needs. The free person is one who knows the ideal for which they strive, and they set this ideal self as the goal of their endeavours. They know who they are and who they wish to become. To live the life of a 'free person' is to attain 'the highest thing we can hope for' – to flourish and to find happiness itself.

———

I decide to force the detour. But, I realize, I must do it fast. I sign up, pay the fees and lock in. Because once paid, I know there will be no turning back.

We've arrived in Paris via Ireland, where our second child was born. I leave Zan and our two children in our Parisian apartment in the 16th arrondissement and take the train across town. I'm clutching a human-sized mannequin on the Paris Métro, my arm warmly wrapped around her cotton frame. Two children point up at me as though I were oblivious to the frivolity of my endeavour.

In modern-day society, self and identity are founded on what we have, or what we own, thinks the German social psychologist Erich Fromm. We craft our ego and manage our identity by working on our list of 'haves' – such as our career, our possessions, our health, our talents. Sometimes we tinker with our image by changing the brand of car we drive, taking up a new sport or switching jobs. Sometimes our image and sense of self is bolstered by a pay rise or a new personal connection. But our relationship with the world, Fromm argues, is one of possessing and owning, where everybody and everything becomes our property.

The trouble is, what we 'have' is bound to disappoint us – things break, our careers sag, we get sick, fail an exam, lose money – and when this happens, we get down on ourselves. Our identity and sense of self suffer.

Fromm believes that the dominance of the 'having' mode of existence is apparent in the growing use of nouns and decreasing use of verbs in western languages over the past few centuries. Who are you? My job, my sports, my education, my family, my possessions, my leisure time, salary, appearance, network, image, fame, health, talents and ego. Indeed, if we were to alter the descriptions from 'having' to 'being', replacing the nouns with verbs, the list would be more like the following: working, exercising, learning, nourishing, collecting, playing, earning, grooming, connecting, communicating, existing, living, flourishing and being. Interestingly, the second list, although similar in content to the first, has a very different feel to it. It's a process, a development, a progression. It is not an end; rather, it's the means to journey to some place, a place that never actually arrives, but that's the exciting part. Because in the 'being' mode of existence, our life is one of doing, of living, loving, crafting, creating, exercising. The lightness of the 'being' mode of existence is that it's not about success and failure.

When we engage in life as 'action' beings, it puts a new slant on our goals and aspirations. Here, I am travelling to my new school to engage in crafting and designing. Not to 'become' anything, nor to 'have' anything. Not to 'be' anything. I have decided to study fashion design for no other reason than because I want to use my hands. I want to craft something out of nothing. But I want to do it away from the computer, and fashion is one of the few fields left that has not been reinterpreted by computer chips.

The writer and educator Ellen Dissanayake writes a lot on the activity of 'making', investigating why she, and many like her, have this inexplicable need to make things. This 'making' urge can manifest in building, constructing, sewing, cooking, painting, writing, decorating, fashioning new things from old, gardening, and so forth. It's a desire to use one's hands to create something, anything.

This urge 'to make', Dissanayake believes, is genetically hardwired into our bodies, passed down from our ancestors well over 200,000 years ago. Even newborns apply their incredibly dexterous hands to grab, touch and move objects about in their environment. We are predisposed to be tool users and makers, she insists. It's in our DNA. 'Anthropologists, who like ourselves come from modern and postmodern societies, where the arts are generally considered to have no function, are at pains to point out how in earlier or simpler societies the arts are inextricably involved in everyday life, embodying the norms of the group, articulating its deepest values.'

The making urge, stresses Dissanayake, is as normal in behaviour as the human urge to talk. In fact, she regards the human art impulse – the need to make ordinary experiences, of whatever kind, extraordinary – as behaviour on par with language. Making, she thinks, is a way to shape our everyday, mundane reality and transform it into something special. It has enhanced our survival, and always did. 'While I acknowledge the opportunities, comforts and pleasures that the industrial and postindustrial, modern and postmodern worlds have brought, I am very much preoccupied with the psychological and spiritual benefits we appear to have forfeited,' she writes.

There is an inherent pleasure in making, she believes. 'We might call this *joie de faire* (like *joie de vivre*) to indicate that there is something important, even urgent, to be said about the sheer enjoyment of making something exist that didn't exist before, of using one's own agency, dexterity, feelings, and judgement to mould, form, touch, hold and craft physical materials, apart from anticipating the fact of its eventual beauty, uniqueness or usefulness.'

But in a society where 'making' is devalued, where fewer of us make much – if anything – at all, Dissanayake warns of its psychological effects. 'Someone acquainted with human evolutionary history must question whether our species can prosper if so many of its evolved abilities are not fostered and so many of its evolved needs are not met. Making is not only pleasurable, but meaningful – indeed it is because it is meaningful that it is pleasurable, like other meaningful things: food, friends, rest, sex, babies and children, and useful work are pleasurable because they are necessary to our survival as individuals and as a species. A society that devalues making, and making important things special, forfeits a critical component of its members' birthright.'

Making matters. As Dissanayake writes in 'The Pleasure and Meaning of Making', 'More and more it appeared to me that the best and most inclusive way to characterise the human art impulse or "behaviour" was that it is a way of making ordinary experience, of whatever kind, extraordinary.'

———————

Day one at fashion design school, and it's all about finding ourselves. 'Without finding yourself, you are nothing as a designer,' our Danish instructor bellows in military English. The class feverishly sets upon slicing up magazines, tearing out pages, cutting things out. 'Your self-collage,' she says, 'will accompany you on this journey of designing, even,' she pauses, 'on your journey through life.'

We are told to work automatically and not consider why one image is selected over another, but simply follow our instinct or intuition. Our images are arranged on a single cardboard sheet, designed whichever way we like, one sheet for each of us. The days unfold and clouds of thin, glossy paper obscure desks and floors. Thought has long perished. No one dares tidy up or pack away, so immersed are we in unveiling our self. Our cut-outs pile up, some are secured with glue to cardboard, some left aside, or combined, and into day three, we are slower and more contemplative, and it's apparent that something is emerging. There is an uncanny familiarity to the colours chosen, the tone and style, and as I walk into the classroom one morning and see my collage leaning against the back wall, it's as though I've come face to face with the spectre of a relative, or sister, watching me from the other side of the room. There is indeed a familiar quality to my final collage, but also an unknown. Indeed, in the act of assembling myself on cardboard, there emerges something I wasn't quite aware of before.

On the final day our instructor shouts, 'Tools down. Now look. Look at you.' I stare at my collage, and the other students, too, seem somewhat mesmerized by theirs. We attach them to the wall and walk from one collage to the next, and, indeed, there is something distinctive about each work, but nothing personalized, no photographs, no signature, nothing but cut-outs from the same magazines we all shared. Nonetheless, each board is utterly unique. Here, we behold floating flowers, trees trapped in houses, butterflies in bags, baskets of fruit and human faces. Some collages are set apart by a single monochrome colour, or a unifying theme. Others, a kaleidoscope of contrasting elements. Expecting to hear some detailed explanation as to why we sliced up thousands of magazines, losing a week of our life to pinning images to a board, our instructor says with a matter-of-fact certainty: 'Over the week you've found yourself. This is your style. This is your image. Keep it close. And stick to it.' And with that, she closes her bag and gives herself a five-minute early mark to beat the Paris traffic.

We sit in silence, staring at our boards, so familiar – almost us, but not quite.

Waiting for class to start, I watch a student step out of a long, shiny black Mercedes-Benz, wearing a fur coat and matching beige fur hat. She is Russian and hasn't worn the same clothes to class twice. She sports her own driver – who drops her to class and picks her up promptly upon her call – and has numerous nannies for her children. An Eastern European girl stands with me, smoking a cigar, while an American chats incessantly, oblivious to the wealth around her, as though everyone were sharing the same fate.

The Russian beams when she sees us and strides across. Her attire is so spectacular on this drab Paris morning that she casts a shadow over our little group standing in the dim light. Fashion is power. And while we may scoff at such a suggestion, how is it that this epitome of Russian glamour in furs and leather boots makes me feel as though I've suddenly lost two inches in height?

What are you wearing today? Take a look. And then take a look at your immediate surroundings. You are an actor on stage, standing within a setting – and what you wear, the setting, the props, your gestures and speech are all interpreted by others around you, just like they would be in a play. The audience is watching you perform, and they will use these inputs to form a narrative about you.

In the 1956 sociology text *The Presentation of Self in Everyday Life*, Erving Goffman put forward the idea that we guide and control the impression others have of us in everyday life, much like an actor does on stage. And we do this through a range of inputs. Are you wearing a fancy business suit, or gym pants and a T-shirt? Are you standing within a minimalist room with a green pot plant and a hessian mat, or are you sitting on an old sofa on a dusty porch with a cat at your feet? In each situation, others around you are forming a judgement about you, even before you say your first lines.

In his theories on the art of impression management, Goffman explains that there is a front stage, where we act in front of others, and a backstage, where we prepare for our role, or even set it aside for a while. In preparation for the front stage, we may fix or change our appearance, setting and manner; we may clean up our stuff, put on makeup, brush our hair, calm ourselves, and then, once ready, we enter the front stage to appear before an audience, who form an opinion about us. As actors, we try to maintain some consistency in our role; hence it's unlikely we'll whip off our suit and throw on a superhero outfit in its place. To maintain our role, and so as not to confuse the audience, our social status will be more or less consistent, whether we're engaged in work, play, sport, family or social functions.

In 2000, the scholars Alison Guy and Maura Banim interviewed women on why they wore what they wore. The women in the study were asked to keep a clothing diary and to answer questions such as 'what clothing means to me'. Cupboards were thrown open to reveal their current clothing style. The researchers discovered that women typically use clothing to bridge the gap between who they are right now and the person they hope to be in the future. The Russian, therefore, I surmise, is dressed as if she were the CEO of a large fashion chain, which is, I find out later, what she hopes to become when she returns to Moscow at the end of the course. Amid cigar smoke, she candidly talks about tax in France compared with Russia, pulls out her homework, answers her phone as though nothing were at all out of the ordinary. But in her luxurious attire, she is already a fashion great of Paris, not a woman about to enter a building to create a bodice block out of calico.

One day a Chinese student, short in stature and big-bellied, says he doesn't 'get' why I'm doing the course. 'You are too old,' he says, returning to pinning his dress form.

I am a little crestfallen. Too old to try anew.

I wonder what age the cut-off is, and surmise it must be early twenties, because by mid-thirties, I'm far too old by his estimate. If I'm in my thirties, then I should be on the path already – having chosen the occupation just out of school. What a daunting challenge for the poor school-leaver, I think.

I've never seen life like that, as a one-lane freeway. And, according to David Epstein, writing about early specialization versus generalized education, I am better placed by being like that. See life as an eight-lane freeway of multiple career streams, don't narrow your focus, especially in the early years, he advises. Unless, of course, you want to be a world champion chess player or golfer, in which case you're better placed keeping your talents narrow. 'We are often taught that the more competitive and complicated the world gets, the more specialised we all must become (and the earlier we must start) to navigate it,' he writes in *Range: How Generalists Triumph in a Specialized World*. But in myriad fields, from science to literature, generalists with wide interests trump the specialists. 'Nationally recognized scientists are much more likely than other scientists to be musicians, sculptors, painters, printmakers, woodworkers, mechanics, electronics tinkerers, glassblowers, poets, or writers, of both fiction and nonfiction. And, again, Nobel laureates are far more likely still. The most successful experts also belong to the wider world.'

In his book, Epstein demonstrates how children who sample a range of instruments are typically better musicians in later life than those whose parents selected the violin for them at, say, age two, and drilled them with hours and hours of daily violin practice. Of course, the specialist child with the head start will be a star performer at age eight, but will they be the lead violinist in the orchestra come age 35? Epstein notes that exceptional musicians often come from unstructured musical backgrounds, where much is sampled and specialization only comes about much later, when the child decides one day, 'I really love the cello more than anything,' and specialized practice accelerates. From that day onwards, the smitten musician will pour her heart and soul into practice, and this zest for the instrument is what will propel her to greatness. Not the tedious hours of chirping away on the violin at age two, much to the chagrin of pushy parents.

———

Much like a tapestry, we tend to view life as having a narrative, a colour scheme and a general purpose, where the disparate parts come together in some meaningful way. A crafter, having suddenly arrived at the mid-point of a tapestry, is loath to make some dramatic change, like switching the colour of the thread, or turning a country scene into a cityscape. It's this continuity, this need for consistency, that prompts some to look at life with uncertainty, confusion even. If life is a trajectory with a beginning, a middle and an end, what happens when one's tapestry of life demands a new thread?

In *A Glorious Freedom*, Lisa Congdon reflects on her own experience of ageing. Congdon began her illustration career at 40; she started writing at 42 and published her first book at 44. At 45, she got married. Congdon, a self-described 'late bloomer', went in search of others with a similar fate. Her book tells tale after tale of women who refused to hit mid-life with a whimper. Women like Stephanie Young, an established magazine writer and editor with a 30-year career in publishing. As she walked through Central Park one day with an old school friend, the friend said to her: 'If failure were impossible, what would you do with your life?' Without a pause, Young replied: 'I'd quit my job and go back to medical school.' At so it was that at the age of 53, Young packed up her life in New York and headed for Dominica. While no American school would take her – she was 'far too old' to study – she was accepted by. Ross University in the Caribbean. 'It's like I took a leap off a cliff, and the free fall is exhilarating.' At 60, Young began her medical career as a doctor.

What's most refreshing in reading the interviews in Congdon's book is the sheer brashness of these women to say, 'To hell with it' – like the writer Caroline Paul, who took up surfing at 49. 'It probably wasn't the best use of my time, energy, ego. But, what the hell,' she says. When Paul wasn't surfing, she was watching surfing videos and doing practice jumps at the gym. The author Cheryl Strayed, famous for her memoir *Wild*, published when she was 43, writes: 'The fear of getting older is the false notion that one's power was rooted in the things that youth offers us – namely, beauty. My advice would be to see that for the lie that it always was. Our power was never about how pretty we are. Our power is about how we live our lives.'

And that's exactly what the women in Congdon's book prove, whether it's completing a triathlon at 82, as Sister Madonna Buder did, or becoming a collage artist at 72, or selling a successful dental practice at 50 to become a full-time writer, like Zoe Ghahremani, or first picking up a paintbrush at age 76, as Grandma Moses did. These women didn't let age get in the way of changing course. And no field of interest seemed to be off limits. As one interviewee noted, the possibility that one can 'do anything' becomes addictive after a while, as it did for Paola Gianturco, who, at 55, having left her senior position in advertising to take a year's sabbatical, found herself on the back of a Toyota pickup truck 'shooting the sun going down' with her camera, and realizing with a start that it was the happiest she'd ever felt working, and that she was never going back.

There's plenty of research into the natural and evolutionary trough of middle age, a phenomenon also found in chimpanzees, orangutans and great apes. It's a U-shaped pattern, which bottoms at the midway point before gently ascending again. It's not to say that getting older is easier – in fact, many people experience more hardships as they age, more health worries, more financial concerns – but for some reason it's also accompanied by a more accepting disposition and less regret. The Impressionist painter Ilona Royce Smithkin, at the age of 95, stated that it wasn't until she was in her eighties that she started to give herself credit for her accomplishments. 'There are different ways to be happy,' she said. 'If one doesn't work, try another . . . there are lots of doors in life and lots of potential, if you are open.'

I'm scooting through the streets of Paris on a Vespa, studying full-time, my bag bursting with calico, pattern-making supplies and chalk. I'm doing fashion to embark on Fromm's concept of 'being' – doing it for the sake of doing it, nothing more. Fromm warned about our increasingly purpose-orientated culture, where activities, once pursued for the sheer love, or delight, are shunned in favour of instrumental pursuits undertaken to meet some target, goal or financial gain. For instance, we read books to improve our website's SEO ranking on search engines or our assertiveness skills for a hoped-for pay rise; or we read up on entrepreneurs or celebrities to somehow learn the trick to become one ourselves. I decide to pursue fashion solely for the frivolity of making a calico dress that I will never wear, and to draw hundreds of Barbie doll-sized drawings that will be kept in a cardboard folder.

It's not long before we are caught up in the Ted and Jackie circuit. Ted and Jackie are two writers living in Paris. Ted, an Englishman who writes long, unwieldy articles for prestigious journals, is married to the Irish-born Jackie, who has a blog that she is earnestly committed to while simultaneously writing her first novel.

Their apartment, on the second floor of a classic Haussmannian, faces a road junction, but is surprisingly quiet, and it is here we meet the couple's four-year-old son, who has just returned with the nanny from the park. The walls of the apartment are lined with books, and Jackie and Ted share an old school desk in the spare room to write, both facing the street below.

The dinner is rushed, and small plates are almost thrown on our laps. There's a muffled sound of voices from the kitchen, and the dishwasher is slammed shut. 'You could have actually helped when I asked you about two hours ago,' Jackie hisses.

The potatoes are overly crisp, there is no knife for the butter and there are no spoons. The soup bowl is plonked in the middle of the table. Ted quells the tension by graciously pouring us both a wine. He says, in jest – although I guess from Jackie's reaction that it's a slight – that Jackie has been too busy writing her blog this afternoon to cook a banquet for us.

Jackie was writing for an online magazine, but the work had recently fallen through. 'It was awful stuff,' says Ted with a grimace. 'She was writing about things mothers can do in Paris with their children. I mean, what sort of person needs to be told what to do in Paris? You were smart to get rid of that gig,' he says, turning partly towards Jackie, who nods miserably in agreement.

'In honesty, I've had the roughest day. My editor called at 6 this morning, seriously, asking for a paper that I've almost finished, but not quite,' he says, looking briefly out the window.

Ted's work takes him around Europe, from Istanbul to Antwerp, on assignments. He's often not away for long, but the interruption can happen at any time, which means that Jackie tends to pick up their son from school and is the one permanently on call.

Later that week on a walk along the Seine, Jackie says, 'I said to Ted the other day that I'm not bitter about his success.'

'Oh, really,' I reply.

'I mean, I know it has been a sacrifice, from my point of view. If I were able to put in the hours like he can, I'd be successful. My novel would be finished by now. But we've got commitments. We've got a child to look after. Someone has to do the shopping, and if I don't do it, we would all starve.'

'Yes,' I say, frowning.

That weekend we take a trip outside Paris, renting rooms in a stone mansion. We go for a walk in the forest, and I walk ahead with Jackie, with the prams, while Ted and Zan trail behind.

'Some of these trees are over 300 years old,' says Jackie. We look up and can barely see the branches at the top of the trees circled by the midday sun. Underneath the canopies of these monstrous specimens, it's cold and damp, and I pull the blanket over the children's legs. I shudder and look ahead for light, but the canopy is thick for what seems like miles ahead.

It's a sunny day, but here in the shadows a deathly chill pierces our skin. I take off my sunglasses to view pools of water that have collected, but I can't remember the last time it rained in Paris. The leaves are so sodden that they bounce underfoot and, unlike in the gardens we walked through earlier, there are no roses or flowering shrubs, just sodden leaves and pools of water.

'I suppose nothing can grow under those enormous limbs of a tree. They take all the light,' I say.

'Yes,' says Jackie. 'The smaller ones can't flourish because they can't reach the light. And even those trees there, you can see they're struggling. They aren't as full as the larger ones, because they're always competing for light but never receiving enough.'

'If this tree here,' I say, pointing to a pretty-limbed ash stuck underneath an ancient birch, 'if this tree were moved say 100 metres that way, closer to that pond there,' I point to a clearing lit up by the bursting midday sun, 'it would probably be twice the size it is now. But its whole life it has had to compete with these bigger trees, and they're just not going to let it flourish.'

We too, I surmise, are like trees competing for light within a dense forest. Sometimes we can't grow as a result of being crowded out by those around us, or because someone or something is taking our light. Relationships, both good and bad, affect us – we do not stand alone.

CHAPTER 13

Birth-death

'So as not to feel the horrible burden of time that breaks your back and bends you to the earth, you have to be continually drunk. But on what? Wine, poetry or virtue, as you wish. But be drunk.'

—Charles Baudelaire

W E TRAVEL TO A château three hours south of Paris. The owner dashes down the driveway to greet us, wearing slacks and a royal blue blazer. Henry is Canadian, lives in Paris, but delights in spending weekends and holidays at his château, which he has been renovating for years, his 20-year-old pink convertible Rolls-Royce tucked within a makeshift carport, modern art upon crumbling walls. Henry is known for buying extravagant wine, for week-long parties at his château, and for travel – winging from one party or occasion in the world to the next. Inside, an Australian builder works full-time on a scant budget, peeling paint from the ceiling, while our friends – an Australian couple and their three-year-old son – live in the renovated wing with the windows painted shut.

The Greek philosopher Aristippus, too, was a lover of fine things, like shopping and travelling. He would have commended Henry on his château purchase and designer sports jacket. When Henry dines with friends, a $1,000 bottle of red wine is seen as a social good, and Aristippus would be all applause.

When Aristippus came to Greece for the Olympic Games, he enquired after Socrates, so desperate was he to meet the philosopher guru. In search of Socrates, Aristippus soon left for

Athens, not knowing at the time that he was destined to become Socrates' disciple.

Aristippus was a hedonist, a lover of pleasure – and eventually this philosophy of life put him at odds with his mentor Socrates, who saw wisdom and learning as the ultimate good. For Aristippus, pleasure was the supreme goal; it was not only wise but right for someone to manipulate circumstances to their own benefit. For this reason, Aristippus was the first of Socrates' disciples to take a salary for teaching philosophy – designer jackets and expensive wine must be purchased somehow! Aristippus later founded the Cyrenaic school of hedonism, named after his birthplace, Cyrene.

The château owner, too, is a hedonist, an aesthete, a lover of pleasure. 'The art of life lies in taking pleasures as they pass,' wrote Aristippus, 'and the keenest pleasures are not intellectual, nor are they always moral.'

We have a coffee from his commercial coffee machine in the newly painted kitchen, oddly modern within crumbling stone, but the stone floor is original, and the cornices have water marks and darkening paint around them.

Henry hands out cups of a dense health tonic, a mix of kale and mint, and we stand awkwardly drinking the brew within a damp side room, the children having long disappeared. I worry about the gaping holes in the floorboards, and about wells and dungeons, and within its humungous girth – the château has four separate wings – there are entire ramparts that are still unrenovated, walls barely upright, keyholes exposed to the skies.

Henry takes us on a tour of its skeletal frame, its paint weeping like decayed skin. 'The family were going to knock it down, it required too much of a Theseus overhaul to put it right,' he says. Like the ship of Theseus, which was rebuilt plank by plank, the château's window frames, doors and suspension walls are being replaced piece by piece. The roof itself cost an eye-raising 200,000 euros, but still, even with the modern kitchen and the fluorescent paint, like a death perfume, the château refuses to relinquish its past.

The Canadian hopes to re-create the château in a way that's more akin to his upbringing and his professional life in the software business. But I fear that the château has its own ideas, seeped within its moss-eaten grounds, and that no matter how much it is retouched, repainted and replaced, it will keep close to its origins. We too can change into new clothes or update the car, but much of us remains, too many years, too much time – and then there's us, from the beginning when we were born, with our genetic coding and hereditary traits, our looks, voice, smile, our fears and passions. And, like us, the château, with its well, its underbelly, its stone ramparts, its position facing north-west and its neighbouring mansion houses, can only change so much. The château already sports a new kitchen and coffee machine, and its brand-new slate roof certainly glitters in the sunshine on a day in mid-June, but is the château a new château, or is it the same with just some parts replaced?

We sit on picnic blankets drinking champagne in the sun, surrounded by beanbags, French sofas and a Persian rug on the moist undergrowth, the building overshadowing the small figures on the lawn and on a swing in the woods. The château is now witnessing a new history, new faces. Improvements, indeed, create change. We, too, have the power to improve on what we've got, to polish and replace, to keep nice, to look after, while realizing, too, that, just like the château, we are embedded in our history, our place and time of birth, our neighbours and friends – this cannot be erased, and neither should it.

As the sun goes down, we drink on the lawn and graze on a platter of fruits and cheeses. Music pumps from a window on the third floor, and Henry dances from a window, fists pounding the air, shoulders circling with the beat. The little girls are tired from racing around, and I put them to bed in the room with the new paint, leaving the window open for ventilation. Below, I hear Zan and the others talking, yelling among themselves, bottles rattling, and singing, and more music turned up with the quickening beat. I retire to bed, nervous about leaving the girls alone on the third floor in the endless halls of the château, half collapsing upon itself. As I drift off to sleep, I hear pounding feet upon the floor below, cupboards opening and closing, screaming – more bottles tinkling on the lawn – and when I awake, I know not when, eerie silence. For some reason, my heart is pounding.

In Kierkegaard's *Stages on Life's Way*, in a section entitled '*In Vino Veritas*', a group of revellers share an impromptu banquet, a celebration of the immediacy of enjoying the moment. Neither planned nor retained, the banquet represents the impermanence of life, for at the end of the night everything is destroyed; the host, Constantine, to signify the end of it all, symbolically throws a glass against the wall. While Henry, by all accounts, seems to be having a marvellous time of it, Kierkegaard seems to suggest that the life of hedonism will lead to despair, unless the hedonist transitions to a more ethical stage of existence.

For some, I agree wholeheartedly that partying until the end mightn't be enough; but not for everyone. For those with the means to be aesthetes, like Henry with his trust fund, his redundancy cheque and his good fortune to be born a good-looking male in a well-paying field, one could say he is blessed to live the aesthetic life. But even so, the aesthetic life still has to be worked at, new pleasures found, logistics organized for their attainment, forever coming up with the next pleasure hit, whether that's in the form of a new luxury antique to acquire or a new travel spot or a new friendship, and then finding the means to continually fund it all as hedonistic pursuits take up more and more time and cost ever more money. One can become travel-weary from having so much pleasure, exhausted by the chase. 'With the possession or certain expectation of good things,' writes the German philosopher Arthur Schopenhauer, 'our demand rises, and increases our capacity for further possession and larger expectations.'

However, the person who attempts to gain happiness by having higher and higher pleasure hits will require even higher hits just to sustain happiness levels. When the highs from the château and the Rolls-Royce subside, and the $1,000 bottle of wine becomes par for the course, further pleasures must be sourced. It's for this reason that a billionaire will finally blast into space as the last act of hedonism. When you already have everything that Earth has to offer, what next? Mars, anyone?

'What applies to drugs applies, also, within limits, to every kind of excitement,' writes Bertrand Russell in *The Conquest of Happiness*. 'A life too full of excitement is an exhausting life, in which continually stronger stimuli are needed to give the thrill that has come to be thought an essential part of pleasure. A person accustomed to too much excitement is like a person with a morbid craving for pepper, who comes at last to be unable even to taste a quantity of pepper which would cause anyone else to choke. There is an element of boredom which is inseparable from the avoidance of too much excitement, and too much excitement not only undermines the health, but dulls the palate for every kind of pleasure, substituting titillations for profound organic satisfactions, cleverness for wisdom, and jagged surprises for beauty . . . a certain power of enduring boredom is therefore essential to a happy life.'

The seventeenth-century thinker de Spinoza, too, was critical of the high life, mainly because it distracted one from that which was purely good – namely, knowledge. For Spinoza, hedonism diminishes one's *conatus*, or power in body and mind. In other words, the party life can become addictive – and too much drinking, too much frivolity can turn us into babbling messes. Everything in moderation, as they say.

Thorstein Veblen, in *The Theory of the Leisure Class*, studied the behaviour of the wealthy and concluded that even the well-off, who can afford to buy whatever they please, are typically unhappy because of this perpetual jostling for status. Veblen noted that the rich cultivate unproductive desires, like playing golf and having extravagant parties, as a conspicuous display of their freedom from work. The problem with these hollow pursuits is that they fail to deepen skills or understanding and therefore invariably lead them even further from true happiness. Or, as Henry Thoreau put it: 'The value of any experience is measured, of course, not by the amount of money, but the amount of development we get out of it.'

What's more, these days the aesthetic life can be full of hedonic angst when we discover via social media that others are supposedly living more pleasurable lives than we are. People post an image of their smiling face at après-ski in the Andes, only to discover with quiet resignation that others are lounging about with rattlesnakes in Costa Rica.

The château falls into a deathly stupor. I climb out of bed and wander to the window. The outside lights throw a gloomy pallor upon bottles, plates and rugs on the lawn, but there is no sign of anyone.

I sit on the window ledge and think about where they could be within the château, which room they'd choose within its 40 or so possibilities. For some reason, as I look at the little girls sleeping, I think about the term *shoji* in Japanese Zen, which roughly translates as 'birth-death' – no separation between life and death other than a small hyphen. How close we all are to the other side of the line.

I'm thinking, what would happen if they'd all died – the partygoers? Drowned in the river, hanging by the neck from the swing in the woods. Or, having stumbled into a crypt in this vast château, muffled voices still singing the party song, and then – like a flicker of light from a candle – puffed out. No more.

Zan opens the door ajar. 'He almost killed me,' he says. 'He just grabbed me and threw me to the grass.'

After some moments, I realize he is speaking about the other Australian, the one whose child is sleeping about 20 rooms down from us, in another wing.

'But why, what did you say?'

'Nothing. We weren't even talking,' Zan replies quickly. 'He just stood up and tackled me, and we rolled down towards the woods.'

'What did the others do?'

'Nothing. They just thought it was a game or a sport. They kept drinking. But he had his knee on my neck, holding it there. I couldn't breathe. I couldn't yell, I couldn't tell the others either, because they were so far away. The only way I survived was, I . . . somehow summoned the strength to throw him off me . . . and, I dislocated his finger – and it was at a complete angle.'

'Oh,' I say, almost in disbelief.

'He screamed in pain, and then I pulled it back into line, in the kitchen. His girlfriend is going to be annoyed with me in the morning.'

'Yes, she will be.'

I am in a large private hospital in Paris. I wait in line behind a row of women in different stages of pregnancy. Here we are patiently anticipating the 'birth' part of the *shoji* description. The baby, likewise, waits for its turn to step into the world.

This will be the first time that I have seen the growing child in my belly, three months on. I am tired from a few fitful nights of sleep, full of troubling dreams. The other women in the waiting room seem relaxed, comfortably reading magazines. In contrast, I dance in my seat restlessly, nervous about seeing who it is that is attempting the first part of that equation.

Over more than 30 years, teacher Frank Ostaseski sat with thousands of people on the precipice of death. 'Some came to their deaths full of disappointment,' he writes. 'Others blossomed and stepped through that door full of wonder.' When contemplating death from such a close perspective, Ostaseski came up with principles for coping with death, which, he says, are surprisingly relevant guides to living a life of integrity.

One of the principles of death that Ostaseski stresses is 'don't wait'. 'If we listen closely,' he writes, 'the message we hear is: "Don't wait."' Seated beside the dying, those with a matter of weeks, or hours, or even seconds left, Ostaseski found himself thinking that we all need to speed it up a touch, to dive into that which we want to do. 'Don't wait' – for we hardly have enough time as it is. He quotes Zen master Shunryu Suzuki, who pondered the word 'patience' a little more: 'It implies we are waiting for something to get better, we are waiting for something good that will come.' Instead, when it comes to acknowledging the finiteness of a life, we might need to exercise a little impatience, to start taking note of how we are living our lives, and whether we are prioritizing that which matters most. Although it's a cliché, if you knew you only had a few weeks to live, what would you do differently? This is the thinking that Ostaseski suggests we should take on a little more in our everyday life, an urgency that makes us act. In other words, we should have a little more impatience to begin the things we've always wanted to do. Of course, once begun, everything then takes time – and patience is definitely the trait that's required to nurture and grow our talents. But we need, at least, to start out on the journey. And the best time to do so is now.

This concurs with the thinking of Seneca, who said: 'It is not that we have a short space of time, but that we waste much of it. Life is long enough, and it has been given in sufficiently generous measure to allow the accomplishment of the very greatest things if the whole of it is well invested. But when it is squandered in luxury and carelessness, when it is devoted to no good end, forced at last by the ultimate necessity we perceive that it has passed away before we were aware that it was passing. So it is – the life we receive is not short, but we make it so, nor do we have any lack of it, but are wasteful of it.'

At the allotted time I am shown into a cavernous room, where I lie on a reclining seat. A cinema screen engulfs the opposing wall, alongside an assortment of machines and cords that match the white coat of an officious paediatrician who prepares silently, rubbing gel on my stomach and hooking me up to the ultrasound machine.

So here we are, anticipating the movie of the moment, the baby's life projected on to the cinema screen, its hidden cave a stage set for an eager audience. Will it be a boy or a girl? Are its dimensions, its hands, legs, arms, as they should be? What is the pace of its beating heart?

The baby will be measured, assessed, viewed from every which way. The paediatrician may attempt to move the baby from side to side and push on my stomach to get a better angle, waking it from its slumber – ordering it about.

The second principle that Ostaseski learned at the bedside of the dying was to 'welcome everything, push away nothing'. We don't have to like what is arising, he continues. 'It's actually not our job to approve or disapprove.'

Ostaseski notes that we like certainty, we like the familiar. 'We love to have our preferences met,' he writes. 'In fact, most of us have been taught that getting what we want and avoiding what we don't is the way to assure our happiness. Inevitably, though, there are unexpected experiences in our lives – an unanticipated move, a job loss, a family member's illness, the death of a beloved pet – that we want to push away with all our might. When faced with the uncertain, our first reaction is often resistance. We attempt to evict these difficult parts of our lives as if they were unwanted houseguests. In such moments, welcoming seems impossible or even unwise.'

Is he saying, then, that you should let life walk all over you? Just accept things as they are? Your best friend takes your husband, your boss accuses you of something you didn't do. Are we just to roll over and welcome it all? Not at all, Ostaseski insists, but being open and receptive to what is happening around us gives us options. 'We are free to discover, to investigate, and to learn how to respond skillfully to anything we encounter. We can't be free if we are rejecting any part of our lives. With welcoming comes an ability to meet and work with unpleasant circumstances. Gradually, with practice, we discover that our wellbeing is not solely dependent on what's happening in our external reality; it comes from within.'

Ostaseski calls it a 'fearless receptivity'. And, I suppose, this is something that he would no doubt have experienced with his patients: of those who receive a bad diagnosis or find out that there is nothing that can be done to extend their life, the ones who flourish in their final days are those who accept things as they are, who don't run.

The gel is cold on my stomach, and before me on the cinema screen an even wider room is projected – wider, it seems, than the one in which I lie. My eyes scan the perimeters, searching, seeing lines, dashes, black smudges, and I wait for the woman to report on what she sees.

There's a shuffling, and then she stops and moves to the other side of the room. She picks up a folder.

I search the screen, but can only see a white backdrop and a group of grey lines like a pencil drawing of a ball of wool. 'How many weeks old . . . ?' Zan asks, trailing off, peering at the image.

There's a silence. Zan adds, 'It's too small, isn't it?'

She nods to the back wall. She looks at the screen, squints her eyes, and then suggests six weeks.

I still don't understand. And then I think that six weeks is less than twelve. But what does that mean? I can sense it, that second part of the equation – the other side of the hyphen – and it has a taste to it: gritty. Still, nothing has been said, and I don't know why she is not talking and has given up on me. She fills out a form, and still doesn't say anything, and I can feel the glue tightening on my stomach. The little cave, still exposed, a miniature graveyard.

Exiting, I nurse an ultrasound, a bundle of forms and a lead pencil, and traverse a hall of women blessed by fortune. In a separate room we discuss the removal, the procedure – and I am crying, as though I may never stop.

Ostaseski's third principle of death is to 'bring your whole self to the experience'. He thinks that it's the tough times of suffering and vulnerability that are the most valuable. Although we want to look good, to be seen as capable and strong and well dressed, rich and famous and all those things, it's these times of hopelessness, anger and ignorance that are often the meaningful moments. 'We need acceptance of our conflicting qualities and the seeming incongruity of our inner and outer worlds,' he notes.

———

When asked 'What makes you happy?' most people will list things such as financial security, good health, a hearty meal, time with friends and family, and so on. Few will say, 'I am most happy when sitting alone in an empty room.'

Happiness for many, therefore, hinges on circumstances. 'I am happy when people are nice to me, or when I make money, or win competitions, or take a holiday, or buy nice things.' Happiness hinges on something occurring that is pleasant, which means that in its absence, we may experience the opposite of happiness – boredom, disappointment, listlessness, frustration.

The French Buddhist monk Matthieu Ricard says that this is a common error when thinking about happiness. When our happiness relies on something external occurring, that's not happiness, but pleasure, he thinks. We experience pleasure from eating chocolate or watching the sun set over the ocean; we gain pleasure from buying a house and decorating it or by landing a new promotion at work. Pleasure, however, is exhausted by usage. 'It is almost always linked to an activity and naturally leads to boredom by dint of being repeated,' he notes. 'When repeated it may grow insipid or even lead to disgust.'

Authentic happiness, instead, is not linked to an activity – rather, it is a state of being. 'While ordinary pleasures are produced by contact with pleasant objects and end when that contact is broken . . . lasting wellbeing is felt so long as we remain in harmony with our inner nature.' Ricard argues that happiness is a skill that must be learned, but many of us are so intent on being successful in our lives by 'making' a career, a family or a home that few of us manage to master even the most rudimentary steps in the happiness handbook. We neglect to develop skills such as altruism, patience and humility. We 'tell ourselves that these qualities will come to us naturally in the long run, or that it's not a big deal and that we've gotten along just fine without them up to now'. However, happiness, like any art worth learning, requires commitment to training the mind and developing traits that will enable us to flourish, no matter what transpires.

CHAPTER 14

Barcelona, Spain

'The more time you spend attending to the things that make you happy, the happier you will be. Change what you do, not what you think.'

—Paul Dolan

OUR FURNITURE IN OUR apartment in the 16th arrondissement is packed up and placed on a truck, and the rest of our belongings are in the car, along with two small children, the younger one white-faced and in tears. We head south, out of Paris, and hit traffic at a crawl. There's a retching sound from the back; the toddler vomits. Sandstone-coloured flakes hit the back windowpane, the front seats and the floor. But we're on the freeway proper now, moving at running pace, and there's not much we can do but sit until we're freed from the traffic's embrace.

By nightfall, we have arrived at an old château where we are lodging, and we climb the stairs to the second wing. It's as silent as a graveyard, and deadly dark as we unpack. Using the dim glimmer from a table lamp, I place the toddler on the bed. She rolls, and I turn to find her sleepsuit, and she rolls again, and tumbles – thud – a fair smack upon the château floor. There's a stirring downstairs, the owners alert to the peculiarity of this deadweight noise, and we scurry and panic over the toddler lying flat against the stone floor, her cries loud enough to wake the dead.

At the sun's first rays, through a window I witness a sea of dead sunflowers, each yellow frame outlining a skeletal face, eaten out like decayed flesh. Breakfast is presented in a spacious dining room, where it is graciously, teeteringly, laid upon linen, with cheeses, croissants, breads, hams and hot chocolate. We eat alone, looking out upon the blackened sunflowers, gathering our thoughts, before the host pokes her head in and enquires as to how we slept. She had heard the thud from overhead and the baby cry. 'Was everything OK?'

We leave through the château gates, wishing to stay longer, but, like gravity, there's that push of momentum compelling us onwards, never letting us be, always driving us to keep seeking.

It's in the high 30s when we enter Barcelona's old town and stand in the streets, straddling puddles on centuries-old cobblestones. From the rear balcony of our apartment, we face another balcony that is a sea of pot plants, tangled wires, TV sets and air-conditioning vents. It almost touches ours, and the owner of the apartment to which it belongs paddles out at odd hours wearing a singlet and shorts, a woollen beanie on his balding head, his rounded belly intent on reaching ground level. The mass of objects in his home leave him with little space. He takes a drag on a cigarette while seated upon a crate pressed between an old refrigerator and an outside clothesline.

At lunchtime, he reads the paper under the intense midday sun. After some moments of awkward silence, we get talking from our respective balconies. I soon find out that he is a truck driver working shifts – some weeks on the road from Barcelona to Madrid, other weeks down at Bari on the Adriatic Sea. On his journeys, he seeks. I envisage him driving down the *autovías*, his head nodding from the driver's window, his eyes scanning – old computer monitors, washing machines, bits of machinery for his truck, an antique organ. And then he lugs them back to his apartment, squeezing them in between bookcases and old record players. He says that one day, he likes to think, he'll have more time to fix them up, repurpose them, bring them back to life. Like a night doctor working on the dying. But shift work is so exhausting that during his periods of no work, he finds himself with a newspaper on his knee, or enjoying the odd beer with his mate, and then it's time to return to the road again.

I watch my neighbour as he squeezes his square frame between the outdoor fridge and a cabinet, and I think, 'He just needs to clear the decks.' I feel like leaping across to embark on an exercise of clearing, of picking up, packing, sorting, taking objects down three flights to the foyer and out the door.

We're encouraged to seek. Be it ideas, inspiration, news, consumer goods or experiences. We drive around our life looking for the new and taking it in. But all of these ideas and stuff eventually build up, clogging our mental pathways, obscuring our view, causing chaos and confusion, until we're immobilized and all we want to do is to leave the lot, shut the door and walk away.

In seventeenth-century Europe, some time before the advent of our modern tools of reminiscence such as cameras and hard drives, cabinets of curiosities served as memory stores. Objects sourced on journeys were stored in wooden display cases for safekeeping – polished stones, coral, mineral specimens and preserved animals. No longer lost to the mind, memories could be recalled by observation – a wildflower and a shell, a feather and a skull. But just like a cabinet, our mind can only hold so many memories. It takes in some, while discarding others. And while vivid and strong memories remain with us forever, the more delicate memories are the first to wilt, wildflowers tossed aside to make space for old television sitcoms and fading celebrity faces.

'Which weeks do you like best?' I ask. 'The weeks on the road or your time off?' He thinks for a second, his head cocked at an angle, his brow furrowed. 'When I think of it,' he says with some alarm, 'I'm probably happiest on the road.'

We find an unfurnished apartment in Las Ramblas and enrol the girls into an alternative preschool about 20 minutes out of the city centre. The apartment sits between Las Ramblas on one side and a brick wall on the other.

It's a time of no work. But to not work, what does one do? I find myself on the internet, searching, a form of mentalistic hedonism. With no schedule to attend to, my mind drifts to the things I don't own, like my own home, or I start to think about my lack of purpose in life. During school hours, I start to fret about the children. Has something happened? I find myself thinking about illness and ageing, about not eating properly, or not living properly. But mostly, I'm worrying about the children, and can't seem to purge these catastrophic thoughts from my mind, try as I might. Suddenly, a worrying thought arrives, and I spend the following hours, or even an entire day, trying to distract myself; but the more I try to redirect my thoughts from this lurking concern, the bigger it seems to grow.

'Men fear thought as they fear nothing else on earth – more than ruin, more even than death,' writes Bertrand Russell. It's true, there is nothing more terrifying than being the victim of one's own thought patterns, which, as Russell comments, 'is merciless to privilege, established institutions, and comfortable habits'. Anarchic and lawless as they are, you cannot escape your own thoughts – they will track you, no matter where you hide, no matter how far you travel in your quest to rid yourself of them. And regardless of how safe and secure, successful or triumphant you feel, irksome thoughts are apt to gatecrash any joyful moment. 'Thought looks into the pit of hell and is not afraid,' Russell warns.

Fear, or anxiety, is caused by nervous system arousal. When we were hunters and gatherers, it was important to fear the unexpected, such as the sudden presence of a buffalo racing towards us at great speed, or the legs of a poisonous spider. For survival, we learned to flee – to get away, our heart pumping. The fear response has saved many an ancestor from a pickle. But today, in our highly-controlled world, this response is often misdirected. We can fear an unwashed cup, a passing thought, even the unexplained tensing of our shoulders, as we once feared the plague or an advancing army. 'To escape from nervous fatigue,' argues Russell, 'is a very difficult thing.'

The toddler has a tendency to launch food into her mouth, forgetting to chew. Entire bits of chicken get thrown in, and then she's suddenly red-faced and gagging. Nights out at dinner in Barcelona are accompanied by chairs toppling over as one of us reaches to thump her on the back, or even, once, to scoop the chicken from her throat with a finger. During lunchtimes, I'm jumpy. Has she eaten already? What are they serving for lunch? Hopefully not chicken. Was it pasta with chicken? Or just pasta? Entire mornings could be spent in such fretful rumination.

Chaos, not order, is the natural state of our mind. When no external stimulation engages our attention, thoughts drift randomly – and thoughts, when the mind is idle, are likely to be depressing. Worrying is a natural state. We will turn to negative thoughts as surely as a 'compass needle turns to the magnetic pole', Mihaly Csikszentmihalyi writes in *The Evolving Self.*

For the human species, negative thoughts have been key to our survival. If we'd all lounged around in our caves thinking life was positively dandy, we would've either been munched to death by predators or starved to death. Survival required us to dwell on what could go wrong, because inevitably things did. More bad things happen in our lives than good ones, simply because 'the kinds of outcome we define as "good" are generally rare and unlikely', notes Csikszentmihalyi. Finding a purposeful occupation, buying the house of our dreams, meeting the love of our life, these things happen, at best, once in a lifetime. On the contrary, disrespectful neighbours parking over our driveway, vexing teenagers and illness scares are the ordinary stuff of life.

'While negative feelings last, they take over our consciousness and make it difficult to control thought and action,' Csikszentmihalyi writes. And so here in Barcelona, without work, without children to care for during the day, lacking a purpose,

I am anxious most of the time. 'Depression, anger, fear, and jealousy are simply different manifestations of psychic entropy,' Csikszentmihalyi adds.

Worrying thoughts are indeed tricky to shake. Most men and women, laments Bertrand Russell, are quite deficient in control over their thoughts. 'They cannot cease to think about worrying topics at times when no action can be taken in regard to them,' he writes. 'The wise man thinks about his troubles only when there is some purpose in doing so,' he continues. 'At other times he thinks about other things, or, if it is night, about nothing at all.'

Russell believes that by cultivating an orderly mind, we can increase happiness and efficiency. 'When a difficult or worrying decision has to be reached, as soon as all the data are available give the matter your best thought and make your decision; having made the decision, do not revise it unless some new fact comes to your knowledge. Nothing is so exhausting as indecision, and nothing is so futile.'

The American philosopher William James agrees: 'If you believe that feeling or worrying long enough will change a past or future event, then you are residing on another planet with a different reality system,' he writes. Although this seems simple enough to understand, we rarely take this advice. I'm not sure, but I feel it's due in some part to this belief in the rational head of ours, that most things can be just 'thought out', which has the unintended effect of exacerbating problems, not alleviating them. I think about the truck driver, and in some way this explains why he finds 12-hour days of driving preferable to his days off. On the road, life is mapped out. With clear pointers and time frames, his mind can lie at rest. If only, I think, he could find comparable solace of mind when at home in his apartment. But then, as the French philosopher Blaise Pascal says, this is perhaps a futile request. As he quips, 'All of humanity's problems stem from man's inability to sit quietly in a room alone.'

It's early spring in Barcelona and the gardener in the park is pruning the trees with vigour, cutting them down to a stump, lopping off dead branches and flower heads. By pruning the trees, by cutting back, he exposes the plant to more abundant air and light. Water and nutrients are redirected away from exhausted areas towards opportunities for growth. He searches for non-essential branches that do not make up the tree's skeleton and removes them from the node, slicing them at an angle.

I think it might be prudent to do something similar, a form of 'dream pruning' if you will. I consider it to be about knocking off certain activities or habits that are taking up time, sapping energy and inhibiting opportunities for growth. So, rather than adding more goals to a sheet of paper, back in the apartment I start to list all my goals in full and begin to scratch some of them off. I place a large line through a goal or activity, eliminating it, which, I hope, will bring me to a final, more treasured list.

But when it comes to some goals, even ones that have not yet been attempted, I find it difficult to put a big line through them. Even goals towards which nothing has been accomplished, nothing even started, goals that have just sat there on my to-do list like the loyal friends I take for granted – it's those goals that I hesitate over with red pen in hand. Why do we have such goals in the first place, when the thought of removing them fills us with great angst, as though it's an attack on our very identity? How can that be, when the activity is not yet even in motion? A goal has perhaps shaped my dress code, my life preferences, but I've still not managed to do anything about achieving it. It's an interesting experiment to spend a week eliminating such treasured goals. And to go on with life without them. Of course, nothing will change. But, I think, could this goal or dream be holding me back? Or, rather, is this the goal that I must seek? Is this the goal that's pointing me in the direction of self-actualization?

The art school is on the third floor, accessed via a winding staircase. It resembles a gymnasium more than an art school. Students do their work at stations – either drawing a jug sitting on a bench in front of them or sculpting a face from a photo – while a teacher wanders about with a watchful eye. The teacher speaks in Catalan most of the time, and I don't understand a word of it. Occasionally, she pats me on the shoulder during her rotation and speaks to me in Spanish. Apparently, I gather, I need to spend more time focusing on negative space.

If you're someone who draws, then you'll be familiar with negative space. It's the bit that you're not drawing, or the space surrounding the object rather than the object itself. As far as drawing is concerned, once you begin to see negative space clearly, the object opens up and reveals its inner workings. It suddenly becomes easy to draw anything. A line that once looked like it was vertically straight is in fact, you realize, slightly on a diagonal – which becomes clear thanks to negative space.

In life, we may see negative space as those parts of ourselves that are missing or incomplete – such as the love of our life, a career that expresses our true identity, financial security, good health, loyal friends, children or time to relax. It's often these missing areas of our lives that we blame for our inability to find true happiness. But let us think of it another way. If the negative space is what forms the whole in a drawing, then for us, too, this negative space is what shapes our life and makes us unique. If you learn to see the negative space as that which forms you, then how does this shift your perspective?

In 1989, days before the magnitude 6.9 Loma Prieta earthquake hit the central coast of California, Susan Nolen-Hoeksema, who worked in the psychology department of Stanford University, handed out a questionnaire to 200 students. Nolen-Hoeksema, a researcher into predictors of depression in children and adolescents, wanted to find out how much her Stanford students thought. Did they ruminate a lot? Did they tend to overthink things?

The earthquake, which hit downtown San Francisco particularly hard, lasted just 15 seconds, but it was enough time to destroy bridges, buildings and freeways, and many fires blazed throughout the Bay Area. In the ensuing chaos, Nolen-Hoeksema was able to locate 137 pre-earthquake questionnaires undertaken by her students just days before; she then hastily followed up with a separate depression questionnaire. Based on her research into depression, Nolen-Hoeksema had a hunch that some students would fare better than others in the days and weeks following the earthquake. While all the students would be rattled for a time, she predicted that some would move on, while others would struggle to regain ground.

Similar findings were obtained in her Bereavement Coping Project, a five-year study into people who had lost a loved one to a terminal illness, such as cancer. Nolen-Hoeksema and Judith Larson, a specialist in bereavement counselling, interviewed nearly 500 people – including older women and men who'd lost their spouse of more than 50 years, younger people who'd lost parents or siblings, and mothers who'd cared for their dying children. While nearly all those interviewed experienced some depression-like symptoms around the time of their loss and over the course of the next year and a half, for some people these symptoms were overwhelming. But they weren't for everyone. Some were able to pick up and move on.

What causes depression? Why are some people able to overcome negative events, loss, disappointment and illness better than others? In her lifelong study, Nolen-Hoeksema pointed her finger at one fairly universal trait that depressed people share: overthinking. And women are more likely than men to overthink. In *Women Who Think Too Much* she writes: 'Women can ruminate about anything and everything – our appearance, our families, our career, our health. We often feel that this is just part of being a woman – that it's a reflection of our caring, nurturing qualities. This may be partly true, but overthinking is also toxic for women. It interferes with our ability and motivation to solve our problems. It drives some friends and family members away. And it can wreck our emotional health. Women are twice as likely as men to become severely depressed or anxious, and our tendency to overthink appears to be one of the reasons why.'

She defines overthinking as the habit of going over and over negative thoughts, 'examining them, questioning them, kneading them like dough'. For example, let's say your boss made a critical comment about you, and for almost the entire next day, you rant: How could he say such a thing? I do nothing but work! 'But when we are caught in overthinking,' writes Nolen-Hoeksema, 'these questions just lead to more questions.' She terms this the yeast effect. 'Just as yeasty bread dough will double in size after it's been kneaded, our negative thoughts expand, grow, and begin to take up all the space around them in our minds.'

Nolen-Hoeksema distinguishes overthinking from deep thinking, or constructive thinking, that looks for solutions or tries to come up with positive ways of handling a difficult situation. It's inevitable that we will face conflicts in our life and be forced to make decisions, and these times necessarily require a certain amount of thinking. To not think about anything at all would be irrational and irresponsible. However, what separates overthinking from constructive thinking is that overthinking is overlaid by negativity, and therefore gives a distorted view of our problems and how we can go about fixing them.

So how do you stop yourself from overthinking? According to Nolen-Hoeksema, you need to stop your running train of thoughts in their tracks, even if that involves holding up a visual 'stop sign' in your mind when you catch yourself overthinking. Yell, 'Stop!' in your mind if that works for you. And then quickly distract yourself with something else to do – chatting to a friend, tidying your house. And if that doesn't do the trick, the best solution by far is to exercise, preferably outdoors: running, walking, even gardening. What overthinkers need to remember is that overthinking is not how you weed out your problems. 'The sense that you are gaining important new insights can make breaking free from overthinking very difficult,' Nolen-Hoeksema writes. But you 'have to recognize that overthinking is not your friend. It is not giving you deep insights. Instead, it is stealing away your power over your own thoughts and feelings. It is lying to you and seducing you into thinking and doing things that are not in your favour.'

I find that the art classes are helping. During class, my mind is quiet – content in its obsession with outlining the world around me on paper. At night, I draw, anything – the oversized kitchen with the Spanish tiles, faces from books, a pot plant. I'm not fussed, one object is no better to draw than another.

I impose order on my wandering mind. As Horace says in *The Epistles*, 'It is reason and wisdom which take away cares, not places affording wide views over the sea.' Activities like jogging, painting, mending, fixing, baking and cleaning the house are good in this regard – by channelling energy towards a specific task, with clear goals and feedback, we can avoid our natural inclination to dwell on the negative.

In the paper 'Reduction of Cortisol Levels and Participants' Responses Following Art Making', Girija Kaimal, Kendra Ray and Juan Muniz measured the cortisol levels of 39 healthy adults ranging in age from 18 to 59 years before and after 45 minutes of doing art. The participants were asked to create any kind of imagery using clay, collage or markers, and after 45 minutes a second saliva sample was taken and transported on ice to a certified lab at the university for analysis. The study found that for around 75 per cent of the participants, levels of cortisol – which is a stress hormone released by the adrenal glands when the human body comes under stress – were lower after making art, and it didn't seem to matter what kind of art they engaged in, or whether they'd had any formal art training. 'Our pilot study provides preliminary evidence for the use of art making for lowering cortisol, a proxy measure of stress, among healthy adults,' noted the authors. There are numerous proven benefits from doing art – such as enhanced creativity, fine motor skill development and improved hand–eye coordination. But recent studies reveal that doing art also directly lowers stress levels in the human body.

At first, art feels like a frivolous thing to do, as though I had decided to go fishing for six months, but then I ask myself: what is purposeful and what isn't? Must something with purpose make money, or make a 'career', or make a 'living'? Couldn't 'a purpose' be to make one happy, or simply to make one less stressed? Why is it that making art is so laden with guilt?

For many thinkers, hobbies – like art – were not taken lightly. 'To be really happy and really safe, one ought to have at least two or three hobbies, and they must all be real,' wrote Winston Churchill in his essay 'Painting as a Pastime'. Churchill, the Prime Minister of the United Kingdom during the Second World War, was accustomed to working under considerable pressure. 'Many remedies are suggested for the avoidance of worry and mental strain,' he wrote, and he mentioned travel, retreat, solitude and diversion or fun as the typical antidotes to overwork – the common factor in all these solutions being *change*. 'Change is the master key,' Churchill wrote. But the problem with the unruly human mind is that you can't just tell it to stop thinking or worrying. Indeed, you could be bobbing about on a pink plastic dolphin in a resort pool, trying to get some rest and respite, and still be plagued by burdensome thoughts. 'The mind catches hold of something and will not let it go. It is useless to argue with the mind in this condition,' wrote the statesman. 'It is no use saying to the tired mental muscles . . . "I will give you a good rest," "I will go for a long walk," or "I will lie down and think of nothing." The mind keeps busy just the same.' It is only when a new field of interest is introduced and new brain cells are called into action, argued Churchill, that the mind is rewarded with relief and refreshment. Hobbies distract us. For Churchill, it was painting that he used to quell worry and provide mental relief. During a particularly intense period of his career, it was this hobby that came to his rescue. A few experiments with a child's paint box one Sunday in the country gave Churchill a new lease on life. 'Having bought the colours, an easel, and a canvas, the next step was to begin,' he declared.

The other important thing about hobbies is that they distract you from fostering bad habits. A study in 2001 carried out on 139 university students at Bowling Green State University in Ohio asked them to report their eating habits using an Emotional Eating Scale. What exactly, the researchers wanted to know, is triggering their eating habits? Interestingly, the study found that the vast majority of students were eating when bored; in fact, boredom, more than any other emotion, was making students overindulge. This study concurred with a similar finding in 1977, which demonstrated that people ate more when given a boring task to do and ate less when engaged in an interesting activity. So why do we eat when bored?

The emotion of boredom, according to scientists, coincides with reduced levels of dopamine (a neurotransmitter that produces a pleasurable sensation) in the brain. So, in an attempt to boost our dopamine production, we reach for something that will increase our dopamine levels – which, of course, happens when we eat, especially fatty and sugary foods. In fact, eating junk food stimulates our dopamine production in a similar manner to drugs and alcohol. So, on the basis of this finding, rather than following a strict food regime or onerously counting calories all day – both of which are very boring activities – we would be better off becoming fixated instead on improving our 'mental lives' by giving ourselves more engaging and fulfilling activities to do each day. Once again, hobbies come to the rescue.

But these days it is rare to meet a person who has developed skills in the art of leisure. How often do you hear someone say: 'Wow, that person has a remarkable leisure ethic!' A good worker, on the other hand, is someone we constantly hear praised. In contrast, in ancient Rome, and again in the Renaissance, many citizens cultivated leisure as an art. But the leisure I speak of here is not what's typically deemed 'leisure' in popular imagination. Leisure is not what happens simply by virtue of not working. Leisure is not rest, inaction and passivity – quite the contrary. To engage in purposeful purposelessness, and to do it well, is a skill that takes time and practice. As Robert and Edward Skidelsky write in *How Much is Enough? Money and the Good Life*, 'It is often asked: what will people do if they don't have to work? Get drunk or drugged? Spend the day slumped in front of the television?' They continue: 'Underlying this kind of question is the view that human beings are naturally lazy, so that work is necessary to keep them productive, keep them "on the rails", stop them from "going to the dogs".' But they argue that this view of humans – as creatures only motivated by the prospect of money or reward – is unique to modern times. During the Renaissance, citizens were extraordinarily active in politics, literature and the arts and sciences, purely for their love of the activities themselves. When we do something because it gives us pleasure, psychologists tell us that we're intrinsically motivated. 'The sculptor engrossed in cutting marble, the teacher intent on imparting a difficult idea, the musician struggling with a score, a scientist exploring the mysteries of space and time – such people have no other aim than to do what they are doing well,' write the authors. 'They may receive an income for their efforts, but that income is not what motivates them. In our terms, they are engaged in leisure, not toil.'

But these authors claim that the habits bred into us by the modern world have left us unable to enjoy leisure properly. We're either working, preparing for work, commuting to work or recharging our batteries for another round of work. Otherwise, we're just zoning out in front of a screen. What's more, they argue, many of the activities that we deem to be leisure are in fact just another version of toil. Jogging to lose weight, hosting parties in order to 'network', learning yoga to be an instructor – these activities are undertaken instrumentally, with a specific goal in mind. Leisure, on the other hand, is done for nothing other than the sheer joy of immersion. Painting flowers on a ceramic bowl, playing the piano and reading literature are all examples of leisure in action. Indeed, cultivating a good leisure ethic is something we all should be working at.

CHAPTER 15

Byron Bay, Australia

'Know that joy is rarer, more difficult, and more beautiful than sadness. Once you make this all-important discovery, you must embrace joy as a moral obligation.'
—André Gide

I AM PREGNANT WITH my third child, and I am desperate to return home. But not to a city – only a rural region will suffice. The emotions of pregnancy are baffling, but Zan relents and we're on a plane home. We fly direct from Barcelona to Byron Bay, bypassing Sydney. Scenically stunning, Byron Bay attracts people in their retirement, as well as those wanting to relocate or to renovate themselves. Byron is a place that people come to rather than come from. Not just tourists, but permanent seekers looking for something that you can't find in the cities, or for that matter in your childhood home. People who come to Byron are seeking a utopia – a place that can make them or change them.

We find a home in Ewingsdale, a genteel middle-class suburb strangely tacked on to the tourist mecca of Byron. It's separated by a road that in the summer sees queues of traffic five kilometres long, worse than downtown Paris. There's an energy present in the region, dark, heavy. It's not easy to feel at home here.

Living in this new-found utopia brings to mind Arthur Schopenhauer's remark in *Studies in Pessimism*: 'If the world were a paradise of luxury and ease, a land flowing with milk and honey, where every Jack obtained his Jill at once and without any difficulty, men would either die of boredom or hang themselves.' And Byron Bay is no doubt a hedonist's paradise. A place of lazing on the beach, yoga, organic food, shopping at farmers' markets; a place to stretch and sigh, but more importantly, a place to stretch and sigh via social media channels so other people know how good you've got it.

Perhaps it's the vibrations of Byron's many seekers that give it that shady restlessness – people seeking a new way of being, people seeking to be seen differently by others, people wanting to be reborn. And do they? I suppose they do in their own way. And some absolutely prosper in the rich soil of the region. But then again, I think these are the types who were going to prosper anyway – the sons of billionaires, the entrepreneurs with family savings, the heiresses. And the rest work as baristas or in pizzerias, wearing the garb but not understanding why they haven't made the cash too. Even if you escape to utopia, you can't escape basic economics – the social hierarchy is as strong in utopia as it is anywhere else.

But it's the 'lifestyle' people come to Byron for, using the word in a similar way they would if they were talking about a horse or a tree. 'We live here,' they say, 'for the lifestyle.' The Austrian psychotherapist Alfred Adler was one of the first to coin the term 'lifestyle', or style of life. For Adler, however, your style of life was not something that you happened upon, or moved to, or took up; rather, it was something you developed over time, integrating it into your life. As a child you set your goals, and then you gradually acquired a style of life that was uniquely yours. It was not something that you deliberately set out to acquire. Rather, it just happened, evolving as you moved through the years, as your family setting shifted and as events shaped you. For Adler, your lifestyle is unique to your personality and attitude. It's a pattern of behaviour that you unconsciously adopt and adhere to for the rest of your life.

But in the 1960s, advertising agencies adopted the term 'lifestyle' and altered its meaning. 'Buy this lifestyle!' 'Live the luxury lifestyle!' Attached to this new idea of lifestyle was a host of consumer products and services, such as watches, cars and boats, apartments in holiday resorts, and lifestyle communities for the over-fifties. Lifestyle was now something that you chose, like the 'bohemian lifestyle' chosen by the Byron Bay set, rather than what you were by virtue of your unique experiences, thoughts and actions. Following the corrupted version of the word, many people seek lifestyle inspiration from glossy magazines, real estate guides, films and fashion – pre-packaged and mass-produced lifestyle ideas for the general audience. It's why many choose Byron for the lifestyle – they set their future self on the image of swinging upon a boho-inspired macramé hammock chair and eating vegan fare. They've seen that exact lifestyle online and they want it too.

From Ewingsdale, now with three children playing within a garden enclosed by high hedges, we begin to formulate our plans for *New Philosopher* magazine. It's not the time to create a print magazine, and people scoff when they hear of such a suggestion. 'A philosophy magazine out of Australia?' they laugh. 'Perhaps a sports mag, but *philosophy*? What are you thinking?' But we felt that this was too shallow a take on it.

It would be easy to spend months, or even years, weighing up the decision to do, or not do, *New Philosopher* magazine. We could look at the costs, the time, the energy and the risks, and to some extent we do, but we don't need to overcomplicate it. As the late US Secretary of State Colin Powell once said, you can confidently make a choice when you have between 40 and 70 per cent of the information. In his words: 'Get as much information as you can and then pay attention to your intuition, to your informed instinct. Sometimes what my analytical mind says to me is not what I'll do.'

When making any decision in life, it's true that you need to do your research, gather your facts, get a list of the pros and cons. But as soon as you hit some 40 per cent of the information that you're likely to get, then you've got enough to make a choice.

By the time you've got 70 per cent of all the information, then you probably ought to decide before you lose the opportunity, and the motivation too. I'm mindful that with any decision in life, it ultimately rests upon the question 'is this something that I want to do with my life regardless of the outcome?'

In a rainforest, we are invited to Richard's for pancakes. It's his firing day and his new pottery is on display on an inside table. Beautiful sea-blue cups and bowls – we gaze and compare, and then take them to the kitchen, where he bills us on his home credit card reader.

Richard is confidently humble and arrogantly placid. He gives nothing away, until you find out by chance that he helped set up an environmental organization, founded a magazine, sold opals and was a politician. He is a diminutive man, almost monk-like behind his pottery wheel, making coffee in earthenware pots or taking guests through his rainforest, which he has been regenerating for decades. There's more fruit on a single tree than I've probably eaten in a lifetime – scores of plums, enough to feed a township. And his rustic wooden home, its balcony open to the encroaching forest, has no balustrade to secure it, but remains unostentatiously grand.

Richard has, I sense, almost transcended self. In the small hill town of Bangalow one afternoon, I watch him painstakingly steer a row of ants out of the front seat of his car before seating himself in it to drive home. At weekend markets, he sells his pottery under the scorching sun, talking for hours with customers in his plum English voice. He is as at home in a market store as he was in parliament, and it's this state of being that tells me that he is, just like the orchard, in a state of flourishing. The car, the house, the clothes become meaningless, and it's the colour of the ceramic cup or the simple serving of pancakes on a rainy Sunday morning that become royal – as though you were eating caviar in the finest seat in the country.

How do you know if a person has self-actualized? It's evident when the ordinary measures we're taught to use – the house, the car, the job title, the clothes, the success in a particular field – are no longer applied. Imagine hanging by a finger to a cliff face, below you, a gaping void, and at this moment you contemplate what matters most in your life. It's likely to be the same things you'll notice in a person who is flourishing – their kindness, their readiness to be involved, their appreciation of the beauty of nature, their spontaneity, their love of life and, more than anything else, their sense of joy; indeed, that elusive emotion is the hallmark of self-actualization.

We are taught to think that to flourish means to be a success in business, that those on rich lists or celebrity lists, or the top influencers – they are the ones who've flourished. But most of these people are nothing other than competitive types who've found themselves running down a road and they're determined to win the race. You'd know of such types from school – they'd trip you up if it would help them get ahead.

Richard talks about spiders to his guests, seated upon long bench seats, as if it were the most riveting topic imaginable. He is childlike in his enthusiasm. Wearing his fake fur coat, he is somewhat indifferent to himself, to his inadequacies, to his ageing face and creaking legs. He has learned to centre his attention upon external objects – nature, rainforests, pottery, politics. His fascination extends to all that surrounds him, including you, if you happen to be seated opposite him. And to be the recipient of his interest is tremendous. Unfailingly, new acquaintances always ask, 'Where is Richard? Is he coming to the party?'

Is this the secret to flourishing? To set one's sights beyond the self, to the world around us? While yogis and mindfulness experts may do this by focusing attention on the breath and the immediacy of the moment, a similar approach, but one that is no less effective, is to focus attention on objects and ideas and subjects that interest us, to be attentive to those who share our immediate space, allowing us to escape the empire of the self.

To be utterly absorbed in the external environment is an act of self-denial to be sure, but one without the moralistic overtones. Richard is monk-like in his commitment to being present to the outside world, to the ripening plums on his trees, but this is not done out of a resolute resolve to be 'mindful' – rather, it is the after-effect of simply learning to be fascinated and curious about the world. It produces the same result: an immersion in the flow of life, without its jagged edges.

We set up a bookstore in Bangalow, near Byron Bay. We don't want a store, but the space is retail only, which means that the rental agreement demands we sell things. But we don't want to sell anything, so first we think about opening a space, our centre for purposeless purpose, such as drawing, watercolour, sculpture, high reading, activities done for no other reason than joy, and for people to come together. And this place, we decide, won't have a profit motive, but instead a mission to engage in fruitless activities, tiny rooms full of purposelessness, and lots of people busy with the task of creating things that don't matter, like monks building sand sculptures with the intention of destroying them once finished. Within this place, time will stand still and no notification from some gadget will wake people from their reveries.

We then consider the idea of a retail room where people come to sit and read books, good books that they don't normally have time to give much attention to. Instead of engaging in consumerism, they 'high read' for a time, among walls of great minds.

'High reading' is an art that was once reserved for the few. It was practised in monasteries, and in cloistered rooms, palaces and dimly-lit libraries. It was a meditative art that required time, space, quiet and deep concentration. But developing the mental discipline to 'high read' takes time, starting in childhood, when we begin to decode letters and accommodate the white space between words. Meanwhile, our brain circuitry adjusts, and eventually it speeds up the reading process, turning letters into words, and words into scenes, dialogue, meaning and, eventually, ideas.

The human brain is not engineered to high read. Rather, our natural state is more akin to total distraction, like animals – we're forever keyed into our environment, into threats and objects close by. Like other animals, we're naturally attuned to the new and unexpected, shifting rapidly and involuntarily from one object or scene to the next. To sit quietly and focus our gaze on a central point is not something we do with ease.

But high reading alters brain circuitry in complex ways. The visual cortex develops an abundance of neurons dedicated to the task of recognizing and interpreting letter patterns, and as the brain changes, the intellect expands. Maryanne Wolf, in *Proust and the Squid: The Story and Science of the Reading Brain*, writes: 'Much of how we think and what we think about is based on insights and associations generated from what we read. As the author Joseph Epstein put it, "A biography of any literary person ought to deal at length with what he read and when, for in some sense, *we are what we read.*"'

We consider the idea of clearing out the store and opening it as a high-reading room instead. Nothing to buy, nothing to do, simply a space to come in and read. The psychologist William James writes that attention 'implies withdrawal from some things in order to deal effectively with others'. It is, he says, 'a condition which has a real opposite in the confused, dazed, scatter-brained state which in French is called *distraction.*' But electronic communication is slowly displacing the art of high reading. Keyed into distractions, we replace quiet, contemplative and reflective high reading with emails, internet searching and videos. As our practice of high reading declines, our brain circuitry shifts.

There is a concern that in the age of electronic distraction, the art of high reading will once again be the preserve of a small minority, and the great masses of people may never engage with the minds of literary greats such as Tolstoy or Faulkner. If it is true that we are what we read, what happens when we no longer read?

Instead, we decide to buy lots of books and sell them, and to open a bookstore, but only stocked with non-fiction and classics, and definitely no best-sellers, nor any books that come in larger formats with garish covers. In other words, we will specialize in books that almost nobody reads: high-reading books – which doesn't exactly suit a township of hippy surfers.

And so we open the bookstore, which we call *poet*, with minimal fanfare, and showcase our scant collection of old literary giants, grand philosophers and fiction greats from Simone de Beauvoir to Hermann Hesse, the kind of books that everyone complains they've already read. But, we say, why does that mean that they shouldn't be sold? Why does it all have to be 'new, new, new', which is not in the spirit of high reading? And why can't a classic be read more than once?

Browsers enter the store and complain, somewhat confused by our meagre collection of books that most had avoided at school or university – and they complain about our odd opening hours, often shut on busy market days and open early on in the week when the township is empty.

And so, over the months and years, we maintain this store, and our daily sales range from $50 to $230, and then, a few days in the week, we even receive a triumphant note from our store manager saying that we made 'zero sales today'. In peak times, we often – for some reason or another – are closed, and neighbouring businesses look aghast at our business practices. We are anti-capitalist, to be sure, anti-consumerist, and we have a small collection of writing paper and pens – our stance on championing handwriting over technology – that doesn't even capture the imagination of the Steiner adherents. But we spend much time and money on aesthetics – French antiques, statues, heads, beaded dark rich velvet curtains, and signs that look like they'd been there since the beginning of time. It is beauty to be sure, but there is often nothing to buy – aesthetics triumphing over commerce.

In the back of the store, we read and discuss topics for the magazine, as well as formulating our ideas for a second magazine,

Womankind. We listen to people stomping around, oohing and aahing over the beauty of the store, and then promptly leaving, as our revolving sales staff –whoever happens to be on the desk at the time – become more and more despondent in the darkened corner, as sales dwindle to near zero and the books either collect dust or fade from the fierce Bangalow sun.

Outside our dusty compound, a throwback to Renaissance times, the Byron Bay residents live out their modern lives. Eschewing anything that might resemble the corporate, we stage publishing meetings sitting upon boxes of magazines, with overhead lights yanked out of their sockets in our pursuit of natural light through a single window.

I'm in a cab from Sydney airport to a meeting with an executive of a supermarket chain that wishes to stock *New Philosopher.* It's bumper-to-bumper traffic and the taxi driver is swilling coffee and talking at a furious pace. At traffic lights, he grabs a book from the dashboard and reads a few sentences, before placing it down with a shove and accelerating. It's a book about making money, how to be rich and think rich. His English is not strong, yet he somehow ploughs through the book, looking for nuggets of gold, and he turns to me and starts talking, revealing that he's already bought three properties, and his son has even more, and they're doing up another property at Penrith, and renting this property, and they're thinking of buying another one and converting it into apartments, and he's racing through the traffic with this 'grow rich' book on his dashboard, and I can tell he is agitated.

I think agitation is a sign that something is amiss. I know this for myself – if I'm hyperventilating with ideas and running over projections, it normally means I'm uncomfortable. I'm running full pelt down the wrong road. I'd be well advised to stop, take a break and look about at the scenery. Agitation is not a sign of flourishing. Rather, when action feels effortless, when the rational mind calms down, when you don't need to push and shove, that's when the path is right. But this new arrival to Australia is swallowing a new mindset with as much effort as if it were nails, and his body is contorting. As he drives, and clocks up more miles and more dollars, and uses these funds to buy more properties so he can clock up more miles, it's true that one day all he aspires to may come to pass, and he'll no longer need to work as a cab driver, and he'll have more money than he ever dreamed of. But will it have been worth it – for his much younger self to have been imprisoned like this, clutching a book in one hand and the steering wheel in the other? He'll never get younger, and this could be his peak time for health. Between the road and the pages of his book, he hasn't noticed a single point of interest on the trip – and I can see that my conversation is little more than background static. As we swing into the drive of the headquarters, he looks at the building and falls silent. I get out and close the door, and he accelerates away without a backward glance.

The problem with telic activities, which are undertaken for some future goal, is that you live your life in an instrumental manner, forever doing things for some future purpose, and rarely living for now. And goals can keep shifting – once one goal has been attained, another will take its place – like a mirage in the desert, a line in the sand that you're forever moving towards but never actually reaching, and all the while those small moments in between tumble into the black sands of oblivion. There needs to be a balance between these telic activities and the joyful idle moments with no point and no future goal – just the sheer joy of the moment.

However, if you've been conditioned to work and be productive, then idleness can be a tricky activity to begin, and it can easily deteriorate into more sedate activities like watching television, surfing the internet or scrolling through social media, all of which are perhaps idle, but they're certainly not joyful expressions of exuberant living. So, we need to devise ways of participating in idleness that prevent us from falling victim to time-wasting. This is the conundrum of idleness, because telic activities, with their future goal on the horizon, seem so much more meaningful and purposeful than simple joys with no future direction or pay-off. And we want to live a purposeful life, so the telic activities are often favoured. The answer is perhaps to add an element of 'telic' to more joyful pursuits, to give them a little future direction and some purpose, which may be, for example, to submit your pastel drawing to the local art competition. Learning to cook, tending your garden or specializing in a hobby can do the same; however, these pursuits, if you're not careful, will be consigned to the back burner if they're not given a special place in your day.

CHAPTER 16

Clunes, Australia

'True freedom means freeing oneself from the dictates
of the ego and its accompanying emotions.'
—Matthieu Ricard

I N THE ORGANIC STORE on Byron Street, Bangalow, the door
opens and a woman walks in. I've seen her before, thick brown
hair and oversized sunglasses, a conspicuously bohemian dress
and nomadic-style sandals. She walks the streets but never
speaks to anyone, continually alone. At the counter she pays
for a small selection of overpriced organic goods and turns to
leave, momentarily halted by the assistant standing behind the
counter, delaying her hasty exit with a question about a festival
on the weekend, and she turns around, and for a second I'm not
sure whether she doesn't have the words in English to respond,
or whether her speech is impaired, or whether she is just slow
to answer questions. However, at some point she answers softly
that, yes, she'll be there, giving a candid smile before burying her
head in her phone.

Intrigued, I ask around town, and soon it's relayed to me who
this woman is. 'She's huge on social media.' 'She has millions of
followers.' I suddenly realize that this woman is not walking down
a street, she's parading across a stage set. She's posing in front
of #nomadcafe, or visiting fashion store #wanderlustclothing,
entertaining herself at #wellnessfestival and wearing a frock
from #ecodesign, with #radicallydifferent sandals. And as she
moves from one stage set to the next, she posts and her followers

respond to her images with comments such as, 'hotbabe', or 'hi beautiful, hope you're having a dreamy day!' She's in a state of perpetual connectivity, which feeds her ego and sense of self-worth. When her phone pings with requests and notifications, her adrenal gland pumps up its production of adrenaline. She gets an energy high.

Narcissism is the habit of admiring oneself and wishing to be admired. And social media is the largest narcissist factory ever invented. For most people who use the system, the process involves posting a photo, mostly of themselves and aptly termed a 'selfie', in order to garner likes and followers. People who post selfies on the system are rewarded for doing so, triggering them to post more selfies, and this positive feedback loop sets them on a path of heightened self-love.

The problem with narcissists is that their self-love outweighs their love of any other subject matter, whether that be art, sport, business, finance, tulips, angelfish or rare historic Egyptian artefacts, which means that the average narcissist loses their zest and vitality for objective interests and pleasures that someone with less narcissistic tendencies enjoys. The woman from the organic shop could indeed meet the partner of her dreams, but could find herself struggling to love them. 'When vanity is carried to this height,' writes Bertrand Russell, 'there is no genuine interest in any other person, and therefore no real satisfaction to be obtained from love.'

The trouble with vanity, or narcissism, is that the world becomes colourless. Russell uses the example of a narcissistic artist desirous of being famous for their art. This keen desire for accolades stomps upon the joy they derived from the art-creation process – the act of splashing paint on canvas, moving it about, dabbing, smudging, wiping, removing, starting over. Ultimately bored with the process of doing art, they instead turn to quick slap jobs on canvas, finding the process ever so monotonous. 'Vanity, when it passes beyond a point, kills pleasure in every activity for its own sake, and thus leads inevitably to listlessness and boredom,' writes Russell.

For this social media sensation, the technology of her phone has shifted from being a means to an end to being the end itself. Today, her phone determines where she spends her allotted hours and what she does with them – it's her social group, her memory, her ego. It is the operating code of her life. And as she garners 'likes' for one post but not so many 'likes' for another, her stress hormones rise and fall, shifting her neural circuitry, the brain regions that control mood and thought – the hippocampus, the amygdala and the prefrontal cortex. But without social media where would she be? 'The internet has made her life. Without it, she'd be just a woman walking the streets. Now she is famous!' her followers exclaim. But the same could be said for the arms dealer. 'Without dealing, he'd be poor. Now that he deals, he gets to drive a fancy car and wear gold chains about his neck.'

It doesn't feel like much, just a simple glance at our phones or tablets. It is, after all, just a second that we're allotting every time we check. Globally, the average user spends three hours and 15 minutes a day on their phone. That's 1,186 hours each year that have shifted from some other activity, whatever that was, to the phone. Attention devoted to one stimulus cannot at the same time be devoted to another.

On the other side of the algorithm, however – and rarely, if ever, mentioned – are the followers, evidenced by tiny squiggles of text on the far right of a post. If it were possible for these followers to be embodied – real flesh-and-blood humans standing together in a room – they'd be a rather pitiful sight. For who indeed are they following? Most influencers have so few talents that one would struggle to list them on a jigsaw piece. Most are not particularly skilled at anything, neither music, nor mathematics, nor painting, nor engineering, nor philosophy. Neither are they adventurers, physicians, inventors or playwrights. And a further issue is this: what exactly are they influencing? If you were to look at the underlying code of how social media works, stories of upsets, grievances, failure, depression, breakups and anxiety garner more hits than good-news stories (much like the news, which operates on the same principles). So it is that influencers are often the feeders of neuroses. 'Society fabricates types of people just as it fabricates styles of shoes or of clothes or of automobiles, that is, as goods that are in demand,' writes Erich Fromm, adding: 'a person learns already as a child what type is in demand.' Indeed, the influencer is a product of a society hell-bent on banal novelty.

'The phenomenon of celebrity reflects popular longings,' writes the historian Stuart Ewen in *All Consuming Images*. 'In celebrities, people find not only a piece of themselves, but a piece of what they strive for.' Like shadows seeking embodiment, social media users follow those who most closely align with their ideal self. And they wish to fashion the influencer in their own perfect image. This benefits the influencer while that love affair lasts; however, influencers easily fall from grace if that idealized fantasy fails to materialize.

Many influencers come from modest backgrounds, giving everyday followers the hope or dream that they, too, could climb the pyramid and become an influencer someday. And in this consumer culture, where striving for stuff – like branded cars and hooded jackets – is the mark of accomplishment, influencers are fairy-tale illusions of what life could be like if money were no object and days could be filled buying one consumer item after another.

'Celebrities, collectively, supply us with the most accessible vision of what wealth means,' writes Ewen. In the media pages, celebrities and influencers demonstrate what being wealthy looks and smells like. But, as Ewen points out, celebrities hide the relation between wealth and power. Though celebrities are sometimes famously wealthy, consumption serves as the primary expression of their power, and lack of it. 'True celebrities can go to the movies without having to wait in line, can get the best table in the house at a moment's notice. Yet these are essentially consumer aspirations: to purchase without restraint, to enjoy the envious glance of those around them,' he writes. However, when it comes to real power, celebrities have none. 'The names and faces and activities of finance capitalists, transnational corporations, corporate leaders, political policy makers, or those who operate the machineries of mass impression, are – for the most part – unknown, invisible,' Ewen writes.

Celebrities might be the kings and queens of shopping excursions, but the people who operate the levers of society exist in relative obscurity – no celebrity, no fame, but plenty of power. 'The qualities which now commonly make a man or woman into a "nationally advertised brand" are in fact a new category of human emptiness,' writes Daniel J. Boorstin in *The Image*. Indeed, influencers can't fill us with purpose because purpose they have not. They do not extend our horizon because the celebrity or influencer is a commodity, a packaged good with an expiry date. 'We try to make our celebrities stand for the heroes we no longer have – or for those who have been pushed out of our view,' writes Boorstin. 'And we imitate them as if they were cast in the mould of greatness.' We have been willingly misled into believing that fame – or 'celebrity' – is a hallmark of greatness.

Intrigued, I am on her social media page. Her average selfie is worthy of a fashion advertisement. It's stylized, cropped and retouched. Her head is thrown back, her teeth glitter, and a mane of sparkling hair cascades to her shoulders. Beneath the image on her social media page is a number, 43,034 – her day's quota of 'likes'. It's higher than yesterday's quota, of 23,400, but falls short of Monday's quota, of 54,005, when she posted a photograph of herself on the beach. If you tumble back in time through her digital account, there are hundreds upon hundreds of selfies. She's lounging in armchairs laughing, or looking pensively or contemplatively at the ocean, and, more recently, the jackpot posts – bikini shots full of come-hither glances and flirtatious eyes. What was the first selfie? You scroll backwards in time, through 2016, 2010, until you come to a pause, a gap – almost like birth – and behold a photograph of a rosebush. The next image is a snapshot of an artwork, and the following is one of her standing – arm in arm with a friend, happy faces beaming. Her quota of likes on this image is 3. But one day, something happened. Her quota spiked, and her activity monitor shot upwards. People liked what she posted. And the comments rolled in. It's a photograph of her standing in the snow, a faux fur hat pulled over her forehead. 'So cute!'; 'Stunning'; 'I wanna be there'; '#soobeautiful'. Her quota galloped up to 128.

In 2001, the Buddhist monk Matthieu Ricard questioned the clinical psychologist Paul Ekman on the traits shared by remarkably gifted people. Ekman's lifelong study into emotions and non-verbal behaviour had put him in close contact with all sorts of people over decades of research, including people with exceptional abilities. 'What traits do the gifted share?' enquired Ricard out of interest. 'They emanate goodness,' replied Ekman. 'These people inspire others by how little they make of their status, their fame – in short, their self. They never give a second thought to whether their position or importance is recognised.' Predominantly, what Ekman noticed in remarkable people was a selflessness. Above all, he said, they exhibit an absence of ego.

For Ricard, such insights would have been far from surprising. For practising Buddhists, it's the ego that causes mental suffering – jealousy, hatred, envy, greed, pride. It's the ego that's at the ready to be either wounded or gratified. The self 'becomes inappropriate and unhealthy when we consider it to be an autonomous entity,' Ricard writes in his book *The Art of Happiness*. 'Our attachment to the ego is fundamentally linked to the suffering we feel and the suffering we inflict on others.'

Just recently, a string of executives from social media platforms have decried the operating code underlying social media machines. Social media, it seems, alters the way we relate to the world and to others, and not for the better. A 2017 study by the Royal Society for Public Health concluded that social media is more addictive than cigarettes and alcohol. 'The platforms that are supposed to help young people connect with each other may actually be fuelling a mental health crisis,' the study warned. The researchers surveyed 1,500 young people aged between 14 and 24 and found, according to the author of the report, Matt Keracher, that social media makes young women 'compare themselves against unrealistic, largely curated, filtered and photoshopped versions of reality'. When the self becomes the object of focus and worship, any setback or criticism becomes unbearable. A sudden drop-off in 'likes' is agonizingly painful, as is a negative comment, fuelling a resolve to prevent such displeasure in the future. The user, trapped in a feedback loop, works hard to elevate her status and fame. 'So long as the sense of the ego's importance has control over our being, we will never know lasting peace,' writes Ricard.

But how does one wind back to the beginning, where it all began? Back to the rosebush and the artwork and the photograph of friends together, in the days before the lonely selfie? 'Renouncing our fixation on our own intimate image and stripping the ego of all its importance is tantamount to winning incredible inner freedom,' notes Ricard. But there just seems no escaping the feed. This time she's wading in a swimming pool wearing sunglasses – seemingly oblivious to the camera's obvious presence. The comments roll in: '#toohot'; 'beauty lady'; 'pretty lady'; 'you are such a babe'; 'gorgeous'; 'babe babe babe babe'.

It's hard to travel back to the first time any of us logged on to a social media platform. It is difficult to remember what the external stimulus was that triggered us to log on – an advertisement, an icon, a link or a word-of-mouth recommendation? Perhaps it was the nightly newsperson excitedly urging us to 'log on and join in the discussion!' But now, most people automatically do it when feeling bored, lonely or indecisive.

In the 1950s, psychologist B. F. Skinner placed pigeons inside a box fitted out to deliver a food pellet every time the pigeons pressed a lever. Skinner soon discovered that if the lever dispensed food at random intervals, rather than in uniform, predictable amounts, pigeons became agitated, overly excited, hitting the lever repeatedly, over and over again. This is because, in anticipation of receiving a variable reward, the pleasure centres in the brain light up – the neurotransmitter dopamine spikes in the brain.

We log on to our social media platforms for the novel and the unexpected, such as a tantalizing image, a social contact or an engagement. Who could be contacting me? Who likes what I posted? What are my friends doing today? And the more time and energy we invest in posting photos, sharing, following, collecting 'followers', gaining badges or privileges, the more we invest in the product – by posting our thoughts, our favourite news picks, our photo memories – and, as a result, the more committed we become. In *Hooked*, the consumer psychology expert Nir Eyal shows how we become addicted to habit-forming products. The more times we cycle around the 'hook', says Eyal, the more automatic and involuntary the process becomes, until one day logging on to our online accounts is as automatic as brushing our teeth, saying 'good morning', even breathing.

The children are invited to a birthday party at a friend's house on a macadamia farm. It's an old farmhouse, fallen into disrepair. We wander through an oddly grand reception area, past an indoor swimming pool emptied of water but dotted with dead rats, and find ourselves in a living room as electrified as a disco parlour.

There's an eruption of noise, of electronic shooting and laser beams. The father of the children, Ed, stands on a leather pouffe in the centre of the room, his head bobbing close to the ceiling, frantically shooting a plastic gun at samurai warriors on a giant grey screen. Children perched either side of him are immersed in their tablets.

We have lunch on an outside table, and the mother of the children reveals in muted tones that her husband is bored. 'He's bored, he keeps telling me – bored, bored, bored. We have a macadamia farm to run and children to look after. How can he be bored?'

'Imagine,' she goes on, 'if he were born 100 years ago. Now that would be boring. He'd have nothing to watch or think about. On the tractor, I say, "Listen to podcasts." There are about one billion podcasts you can listen to. How can anyone be bored?' She takes us to her treadmill perched in front of the television where she watches midday soaps while exercising. I gaze at the treadmill while thinking about Ed's novelty centre in his brain.

Mark Fisher, a lecturer in philosophy at Penn State, became somewhat stumped by the number of students in his philosophy class who did not read. Not even a couple of sentences. Neither classics nor science fiction nor comic books – not even their academic textbooks. 'They will protest that they can't do it,' he writes in *Capitalist Realism*. How is it that these students can't read? 'The most frequent complaint teachers hear is that it's boring,' writes Fisher. While these students are indeed capable of it, reading is hardly as pleasurable as texting, tweeting, pinning and watching streaming videos, and their brain's pleasure centres continually divert the students away from low-pleasure areas – like reading – towards higher-reward activities.

According to Fisher, 'Many of the teenage students I encountered seemed to be in a state of what I call "depressive hedonia",' which he defines as an inability to do anything other than pursue pleasure. With a disquieting sensation that something is missing, students enter the cyberworld to seek out hits of pleasure and newness to fill the void. 'The consequence of being hooked into the entertainment matrix is twitchy, agitated interpassivity, an inability to concentrate or focus,' he writes. Head hunched over devices, punching into screens, students fail to notice that the actual activity is not so pleasurable after all (well, it's hardly as invigorating as wildly bowing a cello, or riding a bike full pelt down a steep hill); in fact, most students appear withdrawn and sullen when online, but seem incapable of separating from their source of instant gratification for longer than a few minutes at a time.

'One of the essentials of boredom,' writes Bertrand Russell, 'consists in the contrast between present circumstances and some other more agreeable circumstances which force themselves irresistibly upon the imagination. It is also one of the essentials of boredom that one's faculties must not be fully occupied.'

But boredom, apparently, is on the rise – not just on macadamia farms, but in the workplace, in schools and at home. According to Sandi Mann, a senior psychology lecturer at the University of Central Lancashire, in her book *The Upside of Downtime: Why Boredom is Good*, when asked the question, 'What bores you at work?', some 14 per cent of respondents said another person. Even people are boring us these days. So what is the problem? According to Mann, boredom is the curse of the twenty-first century: 'It seems that the more we have to stimulate us, the more stimulation we crave.'

But the problem with relying on more technology to save us from boredom is that, as novel and stimulating as it appears on the screen, it's actually pretty boring to operate – tap, swipe, gaze, tap, tap, swipe, gaze, hmm, gaze, gaze, gaze. 'Although we seem to live in a varied and exciting world with a plethora of entertainment at our fingertips,' writes Mann, 'this is actually the problem; many sources of our stimulation are obtained in remarkably similar ways – via our fingertips . . . We are stuck in a rut of trying to satisfy our need for neural stimulation via exactly the same methods. Instead of using varied activities that engage different neural systems (sport, knitting, painting, cooking, etc.) to relieve our boredom, we are falling back on the same screen-tapping schema for much of the day. Life becomes monotonous, repetitive and routine when it revolves around a flickering screen and a glowing keyboard. The irony is that in trying to avoid a single dull moment, we fill in every spare minute by engaging in routine and repetitive tasks.'

But if tap, tap, tapping and gazing at a flickering screen were as boring as all that, we wouldn't do it, would we? It must be entertaining, otherwise why are so many people constantly hooked up to the novelty machine that is the internet? Mann argues that we mightn't have a choice in the matter. Our brains are hardwired to seek novelty. As she explains, we even have a 'novelty centre' in our midbrains, called the substantia nigra/ventral tegmental area (SN/VTA), which lights up when we see a new image, stimulating a surge in the brain of the pleasure chemical dopamine. 'We are programmed to seek novelty and are rewarded with a feeling of pleasure when we find it.'

Ed hovers between the lunch table and the console, his eyes darting. He finally grabs a beer and disappears inside a nearby shed. The macadamia farm, newly purchased, provides plenty to occupy his time. Evidently, the previous owner let things go: the vines have withered in the intense northern sunlight, matted together like unwashed hair; the grass is knee-deep and squirming with snakes. But already he seems indifferent to it all, as though perhaps he should be doing something else with his life – buying a vacant block near the beach, setting up an adventure business? I think about his reptilian brain, evolved over so many millions of years, designed to deal with a world on simpler terms. He reappears from the shed and stands before the white plastic table dotted with ham sandwiches, cakes and a dozen party pies on a crumpled paper plate. His daughter's strawberry blonde ponytail whips past as he stares into the middle distance, visions of samurai slashers and chainsaw-revving marines overlaid by this morning's feed, a new vacant lot in town, a generous allotment of over 1,800 sq. m with beach views. A real prospect.

While his brain may interpret visions on the screen, his senses of touch, taste and smell are muted – three out of five senses put to sleep. Compare computer work with gardening, for example – there's none of that fetid smell of rich black earth crumbling through your fingers. Rather, keyboards are silvery clean, like a psychopath's dissecting table.

Religious orders understood the power of the senses to uplift us, which explains why they built grand cathedrals for religious services rather than holding them in makeshift sheds. Architectural feats such as vaulted ceilings and flying buttresses are awe-inspiring to behold; we are uplifted in their presence. And similarly, caught within a net of glorious sounds – chanting, music, singing – we're moved, altered, transported someplace else. Our sense of smell, too, is powerful, accounting for most of what we taste. Some scientists claim that we can distinguish ten categories of smell – fragrant, woody, fruity, chemical, minty, sweet, popcorn, lemon, pungent and decayed. We process smell – such as the glorious scent of frankincense and myrrh imbuing church services – in the brain via our olfactory system.

Back in 1954, psychologists at the National Institute of Mental Health submerged study participants in a flotation tank to test brainwashing techniques. Naked, blind and hearing impaired under the weight of water, being in a flotation tank is like being set adrift on the Dead Sea. When our ordinary ways of perceiving the world are cut off, does the brain shift? Does it go to sleep? Or does it bend backwards, arch, contort? When we lose our senses, do we lose a part of ourselves?

Starving participants' brains in the flotation tank provided plenty of fodder for the psychologists. When we're locked out of our senses, apparently, we preoccupy ourselves with our own mental images, mulling things over in our minds. We may go over the past, or think about the future, or we may worry and fret. But when it craves stimulation, anything that arrives – a message, a symbol – is devoured by a desperate and hungry mind. Patients immersed in sensory-deprivation chambers for long stretches at a time eventually suffer from hallucinations and other delusions. Madness, like algae, soon settles in.

In places of low stimulation – such as flotation tanks or, alternatively, when online – any stimulus we receive fills our world. It's why we often say things online we wouldn't dare mutter in places of high stimulation, such as at a dinner party or in a classroom setting. This, of course, explains – at the far extreme – the phenomenon of trolls, those social media addicts, who – cut off from the natural world, no taste, no smell, deprived of sensory experience – become like pigeons pecking at levers to dispense pleasure pellets. Trolls, I see them clad in yellow pyjamas, up against the kitchen bench, punching symbols into keyboards, their teeth bared – alone, miserable, caught up in the loop, but unable to stop. What they need is a good dose of sunshine – outside. They need to find a big dirt patch and to lie down and roll around in it. They need to press their face into the wild earth and turn to the heavens and bellow with lungs ablaze. Upon returning to the kitchen, they'd no doubt feel much better – much calmer, and certainly much less crazed.

But Ed, his eyes lit up by the artificial lights of the online world, is not unlike Mark Fisher's students who could no longer read. The grape-like clusters of nuts hanging on his macadamia trees are in his line of sight, but he gains no reward from them, unlike that tantalizing ping of adrenaline he gains when he searches online. While technology may dictate perception in our modern world, our ancient brains still yearn to return to the way we perceived life for hundreds of thousands of years. We yearn to return to the meadow, the savannah, the Arabian Desert, to sense the grit of earth under our feet, to feel the bristle of heat in the midday sun, to taste the tang of minty tea on our tongue.

The trouble with pictures on the internet is that they offer dreams. And dreamscapes are a more novel and stimulating place to be when compared with the everyday humdrum reality of ordinary life. People who exist in the slow heartbeat of day-to-day happenings, passing traffic, air particles, traffic noise, and the odd fly that's caught in the screen door face moments of stupefying dullness. And so, when weighing up painful reality with vibrant dreamscapes, many dive back into the virtual world of videos, social networks and pretty pictures on the internet.

In prehistoric times, when we humans hunted for our food, there was always something to chase. And this was, as you can well imagine, tremendously exciting. Pursuing a giant elk through a dense forest would have been nothing short of exhilarating, its massive antlers waving up ahead like flags, its slim legs leaping at breakneck speed. Today, the hunt comes in the form of online searching, from news snippets to the odd comment from some unknown person into our machines – and we can get caught up in the thrill of it.

In *Animals in Translation*, the American author Temple Grandin retells the tale of two cats in her friend's New York apartment. For some reason, Grandin, a prominent scientist and animal behaviourist, had a battery-operated laser pointer with her, the type that lecturers use on overhead screens. Grandin whipped it about, the light bouncing from one side of the room to the other. 'You could lead Lilly and Harley around the whole apartment at a dead run,' she writes, 'jump them up on the counter, back down on the floor, up a bookshelf – you could shoot them wherever you wanted them to go. They were so frenzied I had to be careful not to suddenly reverse the motion, because I could throw Lilly into a back flip, she was so focused on that dot.'

Grandin was perplexed. Outdoor cats do not chase laser pointers, she explains. That's because outside cats clearly understand that laser pointers are not food. 'Lilly and Harley aren't allowed outside and were never taught to hunt by their mother, whereas a cat with a normal outdoor upbringing learns what to chase and when,' she writes. 'Outdoor cats also learn to inhibit their chasing instinct so they can stalk their prey and get close enough to catch it.'

Grandin states that Lilly and Harley had gone into what behaviourists call hyper-activation of the predatory chasing instinct. 'They were so mindlessly fixated they could have injured themselves,' she writes. 'I think that happens with laser pointers because cats can see the dot but can't catch it. Even when a cat puts his paws on the dot he can't feel it or hold it. The laser dot probably becomes a *super-stimulus* that keeps on stimulating the chase because the cat can't complete the sequence of chase and catch, so the chase instinct can't get turned off.'

There are interesting parallels between domestic cats and humans engaged with computers, television sets and handheld devices – chasing pixels, flicking stations with a remote control. Like Lilly and Harley, they are so stimulated by the chase of the new television show, email, film, news story, social media message, internet search – experiences that simply can't be felt or held – that the chase instinct can't be turned off.

CHAPTER 17

Bangalow, Australia

'Time is change; we measure its passage by how much things alter.'

—Nadine Gordimer

W E RENT A HOUSE in Bangalow, the hill town just outside Byron Bay where our bookstore is located. It's a white weatherboard with a broad deck overlooking the growing village, flanked on one side by a freeway.

One afternoon we return home to a note on the windscreen of our car, a 'hello' from our new neighbours – a couple with a small child – and within no time we meet them at a children's park. She is tall, blonde, and he is dark haired and intense, and they talk at speed. Within ten minutes we know the story of their lives intimately.

On the return walk from the park, we are perplexed by the number of people who seem to know them in the street, considering that they've only recently moved to the town. People stop, chat, wave. A man walking with a group of friends turns and shouts from across the road, 'Thanks for your advice. It changed my life.'

It's not long before the couple knock at our door laden with DVDs, movies and documentaries that they've appeared in, books that they've co-written, and other forms of identification of their fame and worth. But not having watched anything on a screen for quite some time, we know not a thing about them. One is only famous by dint of being seen. And while actors can increase their degree of fame by broadcasting their image far and wide, viewing those images is still very much a voluntary act. The media's ubiquity in modern-day society is still not quite at the point where those agencies broadcast images into our brains while we sleep, drive a car, or walk to work. We are still willing participants in this game of show-and-tell.

But their relative obscurity in our eyes confuses them considerably, to a point of maddening angst. I can imagine it would be akin to wearing a haute couture gown complete with gleaming red designer shoes and luxury handbag down the main street of a town whose inhabitants love fashion about as much as they love eating stale bread with anchovies for dinner. An $8,000 gown paired with a comparatively priced handbag and shoes would certainly not spark the same chemical rush of awe and lust, jealousy and submission in the inhabitants of such an 'unfashionable' town as it would, say, in a crowd of starry-eyed onlookers watching that person roll up to the entrance of a five-star hotel. I cannot help but think of Arthur Schopenhauer's oft-mentioned quote: 'Wealth is like sea-water; the more we drink, the thirstier we become; and the same is true of fame.'

It does show how what we seek in life happens within a context. We seek fame in the context of a world that watches us, or we seek expensive consumer goods in a world that understands that the items we own are in fact pricey. Remove the audience from a Grand Slam tennis match, and all you see are two stick figures smashing a yellow ball over a braided net. At the end of the day, fame and wealth are illusions. On the other hand, a rock, stripped of its context, is still a rock.

Our bookstore is located at the gutter end of a sloping street. And at the top end sits a café, forever in the process of reinventing itself. Its space is long and narrow, with customer seating in the far recesses. More successful cafés, in contrast, place all the action at the front, visible, attractive, accessible. You wander past and see a couple drinking coffee and eating cake, and you want to take part in that too. The same goes for anything you want to achieve in life. You've got to make it visible, attractive and accessible. You can't push your dreams to the far backroom and presume you'll head down there one day, along the dark passageway to the rear end in the half-light. If you have a dream, it must be dragged to the front room and put on display for everyone to see.

At one point in the evolution of the café, the coffee machine was located midway along the bar. Later, it was moved to a position unnervingly close to the sidewalk. Local produce was added to shelving near the counter, jars of jam and bags of coffee, and sometimes flowers. The food shifted from sandwiches to sushi to high tea and cakes, and with each change, its patrons fell off one by one, until the café, now repainted white with new bench seating, was put on the market with a gigantic real estate sign out front: 'Business For Sale'.

A friend in the restaurant business once told me that patrons don't like it when their favourite restaurant changes. They get accustomed to the menu, the seating arrangements, the placement of the bar and coffee stand, even the waitstaff. And so, should the owner decide to make some changes, such as moving the counter to a new corner position or adding new bench seating, there are the inevitable complaints. Frequently the new arrangement feels so unfamiliar that regular patrons do not return as frequently, or don't return at all. Their favourite café is no longer the same, so they go elsewhere.

Too much change, said my wise restaurateur friend, is damaging for business. Instead, he recommended 'the boiling frog' approach, which involves changes on such an infinitesimally small level that they go under the radar, almost as inconsequential as shifting a chair an inch a day. That way, patrons are not disturbed by too much alteration. If possible, he said, 'keep some things the same'. Some things must stay the same.

The boiling frog metaphor, along with its rather brutal imagery, refers to the fact that if you place a frog in cold water and slowly increase the temperature it will thrash about less than it would if you threw it headlong into a tub of boiling bubbles. Apparently, this popular metaphor is practically flawed, but, regardless, it has some useful insights. Like boiling frogs, we too thrash about in the face of too much change introduced too quickly.

When exhausted mothers come into his clinic seeking help for chronic tiredness and anxiety, clinical psychologist Robert Maurer knows the remedy: exercise. He wants to tell his exhausted, stressed-out patients: 'Get out there! Rise early, before domestic duties begin, and pound the pavement. Just do it!' But for sleep-deprived mothers with almost no time for themselves, such advice is like getting a pie in the face. 'How dare he tell me to exercise when I'm juggling four kids and have to unpack the dishwasher four times each day!'

Maurer knows such advice is just not going to work. The brain of a chronically tired and stressed-out patient is going to set off alarm bells of warning. 'No!' it will scream. 'You are exhausted already. If you expend more energy on exercise, you will fall in a heap!' While the rational, thinking brain (or cortex) may point out the benefits of squeezing in some physical movement each day, the midbrain (or amygdala) will prevent this from happening. You see, any shift in routine, any change, any new idea or opportunity will trigger fear in the midbrain.

Every time you stray from your safe and familiar habits, the midbrain will do its utmost to put a stop to it. It's why we typically fail at changing our routine, instead continuing to do what we've always done, even if it makes us unhappy, unhealthy or uninspired. It's why New Year's resolutions are almost never put into action.

So when the remedy is exercise but the advice feels like a pie in the face, Maurer takes a different course. The secret to motivation is action. For one patient, who owned an expensive treadmill but couldn't bring herself to use it, he had a radical treatment plan. For the first month, her therapy involved standing upon her treadmill every morning to drink coffee and read the newspaper. She didn't have to move a leg. Not for an entire month. The second month, after finishing her coffee, she was ordered to walk on the treadmill for one minute. 'During those early months, her small actions would have struck most people as ridiculous,' writes Maurer in *One Small Step Can Change Your Life*. But what Maurer was doing was changing her habits without her even knowing. Within no time, she acquired the habit of heading to her treadmill each and every morning. 'Soon her "ridiculous" small actions had grown into the firm habit of running one mile each day.' This technique is founded on an ancient Japanese philosophy called *kaizen*, or 'continual improvement'. Instead of wild, sweeping, radical change, one aims for infinitesimally small improvements.

The technique can be used for whatever it is you wish to change in your life: each day you have one less sip of coffee; you draw one line on a page in a sketchbook; you write one word of a poem; you sit at your piano and press a single note; you learn one foreign word. When an action is so small it is laughable, the brain does not go into self-protective lockdown mode. 'Instead of spending years in counselling to understand why you're afraid of looking great or achieving your professional goals, you can use *kaizen* to go around or under these fears,' Maurer writes. 'Small, easily achievable goals – such as picking up and storing just one paper clip on a chronically messy desk – let you tiptoe right past the amygdala, keeping it asleep and unable to set off alarm bells. As your small steps continue and your cortex starts working, the brain begins to create "software" for your desired change, actually laying down new nerve pathways and building new habits. Soon, your resistance to change begins to weaken. Where once you might have been daunted by change, your new mental software will have you moving toward your ultimate goal at a pace that may well exceed your expectations.'

The 'boiling frog' metaphor has similarities to the Japanese concept of *kaizen*. Personal changes ignite two primary human powers – fear and laziness – and when you seek change you will observe these twin powers sitting in the driver's seat of your consciousness. 'I've had the worst day today; this is not the day for me to go for a run, or to the gym. Any other day but today.'

Kaizen recognizes that these forces will rear their heads as soon as you attempt to do something new, or to improve yourself in some way, or to forge your own path, or to follow your dreams, or to say, 'To hell with it, this is what I want to do.' Even if we manage to make the decision to study full-time, or start a business, or begin an exercise programme or whatever it is, sooner or later these twin powers will appear in our lives. The Jungian therapists might label their appearance our shadow – that power to keep us stuck in the same routine, circling in a habitual route, around and around. The Jungian shadow lurks at the fork in the path, ensuring you don't head off in a new and unknown direction. 'What if you lose money on this, or waste your time? It could be a lot of work. And what happens if it fails? You may hate it and end up depressed and anxious. You may not make any friends, or worse, the people you meet may be horrible and be mean to you . . .'

Kaizen teaches us to expect these voices as 'normal' and 'natural'. They're not wise counsellors, but scared children. So how do you turn these voices down a touch, or silence them altogether? Like the restaurateur, *kaizen* advises infinitesimally small changes, so small that you stealthily bypass the voices. Meanwhile, something is working in the background, something powerful, and life-changing, and almost magical – and that's habit.

CHAPTER 18

Hobart, Tasmania

'Whoever prefers the material comforts of life over intellectual wealth is like the owner of a palace who moves into the servants' quarters and leaves the sumptuous rooms empty.'
—Marie von Ebner-Eschenbach

I T'S A HALF-ACRE BLOCK on a hill in Bangalow, and we put in an offer to buy it. It'll mean building a house, fencing it off and planting some trees. 'Putting down roots' is the expression used to describe this scenario. You select an area, square it off, and then put down the foundations of a life.

At dusk on the night before the contract signing, we wander across the small block, envisaging our future here, the children growing up on the hill in lockstep with the newly planted shrubs. The block is marked with wooden stakes, and we pace it out, following the slope of the land downwards, remembering to keep to the dark patches. The light is fading fast, and with no streetlights, the children run at each other squealing. 'Shhhh,' says Zan, pointing up at the building above, an old weatherboard house with a large kitchen window lit up like a prison control room. 'We don't own the land yet,' he warns them.

A shadow moves across the kitchen window, and I look around for the children, who've fallen silent, out of view. The twinkling lights of the town give a celebratory effect, and I think we need champagne – to drink a toast to our future, to deciding once and for all that this is it. We've reached the crest of the hill and we're putting up our flag, at last.

I turn to begin my search for the children, and plod back up the hill, feeling tired. The owner of the block, our neighbour, will be signing the contract tomorrow. I look back up at his house on the hill – at his broad block soon to be cut up into little parcels. He must be nervous too, I think. It'll be hard after so many years of being king of the mountain to share your lot.

There's a piercing scream, followed by the sound of a loud clump of something heavy hitting the ground, and I see, first, a shadow in the window, and then a figure at the door – the owner, looking down at his land, his hand cupping his eyes, and I spot one of the children with a stake raised high, about to thump one of the others, and Zan is hissing at them to be quiet, pulling them into the shadows further, and there's a voice above, almost like a voice from heaven: 'Who's down there?'

I grab the stake from the child holding it and turn to place it back in the hole – but it's now pitch-black, too dark to see my feet, and I'm crawling crabwise along the ridge, my head lowered, searching for the spot in the earth where the stake can reclaim its place, but I can't find its home – it's been devoured by shadows. 'Hey!' bellows the landowner above, leaning down to grab something, and I ditch the stake, grab the hand of one of the children, whose eyes are wet with tears, and we're off, slipping back off the hill, away, out of sight.

My heart is pounding, and I'm thinking, 'Did he see me . . . would he know it was us?', and as I catch up to Zan and the other children, my chest is so tight I can barely breathe. The stake has been pulled out, and now the land, which was clearly marked for sale, has lost its southerly point. I wonder if we can still sign the contract in the morning, and as I continue to fret, I turn to my child, who, head downcast, is feeling responsible for this sudden shift of fortune, and for some reason I start to smile, and then laugh. I pull her arm high in the air as if in victory. 'I agree,' I say, turning my back to the block on the hill, knowing there is nothing we can do now to change it. 'Sometimes you just have to pull up stakes.'

And so, within a week, our rental house is emptied, the land left for someone else to buy, and our bookstore left for a staff member to manage. We pile the children into the van and head south, this time to Tasmania.

———————

A change of scenery will be nice, I think, as I project ahead to what life will be like in our new land. But not all changes in life need be made by setting forth on a sea voyage. I think about a friend of our family, a chain-smoker for well over 40 years who, one day, suddenly stopped. She didn't tell anyone what she was doing. Even her husband, who saw her every day, didn't know what she was up to. She threw her cigarettes in the bin and told herself she'd never buy another pack again. The way she saw it, she was the only person who went to the shop to buy cigarettes, so she prohibited her future self from buying a pack again. To do so was off limits. One day, her husband, furious at her uncharacteristic moodiness, yelled at her in the backyard: 'What the hell is wrong with you?' His wife had gone from a pack a day to zero cigarettes – a monumental shift – literally overnight. What had prompted it? Smoking is not just a habit, it's an addictive one to boot. How can such sudden shifts of behaviour like this happen?

On his deathbed, the Stoic philosopher Marcus Aurelius ruminated on life's stages, what he saw as small deaths of self within the journey of life. Our child self is the first to leave us as we enter our adolescent years, and later our adolescent self will depart once we reach adulthood. Childbirth, divorce, illness, education, moving house or country, the death of a loved one, finding a new partner, meeting a new friend, quitting smoking – these landmarks often herald the emergence of a new self. 'As an old man,' writes Donald Robertson in his book *How to Think Like a Roman Emperor: The Stoic Philosophy of Marcus Aurelius*, 'he faces his death not for the first time but for the last. From the moment we're born we're constantly dying, not only with each stage of life but also one day at a time . . . Nobody is the same person he was yesterday. Realizing this makes it easier to let go: we can no more hold on to life than grasp the waters of a rushing stream.'

The chain-smoker who suddenly quits says goodbye to her smoking self. Between one day and the next, she is changed anew – new actions, new thoughts, even the chemicals in her cells undergo a fundamental shift as nicotine, lead and hydrogen cyanide recede from her body and oxygen is elevated in her bloodstream.

Researchers at Washington University's Olin Business School sought to find out whether significant occasions – such as birthdays, holidays, the start of a new week, month or year, or a wedding, for example – would spur goal initiation. In other words, are we more likely to achieve goals in life if we align them with important dates? So, rather than saying, 'I will quit smoking now,' you instead set out to end your smoking days on a significant day, like a birthday. 'We propose that temporal landmarks spur goal initiation when they signal new beginnings or the start of new time periods,' the researchers write in their paper 'Put Your Imperfections Behind You: Temporal Landmarks Spur Goal Initiation When They Signal New Beginnings'. Temporal landmarks, as defined by the report, act as dates that 'stand in marked contrast to the seemingly unending stream of trivial and ordinary occurrences in people's lives'.

Research has shown that temporal landmarks operate as dividers that separate a person's past, current and future selves. They put distance between the before and after – me before my divorce, and me afterwards – that is, there's a perceived gap or psychological distance between past and current selves. New beginnings open new 'mental accounts' – we attribute negative traits to the old self and chalk up wins on the scoreboard to the emerging new self.

The researchers found that landmarks can indeed trigger new beginnings. Although many scoff at the 'New Year's resolution', these academics argued that temporal landmarks are important for starting new goals, mostly because we predict that our motivation to achieve our goals will be higher following some more monumental date. This finding is not surprising given that our ancestors, way back, lived within a time frame of landmarks

– the winter solstice, the equinox, the closure of harvest and the blooming of spring. The researchers suggested that distressing events such as the death of a loved one or the loss of a job can also propel people to take on new challenges that lead to the emergence of a new self.

I wonder about the brewing of a new self as I lie with my head flat against the pillow as the ferry violently pitches its bow into the stomach of the sea. It has been a long 12-hour journey across Bass Strait and I have spent the majority of it in bed in a cabin, unable to move my head for fear of being sick. Our belongings are in the van, inside the bowels of the ferry – a few computers, clothes and toys, but really we have brought very little of our past life with us other than memories.

As land is spotted for the first time in what feels like days, the ferry horn blows – a deep, trumpeting sound, alerting the township of Devonport that newcomers are about to disembark, expectant faces peering out of rectangular windows, figures moving at pace onto the deck, children jumping. I join the throng, excited at what we will find in our new land. I look at the other adventurers on this sea voyage and think, why are we all so restless? What is it that we hope to find down here at the end of the world? What are we all searching for? So very few of us learn the art of being at rest. What are we so afraid of?

On his 38th birthday, the French philosopher Michel de Montaigne, one of the leading writers of the French Renaissance, who went on to influence a long list of eminent thinkers from Descartes to Nietzsche, retired into the self. Rather than winging himself from one end of the world to the next, as many of us do – in search of I know not what – Montaigne set himself up in his library, positioned in the tower of his family's château, and, in utter seclusion, set out to spend his time reading, writing and meditating. His library was a round room, lined with some 1,500 books and decorated with Greek and Latin inscriptions. Here, in his 'sweet ancestral retreat', Montaigne set out to write his *Essais*, a series of essays on himself and his thoughts, a self-portrait more or less, but also a frank and honest account of humankind. Montaigne, like the ancients before him, viewed the inner life as one worth cultivating, and the inner life, I suppose, does not need new diversions every second to keep it content. In his essay 'On Solitude', from the first volume of his *Essais*, he discussed the value of solitude. He argued that desire for other people's approval and the pursuit of fame prevent many from leading a tranquil life.

As I scan the port town of Devonport, I think about what we've left behind – a life in a small township where we knew almost everybody by name. And now here we are, in a land where we don't know a single face. As I ponder these thoughts some more, my eyes trail two bodies trotting at the ferry's pace along a concrete footpath, arms waving, as if in a celebratory gesture of welcome. I feel somewhat elated, much like a child arriving at a flight terminal and seeing their family after a long stint away. I follow their shadowy figures along the riverbank, two teenage boys in dark hoodies and trackpants, bounding and waving. The children, too, are transfixed, watching the boys as apparitions of what is to come in this new place, with its new people. A quiet lull, after such a long, rough journey across the seas, and we are all hopeful.

The big-bellied ferry makes its final push before skating across the milky waters, and the teenage boys are now flat against the fence, so close I can see the freckles on the taller one's face. So close I can see the pupils of his wild hazel eyes. He faces the crowd on the boat and gives us a middle-fingered salute. 'Youse can all fuck right off.'

When you click your fingers and decide to change your life, as soon as it's done, it's easy to fall headlong into the feeling that you've made a grave mistake. But once the momentum has started, there's no turning back. And so Zan's foot is on the accelerator and we are moving through flat yellow plains, and eventually the simple beauty of the countryside reassures me. We have so little luggage. I think about how nice it is to have so few objects about, almost as light as if we could fly.

I remember once visiting the home of a well-known architect. He had an uncanny knack of manipulating space, so much so that the interior of the house had a sense of the great outdoors: the garden seamlessly flowed into a maze of indoor corridors, tree branches swept across a glass roof. And then, a few feet from the door, a fluorescent pink strobing light show emanated from the underskirt of a tall plastic doll. 'Would you like to do the tour now?' he asked my perplexed face. And in no time, I was swept down a dark corridor to begin the inspection of the house's contents.

House tours are strange events. Paraded through the home of another, one is treated like a patron at a gallery opening. 'See here, eighteenth-century tapestry.' 'Moose head from Norway.' As items are paraded out, there's an expectation to 'ooh and aah', to nod one's head in appreciation: 'Wow, that's beautiful.'

In *The Thing with Feathers*, Noah Strycker happens upon a small hut in the Australian outback. A pile of white stones, bleached bones and green leaves is arranged outside the hut's entrance like some kind of religious altar. 'The whole tidy array was surrounded by an expanse of ground so bare that I wondered whether it had been vacuumed,' he writes.

The owner of the hut eventually made himself known. 'Head cocked, he stepped around the stones and leaves to admire his creation from various angles.' All of a sudden it made sense to Strycker: 'I had wandered into the bachelor pad of Australia's winged Casanova, the serial womanizer of the avian kingdom – the great bowerbird.'

You see, male bowerbirds court their ladies by demonstrating a prowess in architecture and design. They spend up to ten months of the year designing and renovating their bowers, decorating them with objects sourced from the surrounding shrubland. Rocks, bones, shells, berries, leaves, and human trash such as plastic spoons and ballpoint pens are the types of precious items bowerbirds collect to impress the ladies. 'It's hard to look at a great bowerbird's decorated bower, on which the bird had lavished so much time in tasteful arrangement, without seeing artistry,' writes Strycker. 'As I stood sweating in the Australian bush, watching this strange bird move his precious stones and leaves by millimetres in pursuit of the perfect visual pattern, I marvelled at his designs. I wondered: is this bird just carrying out his instinctive duty, or is he an artist?' Indeed, the bowerbird does not waste his time pining for a new bower, in a different place with a different series of objects. He is more creative than that. He sees what opportunities exist before him and then rises to the occasion.

Our fourth baby is born a few months later in Hobart and is carried home to an empty rental house in Sandy Bay. The furniture truck seems to have been stuck at the border for months, and all we have are our suitcases and a couple of mattresses on the floor. When the landlady brings us a small gift, then asks if her daughter can stay a few nights a week 'out the back' in the shed, I'm desperate to find a permanent spot.

While carrying the baby around in a sling, we set up *poet*, this time in downtown Hobart, in an ornate nineteenth-century building, the former headquarters of a printer and book publisher, hiring staff, decorating, re-creating our archaic concept of bookstore and tea house once again. Our new staff seem excited to be joining a bustling publishing house and bookstore – until, that is, they start working within our chaos, where nothing is fixed, everything is in flux. There is no order, no day-to-day planning, and we are just as likely to turn the place into a café or fashion store as we are to sell books. At one point council people are dragged in to discuss the cost of turning 50 square metres of the space into a commercial kitchen, only for that kitchen space to become instead the shelves for clothes racks. 'Good luck with the fashion,' says one outgoing staff member, quitting not long after seeing boxes and boxes of garments arrive and promptly set up front and centre, ousting her carefully selected row of cookbooks.

There's only one staff member, Jess, who has the tenacity to stay on. She steers *poet*, our unwieldy ship, through unruly waters, as 26,000 canisters of tea are delivered from Sri Lanka – everything from vanilla rooibos to mango booster to pomegranate white to banana tea. All the while, the residents of Hobart, driving past on their way to work, or taking the kids to school, are subjected to philosophical quotes about life and death, such as one from Henry Miller: 'It is almost banal to say so yet it needs to be stressed continually: all is creation, all is change, all is flux, all is metamorphosis.'

I understand what Miller is saying here, but sometimes a little permanency is needed. It's why I am intent on finding a fixed abode, a place I can call my own.

From the vantage point of a second-storey window, I move a curtain aside. I breathe and take in the view, a perspective I could be seeing for the rest of my life. I am intent on buying a house in Hobart, and after weeks of searching, I think, this house could be it.

My eyes scan the backyard fence separating the house from the neighbour's yard. I swivel hard, and point. 'That house is . . . is . . . incredible . . .'

'Oh, yes,' the real estate agent says smugly, his eye resting on the neighbour's gabled roof. 'I sold that house last year. You see, back in the day that house was the main residence. This house,' he says with a pause, 'the one you are standing in right now, this house was its stables.' I can't smell horsehair, but I think I could if I tried hard enough. I wander downstairs, a little crestfallen, and out to the garden. The agent shows me the flower beds, and indeed they are a credit to the owner at this time of year. But I'm back gazing at the other house, this time pressed up against the fence, taking in the neighbour's sandstone pillars and arched windows.

On closer inspection, I see a barbed-wire fence surrounding the side entrance; laundry hangs limply on a makeshift rope; the gardens are patchy. But why is it in such disarray? Owning such a grand house, surely one would wake every day committed to the art of maintaining it?

Just to clarify: the house I'm standing in is, as the brochure says, 'a stunning example of Federation, Queen Anne-style architecture, and rooms which once accommodated a gentleman's carriage, horses, and tack now form part of a stunning and gracious family home.' But life doesn't exist in isolation; the house stands amid other houses. And the truth is, the house over the fence is, even in its dishevelled state, significantly better.

This story is certainly not novel. It's a well-known narrative, summed up by expressions such as 'the grass is always greener on the other side' and 'keeping up with the Joneses', that all-too-common tendency of neighbours to copy one another's purchases of flash cars, heated pools and concrete driveways. But these quaint expressions do not reveal the underlying cause of what's going on here. Why can't we be happy with what we have? Why are we always looking over the fence for what appears to be a better life?

As organisms, writes Daniel Nettle in *Happiness: The Science Behind Your Smile*, we need to seek out things that are best for us. To survive, or even better, to flourish, we must be 'constantly scanning the horizon on the lookout for a better environment, a better social network, a better mode of behaviour.' And there should always be 'a little space of discontent open, just in case something hovers into view which is really special,' he writes. If we didn't behave like this, argues Nettle, we wouldn't be very successful organisms. If we had lounged around boasting about our naturally superior DNA, we'd have been wiped out by a more ambitious organism. It could be said, therefore, that our capacity for dissatisfaction is our greatest gift – the motivational force that's seen us conquer just about every other organism on the planet. Into this gap, between what we want and what we actually have, enters consumerism with its dazzling line-up of products. 'Peddlers of nostalgia, spiritual systems, drugs, and all kinds of consumer goods,' writes Nettle, will slip into this space promising to narrow the gap 'between our present contentment and possible super contentment'. Stuff that appeals to our need to signal to others our biological fitness – status, beauty, health or wealth – will tempt us more than stuff that's simply useful to us.

The economist Richard Easterlin asked a cross-section of the US public in 1978 what it meant to live the 'good life'. 'What do you want out of life?' he enquired. He handed them a card listing 24 big-ticket items, such as a car, a television, holidays abroad, a swimming pool and a vacation home. 'When you think of the good life, the life you'd like to have, which of the items on this list, if any, are part of that good life as far as you personally are concerned?' Respondents were then asked to tick off items on the list that they already owned. The survey was then conducted on the same people 16 years later, in 1994, and what was most telling was that, while respondents indeed owned more items (3.1 items in 1994 compared with 1.7 items in 1978), they also desired more items on the list (5.6 items were now required for the good life, as opposed to 4.4 items in 1978). In other words, over 16 years, the gap between what people had and what they so desperately desired remained steady, at two and a half items. They were two and a half items short – eternally, so it appears. This finding suggests that perhaps this gap – this small margin of yearning, this nagging sense of inadequacy – remains no matter where you're stationed in life. While few of us yearn for a Rembrandt etching on our walls, it quickly becomes an 'item' on the list for those with the means to purchase it. While the person on an average salary dreams of a holiday home, the billionaire dreams of a public gallery that bears his name, complete with restaurant and hotel. So, it seems, no matter how hard we run in an effort to hurdle that elusive 'stuff gap', we never actually close it. It's just not in our DNA.

I think about the mansion over the fence, surrounded by washing and wire. I think of the owners huddled inside the opulent drawing room lined with gold-leaf wallpaper debating whether or not they'll open a brewery, go sailing or buy a little hideaway somewhere in Indonesia. All the while, the roses wilt, the dirt patches grow and cracks in the arched windows widen. And the stuff gap remains.

———

One afternoon the children are invited to a birthday party. I can't find the exact number of the house, but its location on the map aligns with an overly renovated double-storey block, now turned into a family home. The gardens are meticulously designed around winding paved paths, framed by a dazzling white fence. In the garage, two luxury cars face the street, gleaming to passing traffic like a car showroom. Upon the fence, a pedigree cat displays the owners' careful taste.

The need to outshine our neighbours is not peculiar to modern times. Perched on a Tuscan hillside in Italy is San Gimignano, a medieval city with multiple teetering towers stretching to the heavens. These towers were bastions of power and prestige for rich families who, in thirteenth-century Tuscany, dedicated their life's energy to a race to the top. Back then, the question of how to outdo your neighbour was fought between San Gimignano families on the basis of tower size. The city, boasting over 72 towers in its heyday, today has a mere 14 surviving pillars of prestige, with the remainder collapsing under insecure foundations.

We tiptoe up the path so as to not to disturb a blade of grass, and at the entrance, a woman opens the door an inch too narrow. I apologize for the intrusion and ask for directions to the party. 'Next door,' she replies with a frown and closes the door an inch further in evident fear of me ambushing her opulent home with my four children in tow.

Cloistered within her mansion, she seems miserly and protective – in obvious contrast to the ostentatious manner in which her materialism is on display in the street. I wonder how much has been sacrificed in her quest for competitive success.

Clearly, Vivaldi is not screaming from speakers in her living room, nor is the smell of fresh bread steaming from the kitchen. It's cold, quiet and dark in her home, and her child peers out from the polished mansion much like the cat on the fence, well groomed and dressed in finery, but silent and still.

This woman has achieved material success – at least relative to her neighbours on this very street – but has she mastered anything else? Certainly not the art of general conversation. Her flowers may bloom in the garden, but she will probably not know the botanical names, having hired a professional landscaper to choose and plant them for her, if not to water them, or at least to set up an automatic watering system, saving her the trouble of watering them herself. While she may feel like a victor, huddled behind the door, she doesn't act like one, having had her senses and intellect dulled after years of steadfast dedication to the attainment of shiny cars. While her 'success' yells from the front lawn, she is notably silent. Had she used this wealth to take up lessons in oration, or cordon bleu cooking, or the manufacture of plastic boat-sized poodles to decorate her lawn, how much more she could have offered her neighbours on the street.

And these cars, too, probably bring nothing but problems – faulty transmissions and scratches from supermarket trolleys. I think: how much better placed she'd have been if this money had been spent on any number of spontaneous pursuits that would have made her much more entertaining for her friends. It's a tad ho-hum to see the rich in matching navy sedans with medals on the front, mere replicas, when this money could have been spent on all sorts of outrageous endeavours.

Geoffrey Miller, a professor of evolutionary psychology, poses the following question: In our consumer culture, what sort of behavioural traits are we most likely to find in others? In *Spent: Sex, Evolution, and Consumer Behavior*, Miller identifies the prevailing trait, unfortunately, as narcissism, which is a pattern of self-centred, egotistical behaviour that combines an intense need for admiration from others with a lack of empathy for others. Narcissists, according to Miller, view themselves as stars in their own life stories, protagonists in their own epics, with everyone else a minor character. 'They're like bloggers that way,' he adds. 'They talk about their lives, careers, and families as if nobody else were in the picture.'

The woman is, according to evolutionary psychology, most likely engaging in 'narcissistic self-stimulation' by using social-display products that are expensive. She is sending 'fake fitness indicators' to signal her wealth, status and taste. The problem with relying on fake fitness indicators, such as luxury cars, jewellery, handbags and the like, is that they're expensive to acquire, onerous to maintain and, according to evolutionary psychologists, pretty hopeless at conveying the biological traits that we humans seek in others anyway – traits like physical attractiveness, physical health, mental health, intelligence and a captivating personality. 'Consumerism's dirty little secret,' argues Miller, 'is that we do a rather good job of assessing such traits through ordinary human conversation, such that the trait-displaying goods and services we work so hard to buy are largely redundant, and sometimes counterproductive.' According to Miller, over thousands of years of human evolution, we've become pretty adept at summing up others; we're pretty darn good at gauging another's intelligence, kindness, conscientiousness, open-mindedness, physical fitness and attractiveness.

Although we like to think that we can deceive others with our branded clothing, our sports car, our debt-ridden, overly ornamented house, our diamond-encrusted watch or our plastic surgery, most people either don't notice, or find these ostentatious displays of wealth and status irritating. 'This raises the question,' writes Miller, 'why do we waste so much time, energy, and money on consumerist trait displays?' As he notes, when the majority of these fake signalling devices are counterproductive – which they are if they come at the expense of cultivating other qualities, traits such as intelligence, physical health and agreeableness – then we're most likely worse off. If you take a moment to think about it, what do you most admire in your best friend? Is it their sunglasses, their boat or their shiny shoes? Or is it some intangible human quality that you hesitate to name, almost like a colour or energy of the human spirit that defies categorization?

As the American environmental scientist Donella Meadows once said, 'People don't need enormous cars; they need admiration and respect. They don't need a constant stream of new clothes; they need to feel that others consider them to be attractive, and they need excitement and variety and beauty. People don't need electronic entertainment; they need something interesting to occupy their minds and emotions. And so forth. Trying to fill real but nonmaterial needs – for identity, community, self-esteem, challenge, love, joy – with material things is to set up an unquenchable appetite for false solutions to never-satisfied longings. A society that allows itself to admit and articulate its nonmaterial human needs, and to find nonmaterial ways to satisfy them, would require much lower material and energy throughputs and would provide much higher levels of human fulfilment.'

CHAPTER 19

Kilkenny, Ireland

'My destination is no longer a place, rather a new way of seeing.'

—Marcel Proust

A STOCK TRADER ONCE told me that successful trading wasn't about the first trade you made. A good trader doesn't care so much care about the initial trade-in, the decision to hit the trigger, to buy or sell. It's what happens next that matters. It's how you negotiate the next part, how well you ride the oncoming wave, and how successfully you exit that matters most. Like life, I think that it wouldn't really matter whether we had set up in Ecuador, Argentina, or even Ireland for that matter; what would matter was how we responded to problems once that initial decision had been made. It could be said that the decisions we often regard as 'big', the decisions that we spend months or sometimes even years deliberating, are not as important as the smaller ones made along the way, such as how we spend our time, the activities we engage in, the people we meet, the food we eat, whether we watch six hours of television or cultivate a garden bed. It's the smaller decisions that make the difference, much like the minor moments in a play guide the underlying plot.

I've always been fascinated by people who one day decide to change. They grab their suitcase, pack up the house, step outside and lock the door. How does that happen? Like most things, it's gradual. Change is always slow, like the time it takes for a tree to reach maturity. We plant it and wish that it could become tall, thick-limbed and full-bodied, but we know that time must pass before we see any visible signs of change.

We're driving through the back streets of Kilkenny, Ireland, past grey buildings edged by a grey skyline. Our children are perched in the back of the hired van, looking out at what could be our new home. We are meeting the real estate agent mid-morning, to view a historic property, Kilfane House, which has fallen into disrepair. We think that this could be it, our place, that which we like to call 'Flourish'. It could be our philosophical commune, the place we have been seeking all along. The children are quiet as though preparing themselves for their new fate.

I am always perplexed by the instinct, or gut reaction, that drives our destiny – where does it come from? Why do we decide to buy one house over another, or choose this partner over another, or this career, or that holiday destination? Our random choices become an electric power grid hooking up various parts of our lives. Yet we rarely spend time considering what power source is connecting our choices, creating this interconnected system.

A steady December drizzle is falling, and in the sparse light we can see up ahead a colossal structure, surrounded by verdant parkland. 'That's it,' I say, softly. Its granite blocks have darkened over the years, from rain, wind and frost, and its gloomy pallor in the surrounding half-light gives it an ominous look. It seems to watch us as we edge over the hill towards it, the interior of the car dimming as we are eclipsed by its shadow.

The children are motionless in their seats, looking out. 'It's spooky,' says one. 'It's grand,' I reply quickly. 'It's magnificent . . . just a little run-down.'

'I don't want to get out,' says another, huddled close to the window.

When we want to change who we are, we feel we should be able to make it happen. We just need to write it down, add in the goals, and muster the motivation and discipline to do it. Why can't we just enforce a new way of being?

The British philosopher Derek Parfit rose to fame with his ideas on personal identity – about what makes us uniquely us, and what makes us no longer us. Parfit explained his ideas on identity by means of thought experiments, which are popular tools philosophers use to tackle unconventional ideas.

One such thought experiment that Parfit referred to was conceived by American philosopher Sydney Shoemaker. Imagine two men, a Mr Brown and a Mr Robinson, writes Shoemaker. Both men had been operated on for brain tumours, and brain extractions had been performed on both of them. 'At the end of the operation, however, the assistant inadvertently put Brown's brain in Robinson's head, and Robinson's brain in Brown's head,' writes Shoemaker. 'One of these men immediately dies, but the other, the one with Robinson's body and Brown's brain, eventually regains consciousness. Let us call the latter "Brownson",' Shoemaker continues. 'Upon regaining consciousness, Brownson exhibits great shock and surprise at the appearance of his body. Then, upon seeing Brown's body, he exclaims incredulously "That's me lying there!" Pointing to himself, he says "This isn't my body; the one over there is!" When asked his name, he automatically replies, "Brown". He recognizes Brown's wife and family (whom Robinson had never met), and is able to describe in detail events in Brown's life, always describing them as events in his own life. Of Robinson's past life, he evinces no knowledge at all. Over a period of time, he is observed to display all the personality traits, mannerisms, interests, likes and dislikes, and so on, that had previously characterized Brown, and to act and talk in ways completely alien to the old Robinson.'

Of course, most of us would agree that the owner of the body is Brown, even though it looks like Robinson. That's because he has Brown's personality and character, his humour, his way of speaking, and his memories – and that's what makes him Brown. Parfit argues that personal identity is nothing other than 'psychological continuity', including memories, personality traits and interests.

To change personal identity, according to Parfit, we need to change our memories, our character, our interests. Let's say that you go to a plastic surgeon and ask them to fundamentally alter the look of your face. You exit the building into the blinding sunshine with a raised nose, chiselled cheekbones and an extended jawline. Are you now a different person? Parfit would say no, you're just the same person but with an altered face. Personal identity is the sum total of your memories of your childhood days fighting with your sister over a plastic frog, almost drowning in the backyard dam the day you graduated from law school, or when you got fired from your job. Your personal identity cannot be so easily shifted by surface changes – a new haircut, an altered style of dress, a new job, even a surgically chiselled face.

It's why people struggle to become someone new. 'I want to become an artist,' they declare, and then wonder why it just doesn't feel real, why it doesn't feel right. It's where the 'imposter syndrome' concept comes from, this idea that you are being a fraud trying to take on new interests, that the real self is hiding under the mask, fretful of being identified. 'How can I go from me now to the me when I am an artist?' they ask. Well, change is simply a matter of degree.

Parfit explains it more clearly. 'Imagine,' he writes, 'that Derek Parfit is being gradually transformed molecule by molecule into Greta Garbo. At the beginning of this whole process there's Derek Parfit, then at the end of the whole process it's really clear that Derek Parfit no longer exists. Derek Parfit is gone. Now there's Greta Garbo. Now, the key question is this: At what point along this transformation did the change take place? When did Derek cease to exist and when did Greta come to exist? If you just have to reflect on this question for a while, immediately it becomes clear that there couldn't be some single point – there couldn't be a single day, say – in which Derek stops existing and Greta starts existing. What you're seeing is some kind of gradual process where, as this person becomes more and more and more different from the Derek that we know now, it becomes less and less right to say that he's Derek at all and more and more right to say that he is gone and a completely other person has come into existence.'

The good news is that personal identity is not static, it is continually changing. But you can't become someone new overnight, just as Derek Parfit can't magically become Greta Garbo in an instant. It takes time, and it is a process of moving in the direction of Greta molecule by molecule, becoming more Greta as each year passes.

What can we take from this? For starters, we can learn that we can change who we are, but it'll just take time – time to rack up new memories and new experiences, like the adjustments that Derek made in his transformation into Greta. The person who wishes to become the artist must go about making 'artist-like' memories of going to art classes, reading art books, going to museums and art parties, making arty friends and doing less of what they did before. To undergo fundamental change, the person who wants to go from who they are to who they want to become must create some 'lived-in' experiences, real memories built up over time.

Inside the Georgian mansion, I wander around with the children, weaving between grand reception rooms to a drawing room, its double sash windows opening to a garden, and behind it a light-filled library. The walls are hacked, sliced through, as if paintings and fixtures have been ripped off in a hasty exit. Now, devoid of furnishings, the rooms sit in a state of quiet expectation. Depending upon the new owner, the rooms could be converted into an elaborate family home, or a hotel, or perhaps the outside fertile fields could be transformed into farmland. But the estate is unlikely to become a theme park or a basketball stadium. Its structure, already set down in granite blocks, and its location, within rural Ireland, limit its possibilities.

On the first floor there are eight bedrooms and four bathrooms, while the second floor, as described by the real-estate pamphlet which we were hastily handed upon arrival, has 'many possibilities in terms of additional bedrooms, games room, office, gym or an apartment'. The agent, too, lists the possibilities – but turning the upstairs rooms into a skating rink or luxury department store is not among them. I think, are we too, like rooms in a house, limited to finite possibilities? Based on your childhood history, your adolescent years, your working history, you only have so many rooms – and when you wander around the potentiality of the self, looking for opportunities for change – there's only so much you can do. Of course, with considerable work, the drawing room could be transformed into a magnificent kitchen, but it's certainly not going to be transformed into a bowling alley.

In *The Nature of Explanation*, the philosopher Kenneth Craik introduced the term 'mental model' to explain how our mind constructs models of reality that we use to make decisions about our future. To put it simply, the theories we carry in our heads affect our perception of the world and how we treat it. If our mental model were compared to a house, we only have so many rooms, and we envisage how these rooms could one day be utilized on the basis of our capabilities. Not all of us, for instance, envisage a future where we will be ruling the country, or where we will be the lead ballerina in a production of *Swan Lake*. Rather, we may nurse a dream of living in a cabin in the Alps or of leading a research team into Antarctica. It all hinges on our mental construction of the world, or on that which houses the self.

Every morning Carl Jung sketched a circular drawing, or mandala, in his notebook. The Swiss psychiatrist and psychoanalyst had parted ways with Sigmund Freud, and his nerves were frayed. Jung's first mandala, which he drew in 1916, seemed to him to represent his psychic state at that time. And so, the following day, and for 27 days thereafter, Jung set his pencil to the page and drew another mandala. Rather irritated by a letter he had received, Jung noticed that his mandala drawing that day was off balance and out of symmetry, leading him to suspect that the mandala and his inner state were somehow attuned. 'With the help of these drawings I could observe my psychic transformations from day to day,' he writes. 'My mandalas were cryptograms . . . in which I saw the self – that is, my whole being – actively at work.' The mandala is a symbol of completeness, wholeness and perfection, since all points on the mandala are equidistant from the centre. In Sanskrit, 'mandala' means 'circle' – and in Hinduism and Buddhism the mandala represents the universe or cosmos. Mandalas are found in nature – in the lotus flower, shells, apples, snowflakes and spiders' webs.

For many years the psychiatrist had employed the craft of writing to express his inner life and to channel a nagging sense of meaninglessness that haunted him. However, in 1922, he suddenly realized that 'paper and ink did not seem "real" enough anymore'. Jung felt that he needed something more concrete to work with. So, having always been drawn to the scenic charm of the upper lake at Zurich, he purchased old church land there and set out to build a stone complex to house his inner being. 'That was the beginning of the "Tower", the house which I built for myself at Bollingen,' he wrote. In the early days of building his tower, Jung lived without electricity and running water. He tended to the fireplace and stove himself, and he pumped water from the well, chopped wood and washed his clothes in a tub by the lake. In the evenings he lit oil lamps and walked on the Tower's stone floors. 'There is nothing to disturb the dead,' he exclaimed, 'neither electric light nor telephone.' If a man of the sixteenth century were to move into the house, he gleefully declared, only the kerosene lamp and the matches would be new to him. 'Otherwise, he would know his way around without difficulty.'

Interestingly, in building his home – first the round house, or 'dwelling tower', constructed in 1923, to which a central structure and tower-like annex were added in 1927, followed by a tower-annex extension in 1931 – Jung felt as if he were being reborn in stone. 'At Bollingen,' he cried, 'I am in the midst of my true life, I am most deeply myself.' While Jung admitted that simple living was difficult, he also believed that it was solace for the soul. 'Silence surrounds me almost audibly, and I live in modest harmony with nature,' he wrote. 'Creativity and play are close together.'

Forced to live on limited resources – and using only the materials available to him in his immediate time and place – Jung found himself less inclined to fantasize about some future time when life would be somehow sweeter and opportunities more plentiful. He wrote that there is so much flurry and haste, that 'we live more in the future and its chimerical promises of a golden age than in the present. We no longer live on what we have, but on promises, no longer in the light of the present day, but in the darkness of the future, which, we expect, will at last bring the proper sunrise.' Being outside in the open air, building with his hands, cooking complicated stews in an enormous pot, and scrubbing himself down with a hard brush each morning somehow opened up a world for Jung that had been temporarily buried in his pursuit of the intellectual life.

'We rush impetuously into novelty, driven by a mounting sense of insufficiency, dissatisfaction and restlessness . . . We refuse to recognize that everything better is purchased at the price of something worse.' When asked what clinical illnesses the majority of his patients suffered from, Jung replied that about a third of them weren't suffering from anything at all; if anything, he thought, they were blighted by an aimlessness, or lack of meaning in life – mostly because they didn't know how to live. It was Jung's mission in life, too, it seems, to figure this one out.

———

The real estate agent greets us briskly, before tracking a businessman into the galley kitchen. I think about Jung's idea of the simple life – using one's hands to build or renovate a house, to cook simple stews, to live in modest harmony with nature. But the children, at this moment, have disappeared into the ceiling caverns and I can hear their joyous cries echoing off walls. Why is the simple life so difficult? Why does the modern age drag us into the need to pursue material wealth, or social power and influence? Why can't we pursue simplicity with the same relish with which we seek a promotion at work or the acquisition of a fancy house by the ocean? The French sociologist Pierre Bourdieu believes that we rely on forms of capital to navigate our way in the world – cultural, economic and social capital. We may embark on a course of study to increase our cultural capital (knowledge and skills obtained through education) or a better-paid job to increase our economic capital (material wealth), or we may attend a networking party in the sheer hope of boosting our social capital (social network). Finally, we may dedicate our time to working out at the gym to augment our body capital. So where does the simple life fit into this matrix? Learning to make furniture, or sew one's own clothes, or create the perfect garden is not listed on Bourdieu's map that we humans must navigate; it's a path that fewer tread.

Yet the simple life can offer as much as, if not more than, the other forms of capital – we can learn about ourselves and the world, and then use this knowledge to enlighten our everyday world. For want of a better title, we could call it poetic capital, the capital that makes life more beautiful. There's no guarantee that a degree in accounting, a pay rise or a windfall is going to do as much, but simple pursuits can lead to an improved quality of life. What other activities in life could be classified as poetic capital? Might such activities include the skill of learning a new sport, cultivating knowledge in music, or engaging in some other craft?

A little deflated by the real estate agent's lack of interest, I have a sagging feeling that this is not going to be the home of 'Flourish' after all. But then it suddenly dawns on me that Flourish is not tangible – it's not a dream house or a dream life somewhere in the future; rather, it's our habits and activities and mindset in the day-to-day. It's our slow progress towards realizing our unique gift to the world, whatever that happens to be at the time, which is forever subject to change, much like the weather.

We take some time to wander along the historic woodland paths and hidden fern trails, and it's here that I ponder the Irish gardener and writer Mary Reynolds, who decided one day, after 20 years of landscape gardening, that she could no longer design pretty gardens, which she suddenly viewed as controlled and manipulated spaces, poor versions of the real deal. 'Somehow, somewhere along the way, gardens had become dead zones,' she writes in *The Garden Awakening*. Our need to control and defeat our gardens is obvious from the list of tools required to attack them – mowers, blowers, chainsaws, hedge trimmers, chemicals and pesticides. Gardening, she writes, had become an ongoing effort to 'stop things that wanted to grow from growing'.

In her new definition of gardening, Reynolds realized that she had to understand how to work with nature's energy rather than against it. 'The land had its own intentions. Nature had its own ideas about design and I had to learn what they were,' she writes. Reynolds' forest gardening is a method of gardening that emulates the tiered structure of natural woodland – upper-canopy trees, like nut trees, overshadowing mid-sized fruit trees; shrubs like berries and plants shading herbs and medicinal plants; edible, nitrogen-fixing plants, microorganisms and fruiting fungi interspersed with climbers and vines. 'If we invite Nature to express her true self in these spaces and then work to heal the land and bring it back into balance, something magical happens,' writes Reynolds. 'Nature will embrace you in ways that most people have not experienced for many, many years. A magical doorway opens for us.'

A forest garden, according to Reynolds, is what nature intended, and so the technique of 'forest gardening' is to work with nature – not against it – to create an environment that's self-sustaining, with minimal need for human interference. But when we think about our own garden, or the type of garden we'd like to own one day, few of us think about starting a forest. Mostly, we settle on the merits of a nice, polite lawn, some well-maintained hedges and a row of eternally budding roses. It is not normal, we believe, to dream of creating a mossy woodland in suburbia, a garden screaming with vines, nut trees and medicinal plants.

Working with nature seems to have been Reynolds' motto, and it equally applies to us when thinking about our life's purpose. It brings to mind questions such as: How can I leverage that which is most natural to me? How can I prosper with minimum interference? Rather than chiselling myself into a new look or a new way of being, how can the 'unique me' be drawn out and celebrated? Rather than trying to be someone else, how can you become your best self?

On five acres of ground outside New York City, the flower enthusiast Helena Rutherfurd Ely also set to work on her creation, but for her it was a cottage garden. Gardening inspired Ely so much that she wrote three books on the topic, including *A Woman's Hardy Garden* (1903), which sold 40,000 copies. 'I would make the strongest plea in favour of a garden to all those who are so fortunate as to possess any land at all,' she writes. 'The relaxation from care and toil and the benefit to health are great, beyond belief . . . If you can snatch a few minutes in early morning or later afternoon, to spend among the plants, life takes on a new aspect, health is improved, care is dissipated, and you get nearer to Nature.'

Ely's advice in starting a garden could aptly be applied to any new endeavour in life, from starting a new business to taking up the piano for the first time. 'In starting a garden, the first question, of course, is where to plant,' Ely muses. 'If you are a beginner in the art, and the place is new and large, go to a good landscape gardener and let him give advice and make you a plan. But don't follow it; at least not at once, nor all at one time. Live there for a while, until you yourself begin to feel what you want, and where you want it. See all the gardens and places you can, and then, when you know what you want, or think you do, start in.' Her sound advice is: get advice, make a plan, immerse yourself in it by travelling and visiting places, and most importantly, give yourself time so that nature can take its course.

And, of course, expect bumps in the road because setbacks are inevitable. For Ely, weeds, insects, bugs and foul weather should be seen as challenges to be overcome, rather like the opposition in a sporting match. 'Did everything planted grow and flourish, gardening would be too tame,' she writes. 'Patience and perseverance are traits necessary to the gardener. If a set of plants die, or do not flourish this year, try them again next season, under different conditions, until the difficulties are overcome.'

CHAPTER 20

Back Home

'Our own life has to be our message.'

—Thich Nhat Hanh

W E MOVE OUR STORE *poet* to a new home in a nineteenth-century church in Hobart, a few hundred metres from the old store. In the auditorium-sized space under Gothic rafters we unpack French antiques, books, magazines, fashion, and the remains of 26,000 canisters of tea.

Outside, the wind and rain blow, but the Victorian Gothic church, erected in 1890, faces the onslaught with detachment. Its vast brick back fends off the wind as rain clatters upon its oversized pitched roof. Loose upon the footpath at the front, a steel-legged sign jitters in the subarctic air. On its face it reads: 'Museum of Art & Philosophy'. It is *poet*'s latest manifestation – a bookstore, but this time complemented by an art space.

In semi-darkness, I set myself up in the nave of the church in front of a wheel-shaped stained-glass window. My French wicker desk, teeming with no fewer than 50 books, basks in the blues, reds and greens of intermittent sunlight refracting through the window's hexagram, a Star of David.

In its former days, the church was a branch of the Missions to Seamen, an English association with a presence in every port of the old British Empire, providing care for visiting sailors, and redirecting them, more or less, from the many temptations that were an inherent part of shore life. In this capacity, the church offered good writing facilities, as well as refreshments and games. Back in the day, it also housed a splendid library. Beyond its windows – six along one side and five along the other – was the disease- and effluent-ridden slum of Hobart's Wapping district, where former London convict Isaac 'Ikey' Solomon – the trainer of pickpockets and the inspiration for the shady character Fagin in Charles Dickens' novel *Oliver Twist* – set up shop as a tobacconist.

For Aristotle, the Greek word *'eudaimonia'* – often translated as 'flourishing' – is comprised of two parts: 'eu-', meaning 'well', and 'daimon', meaning 'divinity' or 'spirit'. To flourish is to surpass the material dimension. We are rational creatures who can direct the course of our lives, thought Aristotle, and we have the power to let loose a chain reaction of events, or set in motion a series of happenings that can remake us. To live well and to flourish, according to Aristotle, is to recognize and take control of this rare ability.

The Dutch artist Vincent van Gogh didn't always know he was going to become an artist. He wasn't one of those people who claim, 'Oh yes, I was painting by age two – I always knew I wanted to paint.' For van Gogh, the journey to self-actualization – or, as Nietzsche describes it, the 'violent descent into the pit of one's being' – was torturous. He was tormented, riddled with doubt, confused, and maddened by something he couldn't quite define. He felt like a caged bird, banging his head against the bars. He was aware that there was something within him, and that there was something that he must do – but what was it?

By the time he was 26, van Gogh had tried over a dozen jobs, including art dealer, teacher, bookseller. He then, like his father had done before him, turned to missionary work. In search of that elusive 'divinity' or 'spirit' of *eudaimonia*, van Gogh took up work as a pastor in a poor coal-mining village in Belgium, in the Borinage. 'It's a sombre place, and at first sight everything around it has something dismal and deathly about it,' he wrote to his brother, Theo.

Although he worked tirelessly as a pastor, sacrificing his health in his mission to help others, van Gogh's incessant questioning of his purpose in life was, to his dismay, unrelenting. And constantly shifting and changing his mind, trying this and quitting that, was starting to get to him. 'How many things have been discussed,' he asked Theo rhetorically in a letter, 'that later prove to be impracticable.'

Meanwhile, in the quiet moments away from work, he was drawing with his pencil. He started imitating the works of other artists. And during the winter of 1880, he set out on foot for Courrières, a town over the French border, some 70 kilometres away. He had heard that the French naturalist painter Jules Breton, a native of the town, had moved back. As to why he walked through rain and freezing wind to get there, reduced to sleeping in haystacks at night, he was not exactly sure. 'Perhaps I went involuntarily,' he told Theo, admitting, 'I can't exactly say why.' Undoubtedly, van Gogh was 'following his bliss', and the pilgrimage to Courrières was a symbolic journey – an awakening, or metamorphosis, into a new self. Upon arriving there, he circled Breton's studio, but lacked the courage to enter and introduce himself. He simply wandered around the town for a bit, before promptly heading back home. He didn't need to meet Breton. He didn't need to enter his studio and sit down with the master painter. Nor did he need to organize any form of work with him. Because van Gogh, for the first time in his life, had started walking his own path.

'Wait, perhaps someday you will see that I too am an artist,' he wrote to Theo in his last letter from the Borinage in 1880. 'I don't know what I can do, but I hope I shall be able to make some drawings with something human in them . . . The path is narrow, the door is narrow, and there are few who find it.'

Like van Gogh, the French Post-Impressionist artist Paul Gauguin experienced a metamorphosis of self in middle age. He had enlisted in the French navy, and he'd worked as a stockbroker and as a businessman. Painting was not his full-time occupation until he was well into his mid-thirties. When van Gogh, prompted by his art-dealer brother Theo, urged Gauguin to join him in his rented house in Arles in the south of France – the 'Yellow House' at 2 Place Lamartine – Gauguin was intrigued enough to do so.

In advance of Gauguin's arrival at the Yellow House, the two newly-minted painters exchanged self-portraits, a revealing insight into how the 35-year-old Dutchman and the 40-year-old Frenchman embraced their 'transcendence' into their new roles. Gauguin signed his name in the bottom corner of his portrait, and directly above it he painted in brushstrokes the caption 'Les Misérables', in reference to Victor Hugo's novel. In a letter to van Gogh (a perhaps even more revealing insight into his 'ideal' self), Gauguin described how the novel's hero, Jean Valjean, had been his source of inspiration: 'The face of a bandit like Jean Valjean, strong and badly dressed, who has a nobleness and gentleness hidden within. Passionate blood suffuses the face as it does a creature in rut, and the eyes are enveloped by tones as red as the fire of a forge, which indicate the inspiration like molten lava which fills the soul of painters such as us.' For Gauguin, his ideal self was made palpable upon canvas, as the indefatigable artist, raggedly dressed, buffeted by his creative passion as hot as molten lava, a passion so great it might destroy him.

In turn, van Gogh's self-portrait was sent to Gauguin in advance of the latter's arrival in Arles. It, too, revealed his evolving self, for in it, van Gogh painted himself as a Japanese monk: 'a simple bonze worshipping the eternal Buddha,' he wrote. The Yellow House, van Gogh fantasized from the Café de la Gare in Arles, would become a monastic community of artists devoted to the service of art. Here, they would paint, study and flourish in the solitary south, away from the distractions of ordinary life. 'I have it all planned,' he wrote. 'I really do want to make it – an artist's house.'

In its four rented rooms, van Gogh envisaged artists of the future living an austere but productive life, committed to the single pursuit of painting. It was a religion of the arts, a faith based on aesthetics.

Despite his working period being limited to the ten years preceding his death at 37, van Gogh was prolific. He created over 900 pieces, including paintings, drawings and sketches, working at the eye-wateringly fast rate of one artwork every 36 hours. We humans can be astonishingly productive when we find what it is in life that gives us purpose.

Whenever van Gogh left the cloistered rooms of the Yellow House – at times he did not speak to anyone for days – to take a walk in Arles in order to sketch and paint, he presented as a solitary figure in a long smock and a cheap straw hat decorated with blue or yellow ribbons, a pipe set between his teeth. But van Gogh's new self was not immune to ridicule: local youths would taunt him and throw cabbage stalks at him. We must remember that eight years prior to this period, van Gogh was working as a pastor in Belgium, and since then, his concept of self had indeed undergone a sizeable overhaul. On these walks, he would sometimes be joined by Gauguin, wearing, in his similarly new-found role as full-time artist, the costume of a Breton sailor, complete with jersey, beret and clogs.

Just as celebrities or entertainers may shape the evolving self of a teenager today, literary greats did much the same in the nineteenth century. It was the best-selling writer Pierre Loti who helped shape Gauguin's new identity. Loti's *My Brother Yves*, written in 1883, was a semi-autobiographical tale about a friendship between French naval officer Loti and a hard-drinking Breton sailor during the late 1800s. Its descriptions of Breton seafaring life had stuck a chord with Gauguin's sense of self, which had been brewing ever since his early days in the navy. Loti's books were about escaping from banal, hackneyed European life to exotic destinations like Tahiti and Japan, and his works, including *An Iceland Fisherman*, provided the markings for Gauguin's map of his future life in which, having thrown off his businessman's attire, he took on the costume of a Breton sailor. For van Gogh, Loti's *Madame Chrysanthème* proved equally influential. Involving a romantic fling between a married Japanese woman and a French naval officer, the novel offered insight into

Japanese monastic life. The story must have resonated with the reclusive artist's need for aesthetic flair, for the Yellow House was very much a manifestation of this literary tale.

I'm driving home from work and a bright pink sedan pulls sharply in front of me, the 'P' plate blazoned on its rear. Inside, a young girl flings her pink metal beast through the traffic, and I think, 'Isn't this what youth is all about?' I trail behind her in my silver van – I'm in no hurry – but as I watch her jet ahead, further up the line she slows to a crawl, and then comes to a halt behind big-bellied cars grazing and swaying in the lanes, and, try as she might, she can't get through. 'Ain't that life?' I say to myself. 'We've got all the energy and boldness in the world, but we keep hitting up against the tail of something else. We keep bumping up against reality.'

So much of what we do in life is swayed not just by our vision and goals, but by the obstacles we meet, often involving other people. You might have great ideas and foresight, but you hit up against a lack of money, contacts that disappoint, job interviews that go nowhere, plans that get stymied . . . You're the pink sedan with the energy and will to get ahead, but you keep getting blocked. You know that something better is almost within your reach, yet you do not know how to possibly get there.

The famed mythologist Joseph Campbell said that when we want to get from one place to another in our lives, we first have to overcome an obstacle. That obstacle is not a reason to say that dreaming is hopeless; rather, it is something that should be anticipated, even welcomed, and regarded as a signpost: 'The path ahead is blocked, so I must forge a new one.' Veer off, take the side street, is Campbell's take on it. See obstacles as the impetus to get creative. Praise those who get in your way for making you broaden your horizons. In other words, the obstacles are not forces pushing you off the path, the obstacles *are* the path. As the American politician Frank A. Clark puts it: 'If you can find a path with no obstacles, it probably doesn't lead anywhere.'

At the intersection, still stuck in traffic, I read a sign in a shop window. It's written on a whiteboard, scribbled in messy blue pen by the shop owner and directed towards the passing traffic. The owner changes the message each week, giving residents some pause for thought. This week it reads: 'Every night as I tuck myself into bed at 9 p.m., I whisper to myself, "You're still a rock star!"'

It's true, we all wish we had done more, achieved more. We all wish we had been, or will be, a rock star. The whiteboard message reminds me of the movie *On the Waterfront*, when Terry Malloy laments many of the decisions he made in his life: 'You don't understand! I coulda had class. I coulda been a contender. I coulda been somebody, instead of a bum, which is what I am, let's face it.'

We love our rock stars. We revere the genius. We adore the artist in the prime of life, marvelling at their accomplishments as though they were a divinity, some sort of miracle. But we don't ever line ourselves up against the greats and think, 'Well, you know, one day I will paint like Raphael, or write like Goethe. It'll just take a bit of practice and patience.' If we did, we'd then say to ourselves, 'What nonsense . . . You, paint like Raphael? Are you kidding?' To compare ourselves to the greats feels almost blasphemous.

Nietzsche thinks we separate 'greats' into divine beings to save ourselves from the agony of comparing ourselves with them. We save ourselves the pain of envy. 'To call someone "divine" means "Here we do not have to compete,"' he writes. If they are indeed miracles, they are an 'uncommon accident' or 'grace from above'. It does not hurt our vanity so much to celebrate people who aren't like us.

But what we overlook when we observe the artwork of the great master painters, or anyone who has risen to dazzling heights in their respective field, is the hard work that has been put in over long stretches of time. Nietzsche compares these 'greats' to a mechanical inventor or scholar of history or astronomy whose 'thinking is active in one particular direction', who uses 'everything to that end', who always 'observes eagerly their inner life' and who does 'not tire of rearranging their material'. Genius comes not from innate skill, but from the lessons and talents learned by doing; on the job training, if you will – work.

'The genius, too, does nothing other than to first learn to place stones, then to build, always seeking material, always forming and reforming it. Every human activity is amazingly complicated, not only that of the genius,' writes Nietzsche. But none, he stresses, none is a miracle. As soon as we see the evolution of the artist, the mistakes, the disappointments, the obstacles faced from ill health to poverty, only then does one begin to see that miracles do happen. That we, too, can be a miracle.

This reminds me of an offhand remark made by a radio presenter during the COVID-19 pandemic, a time when many actors left the glamorous city of Los Angeles to move back to their family home to live with their parents, waiting for the wheels of the movie business to turn again. Many of them, fearful of losing their fame during those months away from the spotlight, set up podcasts or took social media shots of themselves for their fans, sitting on their couch with their dog, or in the backyard under an undernourished apple tree. 'You know,' said the radio host, 'they look so un-famous. I mean, under the big lights of LA, they look so glamorous. But at home, they just look so un-famous. I am kind of shocked.' She was being flippant, of course, but underlying her remark was the realization that our modern 'greats' were just ordinary people who'd worked hard and got lucky.

While it's lovely to be admiring of others' achievements, Nietzsche believes that we have it in our power to achieve great feats too. But what you need to remember when setting forth is that, while it's nice to aim for something grand, flourishing takes place in the slow ticking of the everyday.

Many years ago, I watched a documentary on Kurt Cobain, lead singer of the rock band Nirvana, who shot to fame so suddenly that he lost the plot. In an interview about his life, he revealed that he wished to return to the days when the band was just starting out, when they barely had enough to eat, when they were struggling. Through all the glorious moments of being on stage, of being cheered, admired and fawned upon, it was the early days of struggle that Cobain, who tragically ended his own life at just 27, yearned for. The struggling days were his cherished moments. It's somewhat telling that Cobain, the rock star who led the life that many secretly yearn for, turned to a difficult point as his moment of flourishing. This concurs with the view of many philosophers, and with my findings over the past decade of researching this book, that it's the struggle to be who you most want to become that is the essence of flourishing. It's the hiccups and hurdles, the toils and mishaps. And at the end of your life, it's the hardships and conquests that you'll cherish the most. There is no destination.

'The human animal, like others, is adapted to a certain amount of struggle for life, and when by means of great wealth *homo sapiens* can gratify all his whims without effort, the mere absence of effort from his life removes an essential ingredient of happiness,' writes Bertrand Russell in *The Conquest of Happiness*. 'The man who acquires easily things for which he feels only a very moderate desire concludes that the attainment of desire does not bring happiness. If he is of a philosophic disposition, he concludes that human life is essentially wretched, since the man who has all he wants is still unhappy. He forgets that to be without some of the things you want is an indispensable part of happiness.' Indeed, when Cobain could buy whatever his heart desired, and was celebrated for everything he did, or even didn't do, he lost his leap – that seeking drive, which is an indispensable part of happiness. He had it all, so what was left to strive towards? He'd been driving at full pelt on the freeway and abruptly hit a dead end.

To flourish is to struggle to become your ideal self, always shifting, growing, failing, coming up behind obstacles and veering down some unknown street. For Nietzsche, the lot of humankind is to toil, suffer, fail, and fail again; happiness is a rare, fleeting reward once a mountain of struggle has been temporarily surmounted, or an achievement made, but it is rarely encountered on the everyday path. 'You find the burden of life too heavy?' asked Nietzsche. 'Then you must increase the burden of your life.' I must point out here that the 'struggle' I speak of is not the struggle to survive from poverty, war or famine. For many, such great obstacles must be surmounted even before one has the privilege of struggling for self-actualization. Maslow pointed this out in his hierarchy of needs pyramid, with food and shelter being at the base of the pyramid, and self-actualization only coming about when those basic needs had been met.

But struggle also happens in the great swathes of time when nothing seems to be happening, when nothing seems to be going your way. It's the struggle of waiting. And to be fair, it's a skill few of us in the twenty-first century – a time of instant gratification, entertainment and connectivity – possess. We've been accustomed to getting what we want now. Want to travel somewhere? Want to buy something, anything, from around the globe? We learn that plans can all be actioned in an instant. And as the world has sped up, our expectations as to what we can get and how fast we can get it have grown apace. But for those who like to dream – to conjure a future in which they're doing and living the life they've always wanted – often this takes time. 'Waiting is not a very popular attitude,' writes Henri Nouwen in *Waiting for God*. 'Waiting is not something that people think about with great sympathy. In fact, most people consider waiting a waste of time. Perhaps this is because the culture in which we live is basically saying, "Get going. Do something. Show you are able to make a difference. Don't just sit there and wait."'

Anxious types are especially prone to pushing ahead, to being constantly on the move. 'Fearful people have a hard time waiting because when we are afraid, we want to get away from where we are,' writes Nouwen. Perhaps we may view it as the 'flight' component in the amygdala's 'fight or flight' response, the release of those evolutionarily important stress hormones that prepared our ancestors to flee from danger. This anxious need to 'flee' in the modern world can manifest as incessant activity, never-ending to-do lists and constant planning for the future, all of which continue to be derailed, or stunted, in long waiting days when the stars never seem to align. Fear is undoubtedly the strongest human emotion, and, notes Nouwen, 'the more afraid people are, the harder waiting becomes. This is why waiting is such an unpopular attitude for many people.' Rather than taking a seat alongside our inner fears, insecurities and boredom, we move to a different city, or change our career, or even our partner.

When we drove the van around South America, there wasn't a time limit to our trip. But one rule we placed on our travels was that we weren't allowed to plan. That meant that every time I'd conjure up some sort of image of the future – some dream state or idea, some business plan – Zan would remind me that it must wait. Now was not the time to plan. And so I'd turn to the window and watch the fields of Patagonia roll away, putting off the dream in my mind until another moment in time. Now was not the time to plan. My dreams could wait.

Some people successfully work within a state of the unknown, even flourish from it. I think of a friend who doesn't let a state of waiting perturb her – quite the contrary. She is an economist; she writes about a new economic system, painstakingly describing her new system in books. Her system differs from the capitalist mode of resource distribution we've adopted today. She acknowledges that her economic system will not be adopted immediately. Nor will it be adopted in five or even ten years' time. It may never be adopted. But that's not the point. What is of the essence for her is that her theories are 'out there' in the world, that the seed is planted. And one day, when the time is right, her economic theories may suit the nature of the time. Someone, perhaps one hundred years from now, may dust off her books and think, 'You know, this might work.' Her dream state of how the economy could function must find the conditions to support progress. So rather than trying to force change, she understands that she must wait for history to take its course. And in the meantime, she continues to fine-tune her theories.

'Waiting,' according to Nouwen, is 'waiting with a sense of promise.' He continues, 'People who wait have received a promise that allows them to wait. They have received something that is at work in them, like a seed that has started to grow . . . We can only really wait if what we have been waiting for has already begun for us. So waiting is never a movement from nothing to something. It is always a movement from something to something more.'

Although we may feel that nothing is happening, and that our dreams are never going to come true, that we're stuck in doing and living the same life – this isn't actually the case. Because as soon as we have some image of the future, as soon as we glimpse something that inspires us, then something has already shifted in us. Bottom-drawer dreams or New Year's resolutions that sit at the top of our list year after year are an energy source alive within us. And provided that we continue to believe in them, a time will come when, just like my friend's economic theories, the conditions may support progress, and they will be dusted off and embraced. Perhaps one day you will need this dream to get you out of a fix; having it there in the bottom drawer may be your lifesaver.

Of course, waiting can feel passive and lazy because we've been taught to be productive. We think that unless we're getting ready for the task at one hundred miles an hour, then it's never going to happen. But the secret to waiting is to know that if the seed has been planted, then something has begun. 'Active waiting means to be present fully to the moment, in the conviction that something is happening where you are and that you want to be present to it,' writes Nouwen. But it takes a dose of bravery to wait rather than to flee, to sit with your dreams and to nurture them rather than to keep pushing ahead because that's what you've always done. And to realize that, even if your plans don't work out as exactly as you'd planned, there is no grand plan in the end.

I watch the pink sedan up front skate behind a truck momentarily before spotting a gap in the traffic. Elated by the brief opening of space – the opportunity to get ahead – she zips into it with gusto.

Bertrand Russell, to his astonishment, discovered something rather unexpected in the ageing process. The older he got, the happier he got. Now this wasn't something the English philosopher was expecting, especially as ageing is typically accompanied by the diminishment of youthful vitality. Looking into it a little more, Russell pinpointed the root cause of this mysterious happiness that was creeping up on him, and decided that it was due to a diminishing preoccupation with himself.

'Like others who had a Puritan education, I had the habit of meditating on my sins, follies, and shortcomings. I seemed to myself – no doubt justly – a miserable specimen,' he writes. 'Gradually I learned to be indifferent to myself and my deficiencies; I came to centre my attention increasingly upon external objects: the state of the world, various branches of knowledge, individuals for whom I felt affection. External interests, it is true, bring each its own possibility of pain: the world may be plunged in war, knowledge in some direction may be hard to achieve, friends may die. But pains of these kinds do not destroy the essential quality of life, as do those that spring from disgust with self. And every external interest inspires some activity which, so long as the interest remains alive, is a complete preventive of *ennui*. Interest in oneself, on the contrary, leads to no activity of a progressive kind.'

The monk in the monastery may experience a similar fate. By learning to let go of ego and by practising self-denial, the monk fixates utterly on the world around him. Colours are amplified, his senses of touch and smell are heightened. By learning to cut off obsession with self, he will be rewarded. But as Russell discovered, one needn't become a monk to enjoy the fruits of self-denial. Taking an avid interest in external activities will offer comparable rewards.

The Italian-French fashion designer Pierre Cardin by all measures lived an exceptional life. He was another modern-day 'genius', like Kurt Cobain. Cardin built a fashion business that at one point spanned the entire globe, estimating that he dressed upwards of 15 million people. Cardin did not limit himself to fashion, veering into designing furniture, and licensing his brand for sunglasses, ties, even upholstery in cars. An early love of theatre and acting saw him run theatres, supporting young and untested actors such as Gérard Depardieu. For Cardin, the meaning of life was work, and the essence of his happiness was work, but not as most of us comprehend the word. To work was to progress, move forward, struggle, compete; it was a growing up, a growing out; work was 'to be'. 'I work day and night,' he said. 'I'd say that work, for me, is a liberation. I don't know this definition of work because having fun, for me, is work,' he continued. 'I could stop at any time . . . I'm no longer a young man. But I keep working because it's the only reason to be happy in life.'

Unlike Cobain, who stumbled at the finish line of his goal, Cardin didn't ever have 'a goal' in mind, or, at least, if there was ever a goal it was one that forever replenished itself. 'I am always happy with my present, but I am not done,' he reflected. 'I feel that as long as I can do it, why not? It's not dissatisfaction, it's all about going further, like a runner, or a cyclist, or a footballer, or an athlete. In my profession, I like to conquer, to reach the goal, not at all to possess it. That's another thing, possession.'

Tellingly, if there is a goal up ahead, it acts as a mere signpost. There is no end point – merely something to move towards, and sometimes even beyond what he originally thought possible. Cardin sent models down the catwalk of the Great Wall of China at a time when China had minimal contact with the West; in his 'work' he met Nelson Mandela. These activities were not on his list of long-term goals to tick off but arose spontaneously; if a random opportunity appeared to his right, he swung his vehicle into that lane. When documentary filmmakers P. David Ebersole and Todd Hughes turned up at Cardin's flagship store with the unlikely prospect of meeting their design hero and, at most, of getting a photograph of him for their social media page, they offhandedly asked him if he'd be interested in being in a documentary. To their surprise, the 97-year-old replied, 'OK, let's go.'

If there was a grand plan lurking behind all of this, what was it? Cardin replied: 'Well, to fulfil my life, to know that we can be happy while working, while creating . . . As far as I'm concerned, I don't see myself stopping. To wait for what, the end of my life to come? To wait for the day to come? In the end, if we were to think of death all the time, why live?' So, no, it was not hedonism driving him, but a love and zest for life. Cardin surrounded himself with his passions, which, like big pillows, softened the harsh edges of life. How could he be unhappy in a room coloured in every hue he loved? 'I just try to do what gives me pleasure and sometimes I succeed, sometimes not.'

At the end of his life, Cardin purchased a glorious house in the ancient city of Houdan, the house of his dreams, 40 minutes from Paris. He fell in love with it almost instantly. 'Here it is, the house of dreams,' he sang. Interestingly, the 'prize' mansion came at the end of his life. Why not earlier? Because Cardin was too busy flourishing.

Indeed, the importance of living in the present is at the heart of the thinking of ancient philosophers. Don't always look for what you don't have or hope for things to be different to what they are now. 'Do every act of your life as though it were the very last act of your life,' advises the Roman emperor and Stoic philosopher Marcus Aurelius. But how does one reconcile living in the present with the ongoing battle to 'become' – to project outwards towards some future point of self-actualization? The answer is not to 'project out', but, instead, to manifest that condition of becoming in the very present, by doing. The question then becomes not 'How would I ideally like my life to pan out?' but, 'How can I turn my present reality into what I dream?' This is not to push the future outwards, but to bring it into the present. In doing so, you take your dreams and move them into the living room, place them on the coffee table and say: 'How do I take these dreams and release them into the present day?'

We finally buy a property, a stone house in a forest of oversized silver gum trees. It has a view of the river. It's the first house we've owned and it feels eerily permanent – there's relief, but also sheer terror. And so the suitcases remain partially unpacked for months, the walls stay unmarked, and when furniture is added, it's randomly placed as though the removalist truck is due to return at any moment.

But eventually, we settle, and then immediately the question becomes, what next? So we think about extending it on one side, and many ideas are passed about. The new roof of the extension could be gabled, or even peaked in the haunting American Gothic style. There is room to go both frontwards, closer to the view, perhaps with a glassed living-room space complete with a leaning chair next to an open fire, and backwards, higher on the banks – a couple of bedrooms, another bathroom. As a result, we live with this flat piece of dirt for many years – a vacant space that wistfully houses our dreams – and from the kitchen windowpane above the sink, when washing dishes or cutting food, I look at this patch of dirt that becomes home to wild tangled hoses, weeds and empty pot plants. My immediate view is indeed marked by this dream patch, forever in sight, forever lifeless and dormant.

One day we coax a designer in, and then a builder, and we feverishly reveal our dreams of expanding this way and that, not forgetting the extra bathroom and the glassed sitting area overlooking the river view. Like jack jumper ants we dash across the dirt patch, and then it hits. Reality. The bill. It will cost too much for this construction – too much to bear. And so it is that this vacant space forever in our line of view turns from an Aladdin's dream palace to a dirt patch. From dream to reality.

It's from here that things get interesting. We enquire about the cost of walling it in, Tuscan style, and it is well within our reach. And furthermore, it can be done almost immediately. We find a sandstone fountain. And then we plant ivy – and within months the view from the window turns into a fairy-tale oasis, something that we hadn't envisaged before in our wildest imagination.

And that's the trouble with erecting palaces in your mind: you can overlook the magic garden that's staring you right in the face.

Villena, Spain

'Travel can be a kind of monasticism on the move: On the road, we often live more simply, with no more possessions than we can carry, and surrendering ourselves to chance.'

—Pico Iyer

I T HITS: THE RESTLESSNESS. The unease. And within months, the house is packed up, the children are in the van, and we're driving towards the airport in the darkness.

The safety of our home in the Tasmanian forest has been left for something I can't even envisage. We are headed to Villena, a historic town in Spain some 17,300 kilometres away, a walled city under the shadow of the Atalaya Castle.

As the taxi driver tracks the long, winding path out of our property, I sense it – a loss. When we return, I know we won't be the same people who left.

To change, to uproot, is an exercise in destruction. You throw out, shut down, and the destruction is unsettling. You can't just walk out of your life. You have to put a torch to some parts of it first. It's a dismantling of the old self, to be sure.

We closed *poet*, our business, and sold its home, a nineteenth-century church in Hobart. Twelve tonnes of tea, books, French antiques and paintings were moved, sold, given away or left on the sidewalk for neighbours to drag across the street and up to their apartments. I gave our cat to an acquaintance, and as we drove off in our car, I watched it squirm in terror in the arms of its new owner, my eyes flooding with tears, my heart sick with sorrow. Our ducks, which trusted us like family, were put in boxes and taken to a dairy farm to live. Bags of clothes and toys – memories of years living in Tasmania – were left piled in an alleyway next to a charity store. It's a death, there's no denying it. Change is painful.

But when you've been summoned, called to your own adventure, you must make a decision – do I dare? When you take up the challenge to try something new, whether that's to change jobs, or move house, or even country, or whatever it is that is beckoning you, then security will be lost, at least for a while.

Change is unsettling for the human brain, and it will put up a mighty fight against it. The brain wants the world to be familiar and predictable. The brain wants to know precisely what you'll be doing each morning, the mind seamlessly skating across tracks of habits laid down over the years. Deciding to throw out your business, and with it your cat, ducks and possessions, and to pack away, lock up and say goodbye to the confused faces of friends and family puts the mind into a spin to say the least. 'Stop! Find safety!' it will scream. 'Do whatever you can to get back to where you were!' When the mind looks into the future and sees nothing – that, indeed, can be nothing short of terrifying.

What are thinkers from Aristotle to Campbell referring to when they prompt us to follow our bliss? Put briefly, they are talking about our unique quest to find fulfilment. 'There's nothing you can do that's more important than being fulfilled . . . It is the fulfilment of that which is potential in each of us. Questing for it is not an ego trip; it is an adventure to bring into fulfilment your gift to the world, which is yourself,' writes Campbell.

So, what did I discover on my journey over the past 15 years? If I was looking for an answer, for the meaning of it all, what did I learn about flourishing? I learned that it is not a place you can find on a map. You don't enter a town called 'Flourish' and realize that you've made it. Nor is flourish an idea or a concept that you'll suddenly discover on the internet, or when walking in the park at dusk. Your mind is not going to figure out how to flourish one quiet Sunday evening and from then on everything will work out for you. I'm sorry, but a life's path is not linear; nothing in life is ever straight.

Rather, much like the ever-expanding universe – which has neither a centre from which it starts, nor an outer edge towards which it expands – flourishing is an ever-evolving process. Within this state of constant flux, all you can do is push the boundaries, and this, indeed, is what you *must* do. To respond to the call to your adventure is to throw caution to the wind, to step forth, to take chances, and to realize that there's no end point, no destination, no moment where you can put your feet up and know that everything is secure. For us as creatures of the universe, to flourish is an ongoing process of growth where sometimes you fall back upon yourself, but then you pick up the pieces and move forward again.

Whatever you might think, 'flourish' is not a massive bank balance, nor is it a shiny black car or a house that's fancier than your neighbour's. Flourish is not fame, which requires the acknowledged consent of others. Instead, it is a personal journey that doesn't require other people's approval. At the final hour, it's not glittering objects or piles of money that you'll turn to – it's memories, journeys, friendships, love, and the knowledge that you've forged your own path, wherever it may have led you.

SUGGESTED READING

PHILOSOPHY

Arendt, H. (2018), *The Human Condition*, United States: The University of Chicago Press.

Aurelius, M. (2015), *Meditations*, London: Penguin Books.

Baudrillard, J. (2005), *The System of Objects*, London: Verso Books.

Campbell, J. (2004), *Pathways to Bliss: Mythology and Personal Transformation*, Novato, CA: New World Library.

Campbell, J. & Moyers, B. (1991), *The Power of Myth*, New York: Bantam Doubleday Dell Publishing Group Inc.

Camus, A. (2005), *The Myth of Sisyphus*, London: Penguin Books.

Craik, K. (1943), *The Nature of Explanation*. Cambridge: Cambridge University Press.

De Beauvoir, S. (2018), *The Ethics of Ambiguity*, New York: Open Road Media.

Descartes, R. (1993), *Meditations on First Philosophy*, Cambridge, MA: Hackett Publishing Co. Inc.

Epicurus, (2012), *The Art of Happiness*, London: Penguin Books.

Fisher, M. (2013), *Capitalist Realism: Is There No Alternative?* Ropley, United Kingdom: John Hunt Publishing.

Goffman, E. (1959), *The Presentation of Self in Everyday Life*, New York: Bantam Doubleday Dell Publishing Group Inc.

Hadot, P. (1995), *Philosophy as a Way of Life: Spiritual Exercises from Socrates to Foucault*, Oxford: Blackwell.

Heidegger, M. (1962), *Being and Time*, Oxford: Blackwell Publishing.

Kierkegaard, S. (1988), *Kierkegaard's Writings, XI, Volume 11: Stages on Life's Way*, New Jersey: Princeton University Press.

Kierkegaard, S. (2008), *Sickness unto death*, trans, A. Hannay, Princeton: Princeton University Press.

Kierkegaard, S. (1846), *The Present Age and Other Essays*, New York: Basic Books.

Marx, K. & Engels, F. (1987), *The German Ideology: Introduction to a Critique of Political Economy*, United Kingdom: Lawrence & Wishart.

Merleau-Ponty, M. (2002), *Phenomenology of Perception*, London: Taylor & Francis.

Nietzsche, F. (2008), *Schopenhauer as Educator*, Gloucester: Dodo Press.

Nietzsche, F. (1974), *The Gay Science*, New York: Random House USA Inc.

Nietzsche, F. (1978), *Thus Spoke Zarathustra*, London: Penguin Classics.

Ortega y Gasset, J. (1994), *The Revolt of the Masses*. New York, London: W. W. Norton & Company.

Robertson, D. (2019), *How to Think Like a Roman Emperor: The Stoic Philosophy of Marcus Aurelius*, New York: St. Martin's Press.

Russell, B. (2004), *In Praise of Idleness: And other essays*, London: Taylor & Francis Ltd.

Russell, B. (1930), *The Conquest of Happiness*, London: Routledge.

Sartre, J. (1946), *Existentialism is a Humanism*, New Haven: Yale University Press.

Setiya, K. (2017), *Midlife: A Philosophical Guide*, Princeton, NJ: Princeton University Press.

Slingerland, E. (2015), *Trying Not to Try: The Ancient Art of Effortlessness and the Surprising Power of Spontaneity*, Edinburgh: Canongate Books.

Smith, A. (2000), *The Wealth of Nations: Books IV–V*, London: Penguin Books.

Spinoza, B. (2006), *The Essential Spinoza: Ethics and Related Writings*, Cambridge, MA: Hackett Publishing Co.

Thoreau, H. (1995), *Walden: Or, Life in the Woods*, New York: Dover Publications Inc.

Veblen, T. (1899), *The Theory of the Leisure Class*, New York: Macmillan.

Veblen, T. (2014), *Why is Economics Not an Evolutionary Science?* Bristol: Read & Co. Books.

Xenophon, (1990), *Conversations of Socrates*, London: Penguin Books.

PSYCHOLOGY

Csikszentmihalyi, M. (1998), *Finding Flow: The psychology of engagement with everyday life*, New York: Basic Books.

Csikszentmihalyi, M. (1990), *Flow: The Psychology of Optimal Experience*, New York: Harper & Row.

Epstein, D. (2019), *Range: How Generalists Triumph in a Specialized World*, United States: Penguin Putnam.

Fromm, E. (2013), *To Have Or To Be?* London: Bloomsbury Academic.

Gergen, K. (1992), *The Saturated Self: Dilemmas of Identity In Contemporary Life*, London: Basic Books.

Gergen, M. (2000), *Feminist Reconstructions in Psychology: Narrative, Gender, and Performance*, Thousand Oaks, CA: SAGE Publications.

Hollis, J. (2018), *Living an Examined Life: Wisdom for the Second Half of the Journey*, Boulder, CO: Sounds True.

Jung, C. (1995), *Memories, Dreams, Reflections*, London: HarperCollins Publishers.

Khera, S. (2014), *You Can Win: A Step-by-Step Tool for Top Achievers*, India: Bloomsbury India.

Lehrer, J. (2009), *How We Decide*, Boston: Houghton Mifflin.

Mann S. (2017), *The Upside of Downtime: Why Boredom is Good*, London: Little, Brown Book Group.

Maslow, A. (2018), *A Theory of Human Motivation*, United States: Wilder Publications.

Maslow, A. (1962), *Towards a Psychology of Being*, Princeton, NJ: Van Nostrand.

Maurer, R. (2014), *One Small Step Can Change Your Life*, New York: Algonquin Books (division of Workman).

Maurer, R. (2012), *The Spirit of Kaizen: Creating Lasting Excellence One Small Step at a Time*, United States: McGraw-Hill Education.

McKeown, G. (2021), *Essentialism: The Disciplined Pursuit of Less*, London: Ebury Publishing.

Nettle, D. (2006), *Happiness: The Science Behind Your Smile*, Oxford: Oxford University Press.

Nolen-Hoeksema, S. (2004), *Women Who Think Too Much: How to Break Free of Overthinking and Reclaim Your Life*, New York: Henry Holt & Company Inc.

Norcross, J. (2012), *Changeology*, New York: Simon & Schuster.

Ostaseski, F. (2019), *The Five Invitations: Discovering What Death Can Teach Us about Living Fully*, New York: Flatiron Books.

Puett, M. & Gross-Loh, C. (2017), *The Path: A New Way to Think About Everything*, London: Penguin Books.

Ricard, M, (2007), *Happiness: A Guide to Developing Life's Most Important Skill*, New York: Little. Brown & Company.

Robertson, I. (2012), *The Winner Effect: How Power Affects Your Brain*, London: Bloomsbury Publishing.

Rogers, C. (1995), *A Way of Being*, Boston: Cengage Learning.

Schwartz, B. (2017), *The Paradox of Choice: Why More Is Less*, New York: HarperCollins Publishers.

SOCIETY AND CULTURE

Churchill, W. (2013), *Painting as a Pastime*, London: Unicorn Publishing Group.

Dissanayake, E. (1990), *What Is Art For?* Seattle: University of Washington Press.

Ely, H. (2008), *A Woman's Hardy Garden*, Gloucester: Dodo Press.

Grandin, T. & Johnson, C. (2006), *Animals in Translation: Using the Mysteries of Autism to Decode Animal Behavior*, Belmont, CA: Cengage Learning.

Kasser, T. (2003), *The High Price of Materialism*, Cambridge: MIT Press.

Lahiri, J. (2017), *In Other Words*, London: Bloomsbury Publishing.

Meadows, D. H., Randers, J. and Meadows, D. (1972), *The Limits to Growth: The 30-Year Update*, Vermont: Chelsea Green Publishing Company.

Miller, G. (2009), *Spent: Sex, Evolution, and the Secrets of Consumerism*, New York: Penguin Group.

Morris, W. (2008), *Useful Work v. Useless Toil*, London: Penguin Books.

Nouwen, H. (2018), *Waiting for God*, New York: Crossroad.

Picasso, M. (2002), *Picasso: My Grandfather*, New York: Penguin Putnam Inc.

Reynolds, M. (2016), *The Garden Awakening: Designs to Nurture Our Land and Ourselves*, Totnes: Green Books.

Skidelsky, E. & Skidelsky, R. (2013), *How Much is Enough?: Money and the Good Life*, London: Penguin Books.

Stearns, P. (2008), *From Alienation to Addiction. Modern American Work in Global Historical Perspective*, Boulder, CO: Paradigm.

Strycker, N. (2015), *The Thing with Feathers: The Surprising Lives of Birds and What They Reveal About Being Human*, United States: Penguin Putnam Inc.

Wolf, M. (2008), *Proust and the Squid: The Story and Science of the Reading Brain*, Duxford: Icon Books.

MEDIA & TECHNOLOGY

Boorstin, D. J. (1992), *The Image: A Guide to Pseudo-Events in America*, New York: Vintage Books.

Carr, N. (2018), *The Shallows: What the Internet Is Doing to Our Brains*, New York: WW Norton & Co.

Ewen, S. (1990), *All Consuming Images: The Politics Of Style In Contemporary Culture*, London: Basic Books.

Eyal N. (2015), *Hooked, How to Build Habit-Forming Products*, London: Penguin Books.

Knapp, J. & Zeratsky, J. (2018), *Make Time: How to Focus on What Matters Every Day*, London: Random House.

McChesney, R. (2014), *Digital Disconnect: How Capitalism is Turning the Internet Against Democracy*, United Kingdom: The New Press.

McCracken, G. (1991), *Culture and Consumption: New Approaches to the Symbolic Character of Consumer Goods and Activities*, Bloomington, IN: Indiana University Press.

Postman, N. (1985), *Amusing Ourselves to Death: Public Discourse in the Age of Show Business*, New York: Penguin.

Postman, N. (1993), *Technopoly: The Surrender of Culture to Technology*, New York: Random House.

FICTION

Borges, J. (2000), *Labyrinths: Selected Stories & Other Writings*, London: Penguin Books.

Congdon, L. (2017), *Glorious Freedom: Older Women Leading Extraordinary Lives*, San Francisco: Chronicle Books.

Murdoch, I. (1999), *The Sea, The Sea*, London: Vintage Publishing.

Hemingway, E. (1999), *The Old Man and the Sea*, Hemel Hempstead: Prentice Hall (a Pearson Education company).

ACKNOWLEDGEMENTS

I clearly remember the day my English teacher handed each student a copy of George Eliot's *The Mill on the Floss*. He sat on the edge of a school desk, wearing a distinctive cardigan, and read Eliot's words aloud to us. Oh my, oh my, to hear such exquisite writing was a high point of ecstasy for me. It was on par with eating the finest dish in the world. I must thank this teacher whose inspired decision to make us read such a text changed my life.

Flourish would not have come into existence without Zan, my travel companion, best friend and soulmate. So many of the ideas in this book come from our endless discussions and philosophizing on what makes a meaningful life. Additionally, Zan's meticulous editing skills were invaluable in turning the manuscript into a polished piece. He successfully fixed all of my 'odd turns of phrase', as he likes to call them, and his keen eye for detail erased many a typographical error and grammatical slip.

A relative of Zan's used to call us 'the Incredibles'. She'd say, 'What are the Incredibles doing today?' and I used to relish the expression. I felt like a superhero, as if anything were possible. I remember once saying to Zan, 'Are we really incredible? I mean, what does it mean to be incredible? How can we become incredible? What must we do?'

I must admit, it's a nice starting point when setting out on any journey to see yourself as an Incredible, and then to ask the question, 'What would the Incredibles do?' No doubt it makes you push the boundaries, much like what happens when you ask another profitable question, 'What would I try if I knew I couldn't fail?'

This book, of course, would not have been possible without my dearest parents, who are nothing but encouraging, kind and supportive. They have been unfailing in their role as parents to give me a foundation to help me flourish.

For their insights, I'd like to thank philosopher Bertrand Russell, media theorist Neil Postman, historian Stewart Ewen, fiction writer Hermann Hesse and of course George Eliot, whose books I've read and re-read over the years.

I am indebted to my publisher Tomasz Hoskins, whose flexibility and creative spirit assisted with breaking through the perilous days of the mid-point of this book. His positivity was a guiding light in getting *Flourish* to print.

And finally, I'd like to acknowledge my four wonderful children Zola, Escher, Wolfe and Huxley, of whom I am so proud and love more than anything in the world.

INDEX